INTERWOVEN

RACHEL CORR

INTERWOVEN

Andean Lives in Colonial Ecuador's Textile Economy

THE UNIVERSITY OF
ARIZONA PRESS

TUCSON

The University of Arizona Press
www.uapress.arizona.edu

We respectfully acknowledge the University of Arizona is on the land and territories of Indigenous peoples. Today, Arizona is home to twenty-two federally recognized tribes, with Tucson being home to the O'odham and the Yaqui. Committed to diversity and inclusion, the University strives to build sustainable relationships with sovereign Native Nations and Indigenous communities through education offerings, partnerships, and community service.

ISBN-13: 978-0-8165-3773-0 (cloth)
ISBN-13: 978-0-8165-5535-2 (paper)
ISBN-13: 978-0-8165-3814-0 (ebook)

Cover design by Nicole Hayward
Cover art: *Carta de la Provincia de Quito y de sus adjacentes* by Maldonado, Pedro (Pedro Vicente), 1704–1748. Courtesy of the Library of Congress, Geography and Map Division; *Vendors of Quito* by Gaetano Osculati, 1854. Biblioteca Digital Hispánica. Biblioteca Nacional de España.

Publication of this book is made possible in part by the proceeds of a permanent endowment created with the assistance of a Challenge Grant from the National Endowment for the Humanities, a federal agency.

Library of Congress Cataloging-in-Publication Data
Names: Corr, Rachel, author.
Title: Interwoven : Andean lives in colonial Ecuador's textile economy / Rachel Corr.
Description: Tucson : The University of Arizona Press, 2018. | Includes bibliographical references and index.
Identifiers: LCCN 2017048364 | ISBN 9780816537730 (cloth : alk. paper)
Subjects: LCSH: Indians of South America—Andes Region—Social conditions—17th century. | Indians of South America—Andes Region—Social conditions—18th century. | Indians of South America—Ecuador—Pelileo—Social conditions—17th century. | Indians of South America—Ecuador—Pelileo—Social conditions—18th century. | Textile workers—Ecuador—Pelileo—History—17th century. | Textile workers—Ecuador—Pelileo—History—18th century.
Classification: LCC F3721.3.S65 C67 2018 | DDC 980/.013—dc23 LC record available at https://lccn.loc.gov/2017048364

Printed in the United States of America
♾ This paper meets the requirements of ANSI/NISO Z39.48-1992 (Permanence of Paper).

CONTENTS

ILLUSTRATIONS

ACKNOWLEDGMENTS

THE RESEARCH for this book would not have been possible without funding, and I gratefully acknowledge the funding I received from the National Endowment for the Humanities, which provided support for research in Ecuador and writing. I would like to thank as well the American Philosophical Society for support I received from a Franklin Grant to undertake research in the Archivo General de Indias in Seville. A sabbatical from Florida Atlantic University enabled me to finish writing the manuscript.

Thanks to Norman and the late Sibby Whitten, who taught me so much about Ecuador and anthropology. My mentor Norman taught me the importance of history for understanding modern-day cultures. He taught me about ethnogenesis and the intertwined histories of different peoples, including indigenous and Afro-Latin American peoples. I continue to learn from his wisdom.

I am very fortunate to have met Karen Powers, and I thank Susan Deeds for putting me in touch with her. I would not have undertaken an ethnohistorical book project had it not been for Karen's mentorship and encouragement. I have learned, and continue to learn, so much about colonial Ecuador, migration, and ethnogenesis from her, and she has always generously responded to my questions about such matters.

I am grateful to Frank Salomon for comments on earlier papers on the ethnogenesis of the Salasacas. Grace Corr, Chris Ely, Jacqueline Fewkes, and Juan Gonzalez read earlier drafts of some chapters, and I appreciate their advice. I also thank Kristin Block, Carmen Cañete Quesada, Timothy Steigenga, and Christopher Strain for offering valuable advice during various stages of the project. I acknowledge the helpful staff at the Archivo General de Indias in Seville. I am indebted to Rocío Pazmiño Acuña, executive director of the Archivo Nacional del Ecuador (ANE), and her staff for all their help. Elizabeth Fariño, the archivist for the ANE in Tungurahua, was very helpful. Patricio Caizabanda and Fr. Pablo Pilco facilitated my searches in ecclesiastical records. I thank Fr. Fabián Areos, Gladys Almeida, and Patricia Villalba for granting me access to parish records in Pelileo and Ambato, and Fr. Néstor Torres López, director of the archive of the Curia Metropolitana in Quito. I also appreciate the help and advice of Pedro Reino Garcés, the official chronicler of Ambato. While doing archival research in Ecuador, I benefitted from discussions with Alcira Dueñas, Victoria and Michael Hamerly, and Ana Luz Borrero. A special thank-you goes to Espirita Masaquiza, Marcelino Masaquiza, and family, as well as José María Masaquiza, Lidia Jimenez, Violeta Masaquiza, Sonia Masaquiza, Baltazar Jimenez, and Marcia Masaquiza for their hospitality and friendship.

I thank Allyson Carter, senior editor at the University of Arizona Press, as well as Kristen Buckles and Scott De Herrera at the University of Arizona Press, for their assistance throughout the process of publishing. I am very appreciative of the anonymous reviewers, who carefully read through an earlier version of the manuscript and offered highly constructive advice. I am grateful to Milagros Aguirre from Editorial Abya-Yala for granting permission to reproduce a photo from the book *Identidades desnudas*. I appreciate Alejandro Gonzalez, who made the maps for this book, and Hannah Papperno, who helped with the graphics.

Finally, I want to thank my husband, Juan Gonzalez, who supported me every step of the way.

INTERWOVEN

INTRODUCTION

*The alcalde [native authority] of the obraje [textile mill] Juan Challay appre-
hended me in the town of Patate and he put me in the stocks so that I would
turn over a son for the obraje of Pilatos and I, having hidden him [the son]
because he was a young child, had to turn him over, and I did, believing that
due to his young age they wouldn't take him in the obraje, but it wasn't as I
assumed, because they took him.*
—MARCOS CUNAMASI 1661[1]

I N THE seventeenth century, Marcos Cunamasi, an indigenous man of the
town of Pelileo, hid his child to protect him from the *obraje* of Pilatos
(another name for San Ildefonso) but was forced to turn him over. Since his
son was too young to keep up with the workload of spinning a certain quota
(*tarea*) of wool per day, the father went to help him, so that his son wouldn't be
whipped. After a year of working in the obraje, Cunamasi was paid a shirt and
a hat. Such stories are typical for the Audiencia (administrative body) of Quito
in the seventeenth century, where large textile mills marked the rural landscape
of the central and northern sierra of what is now Ecuador. This book is about
the native Andean families who made up the labor force of the textile industry,
about fathers like Marcos Cunamasi and others whose family members experienced forced labor in the textile mill of San Ildefonso. Their untold stories
provide us with a unique perspective on the indigenous historical experience
in the colonial northern Andes. The textile market of colonial Quito developed
to supply cloth to the mining centers of Peru and Bolivia, and it was therefore
linked to the global economy. If we are fully to comprehend the reverberations
of these Andean linkages, we must understand how indigenous families experienced and responded to the pressures of colonial Quito's textile economy. The
aim of this book is to show how indigenous social actors engaged in a variety

of strategies to maintain their families and reconstitute their communities in the face of colonial disruptions.

Through the stories told here I show that the responses to the challenges faced by indigenous people ranged from everyday domestic acts, such as preparing food to send to an imprisoned obraje worker, to long-term historical transformations like the creation of an ethnic community. Analysis of each of these acts provides us with deeper insight to the cultural history of the northern Andes, vividly illustrating how people coped with their circumstances in a town that was dominated by a large textile mill. In what follows I provide a context for the material presented here by describing the setting of San Ildefonso, the diversity of colonial Pelileo, and the significance of this study to Andean ethnohistory.

THE SETTING

LOCATION

The economy of colonial Quito depended in large part on its textile industry and the sale of cloth to the South American centers of Potosí (Bolivia), Lima (Peru), and Santa Fe (Colombia). The central sierra of Ecuador favored the development of the textile industry because its landscape was ideal for raising sheep and it had a large indigenous labor pool. I focus on the indigenous people of one town: Pelileo, the location of San Ildefonso, one of Quito's largest and longest-lasting obrajes. Pelileo is located in the central sierra of Ecuador, in the province of Tungurahua. The modern province corresponds to the colonial jurisdiction of Ambato, where Pelileo was one of nine towns that made up the jurisdiction (figures 1 and 2). The obraje of San Ildefonso was located between the towns of Pelileo and Patate, and the presence of the mill had a major impact on the indigenous people of Pelileo.

THE OBRAJE OF SAN ILDEFONSO

Colonial obrajes in the Americas relied on European techniques of cloth production (figure 3) and various forms of indigenous labor (figure 4), including coerced labor.[2] My research did not yield any drawings of the obraje of San Ildefonso, but there are descriptions of the basic structure of the Audiencia's textile mills. Nicholas Cushner describes the large mills of colonial Quito, based on the mill of Chillo:

FIGURE 1. Map of Provinces of Ecuador.

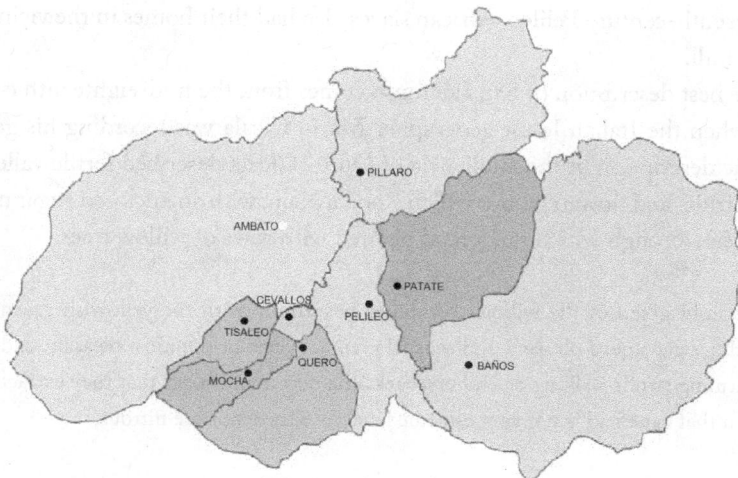

FIGURE 2. Cantons of Tungurahua Province.

The large mill, compared with other structures, was enormous in size, flanked by outbuildings that completed the milling complex. Frequently . . . a sheep run was located close by, as well as farmland and the structures of the farming enterprise. The mill was set close to a stream, since plenty of water was used in the process of making woolen cloth. The cloth-works complex in Chillo was made up of four structures: the textile plant, a one-story building about ninety-two meters long by forty-six meters wide, topped by a lookout post and surrounded by a corridor; the fuller's mill, a much smaller structure; separate building for spinners; and a thatch-roofed hut used as a mill for producing turnip oil. The hut contained a pressing apparatus, a large bronze cauldron, and smaller jars.[3]

The fulling mill (*batan*) of obrajes was "composed of heavy wooden hammers rotating on a hydraulically powered axle that was used to shrink and felt cloth after weaving"[4] (figures 5 and 6). In seventeenth-century Pelileo, there were reports of inexperienced workers, trying to meet their quotas, getting their hands or arms mangled in the fulling mill. Furthermore, the dyers were told that the cloth would only turn out well if it was squeezed before it cooled off after being dyed in boiling water, causing some to burn their hands.[5] One unfortunate dyer fell into the vat of boiling dye and died.[6]

Cleaning the wool took place outside of the mill; inside the mill there were separate quarters for the various other tasks such as carding, spinning, weaving, and dyeing. Around the mill, indigenous families lived in straw-thatched huts, where they had patches of land assigned to them to grow their food. In seventeenth-century Pelileo, African slaves also had their homes in the vicinity of the mill.

The best description of San Ildefonso comes from the mid-eighteenth century, when the Italian Jesuit geographer Mario Cicala was recording his geographic description of the Audiencia of Quito. Cicala described fertile valleys, full of fruits and flowers, above which stood a plain, with an enclosed sugar mill (*trapiche*), through which ran a road planted with rows of willow trees:

> The light green of the willows combines beautifully with the yellowish green of the sugarcane, a pleasing and sensual green . . . one of the most pleasant and charming strolls walking or on horseback. The nectar and sugar that they extract from that canefield is not very esteemed, because the lands are nitrous.[7]

The sugar mills were moved by draft animals. There were many houses and employees, and next to the mill were fruit orchards, fields of alfalfa for the

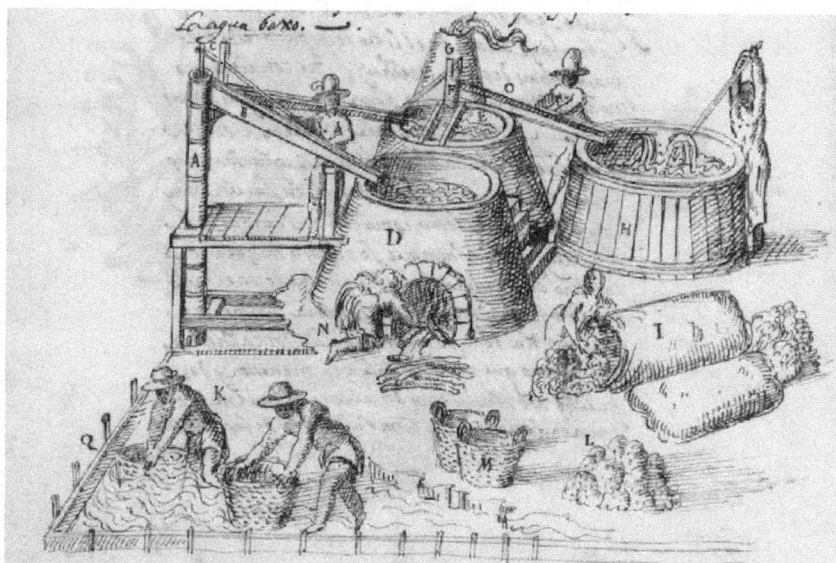

FIGURE 3. Cleaning Wool, Seventeenth Century. From *Los veintiún libros de los ingenios y máquinas* in Biblioteca Digital Hispánica.

FIGURE 4. Obraje of Imbabura Province, Ecuador, ca. 1890. From the book *Identidades desnudas: Ecuador 1860–1920*. Reproduced with permission from Editorial Abya-Yala.

FIGURE 5. Fulling Mill, Seventeenth Century. From *Los veintiún libros de los ingenios y máquinas* in Biblioteca Digital Hispánica.

FIGURE 6. A Fulling Mill of North Wales, ca. 1810.

animals, and "a marvelous woods and exquisite forest." There was the fulling mill to manufacture *paños* (the fine woolen cloth for which Quito was famous) and other wool textiles, where the structure would take advantage of a beautiful waterfall

> that falls from a high rock as if by steps, and after lending its service to the instal-
> lations of the fulling mill, descends to move the two mills below, one of wheat
> and the other of barley, after which the water is finally channeled through two
> aqueducts toward the beautiful and extensive plains on the banks of the river,
> converted into two green grazing fields of exuberant and good pasture dedicated
> to sustaining the draft animals (oxen), mules and horses of the property.[8]

The homes of the hacienda were only a short distance from the fulling mill.

The obraje chapel was beautifully decorated with paintings and statues of saints and the Virgin of Loreto, which was dressed in fine silks and jewelry. The indigenous people would pay for the various feast-day celebrations, including Our Lady of Loreto, San Ildefonso, San Jose, and Corpus Christi. According to Cicala, each afternoon, the foreman (*maestro de paños*) would gather the natives to pray the rosary. Every morning before dawn, he said, about three hundred indigenous youth would gather in front of the large stone cross in the patio of the obraje, where they would sit on the ground, the boys on one side and the girls on the other, while two indigenous authorities called *alcaldes de la doctrina* quizzed them on matters of the Catholic faith, and corrected them when they made mistakes. The daily lessons lasted about two hours, after which they would begin their work in the mill.[9]

Inside the mill, children worked alongside adults, with quotas per pound of wool set according to their age. Children from seven to ten years old had to spin half a pound of wool per day, while the daily quota for adult men and women was a pound per day. If a worker fell short, according to Cicala, he would have to make it up the next day. This description contrasts with an earlier seventeenth-century inspection that describes a situation of beatings and whippings of workers who did not meet their quotas.[10]

Cicala's description portrays San Ildefonso as a village within itself. There were workshops for blacksmiths, carpenters, shoemakers, and a barber, in addition to the manufacturers of wool cloth. There were quarters for the administrator and his assistants, as well as the plantation overseer who supervised indigenous agricultural labor. Cicala estimated a total of thirteen hundred workers in the mill, although he heard it was closer to fifteen hundred. The mill included forty looms, lined up in two rows, with two native workers on each loom. There were separate male and female spinners, each working in their own section, about one hundred women and sixty to eighty men, lined up in rows at their spinning wheels one after the other: "It appears like a true labyrinth to see such a multitude of Indian men and women spinning."[11] In the same room with the spinners were about forty to fifty carders, who would hand over the carded wool to the spinners. Other sections of the mill were used for preparing the dyes and other parts of the process.

Cicala continued with an idyllic description of the indigenous homes. Outside of the mill, beyond the plaza and beautiful gardens, rising above the fulling mill and sugarcane press, there was a slope just below the steep foothills of Chumaquí. There were about two hundred straw huts where the native hacienda workers lived with their families, numbering between sixteen hundred and seventeen hundred people. Each little house had its garden and a patch of land where the family would plant quinoa, wheat, and beans (*habichuelas*); the plots were enclosed by cabuya plants or prickly pear cactus plants, a practice that continues to this day. The indigenous families would channel the water from the

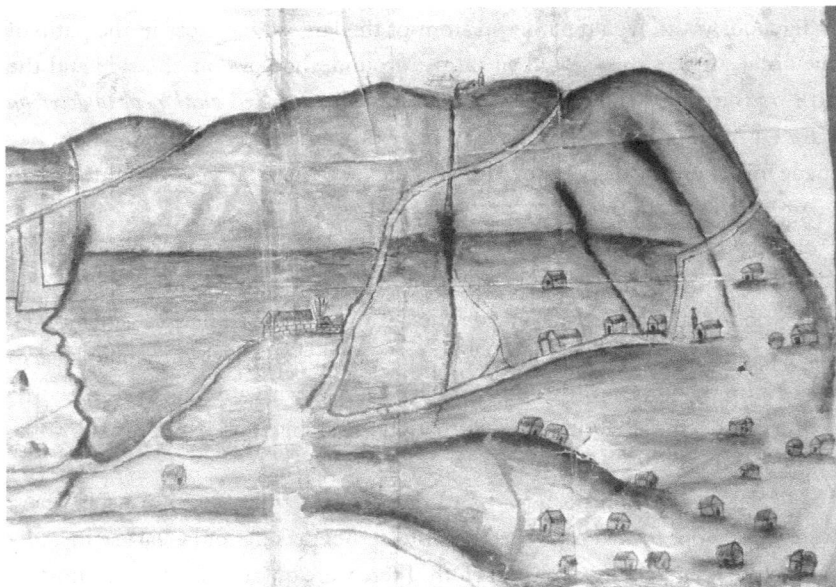

FIGURE 7. Hacienda of Chumaquí, Eighteenth Century. From ANE Mapas y Planos Código ANH.MP.03.11.24.319.

waterfall of Chumaquí to irrigate their fields, which Cicala described as green and fertile. "Everything seems like a little paradise; an enchanting little town with a mild, pleasant climate and very healthy."[12]

While Cicala's writing gives a good, detailed description of the eighteenth-century physical layout of the mill complex, it presents an idealized version of the setting. For the indigenous people it was no paradise. Although experiences differed depending on the owners and individual foreman, obraje labor conditions throughout the Audiencia of Quito were repeatedly described as deplorable, enough to break up indigenous families as people ran away. The chapters in this book trace the indigenous experience in Pelileo over three centuries, as San Ildefonso's ownership passed through different hands, and as people reproduced and transformed their communities.

DIVERSITY OF COLONIAL PELILEO

ANDEANS IN PELILEO'S TEXTILE ECONOMY

I use the term *textile economy* to mean a society based in large part on the manufacture and sale of textiles, which drew from the organizational structure of colonial society, including the regulation of indigenous labor through the encomienda (grant of indigenous labor to a Spaniard), the *mita* (indigenous labor draft), the farm-factory complex, land-inheritance rules, and other colonial institutions and practices. Even those indigenous people who did not directly work in an obraje were affected by the system in one way or another. The term *textile economy* encompasses the colonial society that depended on textile manufacture.

Textile mills had different effects on people who occupied different social positions. I explore the lives of people assigned to different social categories, including African slaves, obraje Indians (those who belonged to an encomienda subject to labor in the textile mill), and non-obraje Indians (those who belonged to encomiendas not subject to labor in the mill). I analyze the testimonies of native elites and authorities as well as those of ordinary men and women who occupied specific social roles within their families (e.g., wives, sons-in-law, fathers). I examine the indigenous history of Pelileo mainly through the stories told by four different sectors of indigenous people. Three of the indigenous sectors discussed in this book—the Pilalata, Chumaquí, and Guambaló—were forced to work in the obraje, and it affected their individual, familial, social and cultural lives. The Pilalata and Chumaquí belonged to the same encomienda and were sometimes referred to as obraje Indians in colonial records, and I use that term throughout the manuscript because the social category to which they were assigned shaped their experience. The Guambaló belonged to a different encomienda, but were also forced into the obraje. A fourth group, the Sigchos Collanas, were *not* required to serve in the obraje, because they had a different status. As the descendants of migrants to Pelileo, they lacked access to lands in the community. During the course of Pelileo's history, the Sigchos Collanas resisted forced labor in the obraje, and they purchased lands from and intermarried with some of the obraje Indians. Through the process of ethnogenesis—the historical emergence of an ethnic group—the Sigchos Collanas re-created themselves as the indigenous Salasacas, who remain as a distinctive indigenous culture of Pelileo today. The families that constituted the labor force of the obraje followed two historical trajectories. Many blended in with Hispanic society and became white-mestizos (people of mixed heritage). Others joined the emerging ethnic community of Salasaca and maintained an indigenous cultural identity.

Focusing on indigenous family and social life in a town that was dominated by a large obraje advances our understanding of the cultural history of Ecuador's indigenous people. People living in oppressive situations, such as slavery, debt peonage, and other forms of forced labor, needed to find ways to survive physically. Yet people also had to survive emotionally, spiritually, and socially. They had to adapt and reproduce their cultural lives, reconstituting households, families, and communities. Recent studies in family history call for closer attention to how families experienced historical events and how individual family choices shaped those events and contributed to the process of ethnogenesis.[13] Such questions are at the intersection of history and anthropology and reveal human adaptability and cultural creativity under some of the most difficult situations resulting from conquest, colonization, global commodity flows, slavery, and other forms of forced labor. Studies that reveal the experiences of African and indigenous families in the Americas bring to life, and humanize, the anonymous mass of "laborers" in particular historical contexts. Examples include Sidney Mintz's work on the cultural adaptations of Caribbean slaves, June Nash's study of the history and culture of families who worked in Bolivia's tin mines, Elizabeth Newman's study of everyday life and culture of hacienda workers in Puebla, Mexico, and Richard Price's study of culture and ethnogenesis among former slaves of Suriname's sugar plantations. Sherwin Bryant's study of slaves in the Audiencia of Quito reveals their strategies for forming families and communities. For highland Ecuador, Erin O'Connor's study of indigenous relations with the state focuses on families in the nineteenth century, with attention to how the hacienda system affected men and women in their relationships to each other. Andrés Guerrero's analysis of hacienda workers in northern Ecuador and Barry Lyons's study of a twentieth-century hacienda in central Ecuador both include indigenous testimonies that reveal the cultural lives of the workers and the range of experiences of indigenous men and women who labored on the hacienda. Emilia Ferraro's ethnography of Peguche provides an analysis of the cultural adaptations of former hacienda workers. These studies enrich our understanding of Latin American history by elucidating the experiences of the families and communities that made up the workforce of plantations, mines, and ranches. The indigenous people's stories that I present here reveal how the presence of a large textile mill affected their relationships with one another, as well as with people of other "races."

RACE, ETHNICITY, AYLLU

"Race" is a culturally constructed concept: a social (as opposed to biological) category to which people are assigned. Anthropologists have shown that although there are not biological races, the social construct of race has had profound effects on the people who are assigned to certain categories—people who are imagined to have certain qualities.[14] I use the term *race* here to refer to the dominant colonial construction of assigning people to the broad categories of "white" (*blanco* or *español*), "Indian" (*indio*), "black" (*negro*), or "mestizo" (blended—usually referring to someone who has both Spanish and indigenous ancestry). These were the most common colonial categories I found in the documentation for Pelileo, and they correspond to the dominant racial categories of modern-day highland Ecuador. Other colonial categories (*castas*) were rarely used in the colonial sources that are the basis for this study.[15] Today most Ecuadorian whites are referred to not as Spanish but as blanco-mestizos, indicating their mixed heritage. There is a history of division between indigenous people and these white-mestizos, who are considered socially superior to both Afro-Ecuadorians and indigenous people. Ecuador's dominant racial hierarchy places whites at the top, black and indigenous people at opposite poles of the bottom, and mestizos and mulatos (who have European and African ancestry) in the middle, with the hegemonic goal of "whitening" (*blanqueamiento*). Figure 8 shows Norman Whitten's diagram of this dominant racial hierarchy.[16]

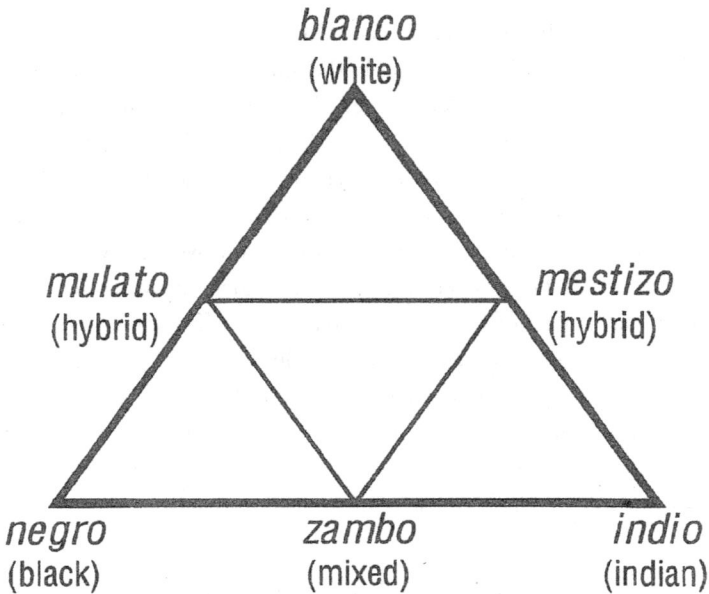

FIGURE 8. Whitten's Diagram of Dominant Racial Categories in Ecuador.

A distinction in identity exists in the Ecuadorian highlands between indigenous people and white-mestizos, and this is an inheritance from the colonial period. Martin Minchom noted that the Audiencia of Quito did not make use of the multiple socioracial categories (called castas) found in Mesoamerica and other parts of the Andes. Rural parish records for Quito used two main categories: indios (Indians) and españoles (Spaniards, which included blacks).[17] Mestizos were classified with whites. Kris Lane explains that "white, or rather *español/a* (or *criollo/a*), identity in large part came to be defined as the opposite of *indio/a*. Among other things, a self-proclaimed *blanco/a*, certainly by the eighteenth century, had to be a Spanish speaker who did not pay tribute."[18] This was not just a class distinction. So stigmatized was the indigenous "race" that nineteenth-century mestizos objected to paying tribute because it would "change their identity and degrade them from citizens to the status of Indian,"[19] and both poor whites and mestizos fought to maintain a clear distinction from indios starting in the late eighteenth century. In an example of the endurance of the colonial legacy of race, in 1981 Joseph Casagrande shared his observation that a financially successful indigenous man from Otavalo (northern Ecuador), a "complete gentleman," still had to endure the insults hurled at him by an "insignificant town *mestizo*."[20]

During Ecuador's nation-building period following independence from Spanish colonial rule, national planners promoted the idea of *mestizaje* (blending) into one nation and one people. However, the goal was not for white-mestizos to embrace indigenous (or Afro-Ecuadorian) heritage, but for black and indigenous peoples to try to "whiten" by embracing Hispanic identity. The goal of mestizaje excluded those who maintained other identities, leading Ronald Stutzman to refer to it as an "all-inclusive ideology of exclusion."[21] In highland Ecuador, indigenous people who maintained distinctive identities and cultures were blamed for slowing down the progress of the nation. The history of racial discrimination, and racist discourse, from white-mestizos against black and indigenous Ecuadorians is a result of the colonial legacy. Despite the stigma, some indigenous people in Pelileo (and other parts of Ecuador) chose to maintain an indigenous identity.

The term *indio* in Spanish is usually glossed as "Indian" in English, although this is considered pejorative by modern-day indigenous people. Throughout the book I use the terms *indigenous*, *native*, or *Andean* to refer to indigenous peoples, unless I am quoting or paraphrasing speech that uses *indio*. I use *African*, *black*, or *slave* to refer to African slaves of Pelileo (negros) in the documents, and *white* or *Spaniard* for whites (españoles or blancos).

The relationships between Africans and native Andeans were complex and varied. Africans were instrumental in colonial governance, including the subduing of indigenous people in colonial Quito, as Sherwin Bryant has shown in his book *Rivers of Gold, Lives of Bondage*.[22] Colonial laws offered special protections to indigenous people, but in practice these laws were often ignored. Colonial policy prohibited black and indigenous people from working together. The stated reason for this policy was to prevent blacks from abusing native Andeans, but some historians argue that it was really meant to prevent alliances from forming between black and indigenous people against the colonial government.[23] Recent scholarship has shed new light on relations between African descended and indigenous peoples of the Americas, and it has challenged the stereotype that black and indigenous relations were inherently hostile. For example, Rachel Sarah O'Toole challenges the stereotype of Andeans as mere victims of African aggression in her book *Bound Lives*, while the chapters in the book *Beyond Black and Red*, edited by Matthew Restall, analyze a range of relationships and interactions among Africans and natives in the Americas.

As these studies and others show, conflict and hostility are overemphasized in colonial reports, and cooperation and amicable relations are underreported.

I expected to find more evidence of cooperation between Africans and Andeans in seventeenth-century Pelileo, when about ninety African slaves worked in the textile and sugar mills. However, all the information about these slaves comes from a 1661 criminal investigation against the Spanish owner. During that investigation, indigenous people gave their testimonies about wrongs they suffered in the obraje, including being mistreated by the owner's African slaves. The testimonies are many and varied and were given by different indigenous people telling their personal experiences, and they should be taken seriously. Unfortunately, those leading the investigation never took the testimonies of the slaves themselves, so the African voices have been silenced out of the historical record. From the indigenous point of view, relations with blacks were overwhelmingly negative. As Jean-Pierre Tardieu has said in his study of San Ildefonso, the owners turned their African slaves into "servile thugs" over the Andeans.[24] To dismiss these indigenous testimonies of their own experiences as mere exaggerations or stereotypes would not only impose our own views on indigenous voices but would also deny the agency of Africans as individuals. Although they were legally slaves, as people, Africans in Pelileo were capable of the same range of behaviors as any other humans: from acts of compassion to great cruelty. It should not surprise us that slaves would take advantage of indigenous people who were deemed socially inferior. Nevertheless, within the indigenous testimonies I pay careful attention to hints of empathy with African slaves, although such hints are rare.

Within the broad colonial categories of "indio" and "negro" were different ethnic groups. I use the term *ethnic groups* to refer to the divisions within racial categories. For example, modern-day Ecuadorians who self-identify as indigenous also have unique identities as Salasacas, Saguros, Otavalos, and so on. While these Andean people all speak the same language, Quichua, they each have a unique style of ethnic attire that reflects their ethnic identity.

The indigenous people of colonial Pelileo were divided into sectors called *parcialidades* by the Spanish, sometimes referred to by the Andean term *ayllu*, which when used in the central and southern Andes can refer to an extended family, kinship group, or community. In the northern Andes, it seems that the term was first applied by Spanish administrators to refer to groups of households headed by local native elites. By the late sixteenth century, the term had become part of colonial discourse.[25] Here I use the term *ayllu* as it was used in seventeenth- and eighteenth-century Pelileo, when *ayllu* and *parcialidad* were used interchangeably, or sometimes simultaneously, as in "ayllu and parcialidad of the Chumaquí." Each of the ayllus of Pelileo had its own chief, called a cacique (or *cacica* for female leaders), who was responsible for forcing his or her subjects to pay tribute and participate in the labor draft. Caciques were addressed with the honorific title *Don* or its feminine form *Doña* for cacicas. In addition to the four groups that are the focus of this study: Pilalata, Chumaquí, Guambaló, and Sigchos Collanas (called Salasacas in Church records), ecclesiastical records report the following ayllus for Pelileo: *forasteros* (outsiders, likely multiethnic), Carpinteros (called Incas Carpinteros in some census records),[26] Puruguayes, and Tacungas.

The relationship between the terms *ayllu* and *ethnic group* for seventeenth- and eighteenth-century Pelileo is not always clear. Those who constituted the bulk of the obraje's labor force, the Pilalata, Chumaquí, and Guambaló, each had their own caciques, but these caciques descended from a common ancestor, so they cannot be said to constitute different ethnic groups. Other ayllus, such as the Carpinteros, Tacungas, and Sigchos Collanas, corresponded to different ethnic groups (see chapter 4). Since ethnic group identity and composition changed throughout the colonial period, and native groups were recombined and reinvented during the colonial period,[27] it is difficult to say whether a given ayllu or parcialidad constituted an ethnic division, although some certainly did. I use the colonial term *ayllu* or *parcialidad* for these colonial divisions of indigenous people, most often by using the name of the ayllu with which the person identified (e.g. "a Chumaquí man" or "a woman of the Tacungas").

These colonial sectors of indigenous people no longer exist. Modern-day Pelileo is a predominately white-mestizo town with one unique indigenous enclave called Salasaca. The Salasacas clearly identify as indigenous, have a distinctive ethnic attire, and speak Quichua as their first language, although most are bilingual in Quichua and Spanish. In the first half of the twentieth century, writers described the Salasacas as "fierce" and defensive against outsiders, and Salasaca oral histories confirm this defensive stance.[28] People questioned the origins of the Salasacas, and writers suggested that they were a mitimae (transplanted population) colony that was moved from Bolivia to Pelileo by the Incas five hundred years ago. Although no writers have presented credible evidence of the mitimae theory, it became a way for Ecuadorians to explain Salasaca uniqueness and traditionalism, including why Salasacas chose to maintain an indigenous identity when everyone around them was engaging in mestizaje (blending with Hispanic society), speaking Spanish, and wearing generic clothing devoid of ethnic markers.

The twentieth-century views of Pelileo as a white-mestizo town with one (somewhat hostile) indigenous ethnic group mask a dynamic history of ethnic diversity and complicated race relations. To understand the history of Pelileo's people, one must go back to a time when Pelileo was a racially and ethnically diverse economic hub around a textile mill that became a town in itself; where indigenous women nursed African slave babies and indigenous men sought refuge from the mill on Spanish-owned ranches; and where people sought to improve their circumstances by seizing opportunities where they saw them: in competition between caciques, in opportunities to run away, and in disputes between Spanish heirs who were coming down on their luck. They also, occasionally, showed compassion for others and had relationships with people of other "racial" groups. Given the social distance between the Salasacas and their mestizo neighbors through most of the twentieth century, these interracial interactions are part of Pelileo's hidden history. Therefore, although the main goal of this book is to show the lived experience of Andeans as they responded to the textile economy, I pay attention to race relations, and especially to little-known stories of cooperation and compassion between people who were classified into the different categories of Spaniard, Indian, black, and mestizo.

The case of Pelileo is a prime example of the interplay of culture and history as described in two works. The first, Eric Wolf's *Europe and the People without History*, calls on anthropologists to understand cultures as part of a world system that has been linked since the sixteenth century. Wolf takes a series of commodities—sugarcane, silver, rubber—and shows how the global demand for these products affected specific local cultures. While Wolf criticizes anthropologists for focusing on local cultures as if they were isolated and ahistorical, he calls on world-system theorists to pay more attention to local cultures.[29] Here, I focus on the effects of global processes of Spanish colonialism, encomiendas, the labor draft, and tribute not only on local cultures, but also on indigenous families. How did the textile market affect indigenous women, men, children, and caciques from the ethnic groups that served in the obraje? How did it affect them in their roles as caciques, catechists, family providers, loyal siblings, or sons-in-law? How did it affect indigenous cultural practices? Through the indigenous histories told here, we see the effects of global transformations on the local peoples of Pelileo.

The second process of historical transformation is explained in Karen Vieira Powers's work on migration and ethnogenesis. In her book *Andean Journeys*

Powers shows that colonial Quito experienced massive migration and disruption of indigenous communities, but that, remarkably, some Andeans managed to maintain unique indigenous cultural traits and identities.[30] This distinctiveness is maintained today through symbols of cultural identity.[31] Such outward symbols in highland Ecuador include clothing, hairstyles, jewelry, language, rituals and customs, and in some cases, kinship and endogamy. By wearing ethnic attire,[32] speaking one's language, and engaging in other cultural practices that mark one's ethnic identity, individuals through successive generations engage in "boundary maintenance."[33] The final chapters of this book show how indigenous migrants to Pelileo purchased land from the obraje Indians and re-created themselves as the indigenous community of Salasaca. Contrary to beliefs that they are remnants from the Incaic civilization from five hundred years ago, I show that the emergence of Salasaca cultural identity occurred through indigenous responses to historical contingencies.

SIGNIFICANCE FOR ANDEAN ETHNOHISTORY: THE OBRAJES OF COLONIAL QUITO

There are several detailed studies of the history of Quito's obrajes. Most of these, however, focus on the economic role of the textile industry in Quito, market fluctuations, Crown policies, and elite obraje owners. All works mention the abuse of the indigenous workers, but place limited attention on the indigenous people themselves. In his 1967 book *The Kingdom of Quito in the Seventeenth Century*, John Leddy Phelan referred to Quito as the "sweatshop of South America." Phelan described the struggles between the Crown's attempts to curb abuses in the obrajes and the Quito officials' insistence on the economic necessity of keeping the obrajes running.

Two major works, written roughly around the same time, provide extensive studies of colonial Quito's obraje economy. Robson Brines Tyrer's 1976 doctoral dissertation "The Demographic and Economic History of the Audiencia of Quito: Indian Population and the Textile Industry, 1600–1800" provides a thorough analysis of the rise and fall of the textile industry in Ecuador. Tyrer's study provides valuable information about labor issues, including the advancement of goods to indigenous workers at inflated prices and use of debt to keep the workers in the obrajes. Tyrer describes the different specialized tasks in cloth production, from shearing the sheep for wool to carding, spinning, weaving, dyeing, and fulling. Tyrer's economic history provides a basis for any study of Quito's textile industry.

In "El obraje colonial ecuatoriano" (1977), Javier Ortiz de la Tabla discusses Spain's inability to control the industry. He was familiar with the elite Spanish and *criollo* (Europeans born in the Americas) families of Quito, and his study of these obraje-owning families is a precursor to his later (1993) work *Los encomenderos de Quito, 1534–1660*. Ortiz de la Tabla traces the links between elite families, who were connected through kinship and marriage and were able to pool their resources. For the case of Pelileo, he shows that the marriage of María de Vera Mendoza, heiress to the obraje of San Ildefonso, to Antonio Lopez de Galarza, an encomendero (a Spaniard with rights to the labor of certain indigenous groups) of Pelileo, allowed them to supply her obraje with his control of indigenous labor. Like Tyrer, Ortiz de la Tabla describes the tasks and specializations in the process of cloth production and the roles of indigenous people in different social positions, including caciques who owned obrajes. He touches on some effects that obrajes had on indigenous families, including the role of women in bringing food to their husbands who worked in the obraje, the loss of male labor in the family's fields, the forced labor of children, and the extreme forms of indigenous resistance to the abuses that they faced. The latter included running away, hiding births, and even abortion. Although I did not find evidence of extreme measures such as abortion in my research on Pelileo, I elaborate on the issues of indigenous family members' responses to forced labor.

Both Tyrer's and Ortiz de la Tabla's studies focus on the important role that textile production served in sustaining the economy of Quito and in allowing Spanish and criollo elites to maintain their status. They also address the recognition, on the part of Quito's colonial officials, that the indigenous population was suffering extreme abuse at the hands of obraje administrators. At the same time, these officials argued that indigenous labor was needed in the obrajes, so Crown orders to demolish obrajes were not carried out, and even the codes that meant to curb the abuses were often ignored.

The link between landed estates and textile mills is explored in Nicholas Cushner's book *Farm and Factory*, an informative study of the Jesuit system of controlling haciendas and textiles mills. The obraje-estate complex was common among other obraje owners: they owned the sheep ranches that produced wool for the textile mills and the estates that produced food, and they could shift labor from the hacienda to the obraje. Cushner had access to some Jesuit archives, so his study provides information about the Jesuit-owned lands and mills. The Jesuits purchased San Ildefonso in 1724 and operated it until their expulsion from South America in 1767. Although Cushner's focus is on Jesuit property, he provides a general background to the obraje system of Quito, including the history of San Ildefonso.

Any economic or political history of colonial Quito necessarily addresses textile manufacture. Kenneth Andrien provides an extensive discussion of the history, policies, and economic and demographic effects of the textile industry in his 1995 work *The Kingdom of Quito, 1690–1830*. There are also articles that focus on specific colonial reports and inspections of obrajes. Two of these outline eighteenth-century recommendations to improve working conditions for indigenous workers. First, Segundo Moreno Yánez describes in his 1979 article "El 'Formulario de ordenanzas de indios'" the mistreatment of indigenous workers according to Don Juan de Luján, Fiscal Protector General de Indios (protector of Indians) in 1737. Luján recommended that the indigenous workers be paid in money, not goods, and said they should be provided with better food. Second, Luis Ramos Gómez's 1998 article "La situación del indio de obraje en la ciudad de Quito según la visita realizada en 1743 por el president José de Araujo" describes the president's inspection of Quito's obrajes and the deplorable state of imprisoned indigenous workers, who seemed to be dying of hunger. Christiana Borchart de Moreno wrote about the "crisis" and decline of obrajes in the eighteenth century and how San Ildefonso survived by adapting to economic changes. Guadalupe Soasti's article focused on obraje owners and merchants in Riobamba. Aside from the large obrajes owned by elite families (obraje dynasties), there were smaller-level obrajes that helped some women to support themselves, as described by Kimberley Gauderman in her article "A Loom of Her Own." Case studies of specific obrajes include Alexandra Kennedy Troya and Carmen Fauria Roma's history of the obraje of Tilipulo and Rocío Rueda's study of the obraje of San Joseph de Peguche.

There are studies that focus specifically on San Ildefonso, including Jaime Costales's master's thesis "El obraje de San Ildefonso," which provides a history of the ethnic groups of Pelileo from pre-Hispanic to colonial times, as well as a history of the obraje from its founding. In their study of the province of Tungurahua, Alfredo Costales Samaniego and Piedad Peñaherrera de Costales describe indigenous deaths in San Ildefonso and speculate on the psychological effects that the obraje had on the local indigenous population. Jean-Pierre Tardieu's article "Negros e indios en el obraje de San Ildefonso" is an analysis of relations between African slaves and indigenous people in mid-seventeenth-century Pelileo.

This study provides a new approach to the existing scholarship by putting the indigenous experience at the center: by emphasizing the actions of people whose lives and families were affected by the colonial system that depended on textile manufacture. Thanks to the existing work on the history of Quito's textile industry, I am able to focus here on the stories of the native people of the town, rather than on the obraje itself, and trace the diverse responses of different members of indigenous society (including those exempt from obraje labor) through three centuries, as people ran away, abandoned or helped one another, and collaborated with one another to sustain themselves.

Previous studies of the history of textile production in Quito, Crown ordinances and their defiance, colonial administration, encomiendas, and the labor draft provide the historical context in which to read and interpret the voices of the indigenous people who gave testimonies. While most studies of Quito's obrajes mention the complaints from the indigenous workers—and colonial reports were highly critical of the treatment of indigenous people—the history of the indigenous experience is full of silences. Michel-Rolph Trouillot speaks of intentional and unintential silences in the production of history and historical narratives in his book *Silencing the Past*. For every recording of an event or story, there is also an omission. The voices of black slaves of the obraje of San Ildefonso were never recorded. Their stories have been silenced, as were the stories of the forasteros who were imprisoned in the obraje and died. Nevertheless, some indigenous workers did get the opportunity to tell their stories, and it is these voices, and the histories they tell, that I attempt to recover. As such, this study makes a distinct contribution to previous studies of the history of the obraje economy by fleshing out the official history with the lived experience of indigenous workers and their families.

OUTLINE OF THE BOOK

My emphasis on native Andean voices and narrative testimonies is made possible by a long criminal investigation, which started in 1661 and included the testimonies of more than 150 indigenous people,[34] against the seventeenth-century

Spaniard Antonio Lopez de Galarza. Galarza was an encomendero, a Spaniard
with a grant of indigenous labor, who managed his wife's obraje of San Ildefonso and forced local indigenous people of his encomienda to work there. The
criminal case was concluded in 1666. In addition to that extensive record, my
research material included obraje account records, wills contained in land disputes, complaints filed by caciques, criminal cases, petitions for mestizo status,
and notarial and religious records to piece together a sketch of indigenous life
in the region surrounding the obraje. The chapters are organized, for the most
part, according to chronological order. The archival sources reveal different types
of information for different time periods, and each of the chapters reveals information about the lives of the indigenous people and the cultural practices that
held meaning for them, such as kinship and gender practices and the political
and religious rituals in which they were engaged. Each chapter shows how
indigenous actors in different social positions responded to colonial pressures
in the context of the obraje economy.

Chapter 1 provides a background to the setting of colonial Pelileo and
includes a brief geographic and ethnic history. Pelileo was already a diverse
region by the time Spaniards began settling there. It had been the location of the
Inca's coca fields,[35] and there were multiple native peoples who were both local
and from Peru. With the arrival of the Spaniards, coca fields were transformed
into sugarcane plantations, and the high grasslands called *páramos* were ideal for
raising sheep to meet the growing demand for wool in the textile industry. San
Ildefonso was founded in 1594, with a Crown license that granted the owner use
of labor from his African slave force and local indigenous "volunteer" workers.
Chapter 2 provides an analysis of the position of native Andeans in relation to
these African slaves, based on the testimonies of indigenous people during the
1661 investigation. These testimonies portray the work conditions, in which Africans were charged with guarding and punishing the native workers. Chapter 3
focuses on how the obraje affected indigenous people's relationships with one
another, according to social positions in indigenous society—native intermediaries, such as alcaldes and labor bosses, and commoners in their familial roles:
fathers, wives, and in-laws. This chapter places emphasis on seventeenth-century
indigenous family and cultural life and how people coped with the difficulties
posed by forced labor in the obraje. Indigenous people used the investigation
to voice their experiences and "unsilence" the deaths of workers in the obraje.

Chapter 4 begins with the early eighteenth century, when the obraje was
owned by the heirs of María de Vera Mendoza. Records from this period

(1700–1727) reveal information about gender and native governance. I analyze three cases in which cacicas fought for the right to govern the natives of their ayllus. Cacicas and their subjects both manipulated ambiguities in colonial laws in order to improve their circumstances and that of their descendants. Chapter 5 is a brief chapter that marks the transition to the mid-eighteenth century. It starts with a general description of the situation of the textile economy of the Audiencia of Quito in the 1730s, and then focuses on the Jesuit ownership of San Ildefonso from 1724 to 1767. This chapter tells the story of Carlos Masaquiza, a Sigchos Collanas man who took legal action to resist being forced into the obraje.

When the Jesuits were expelled from South America, the government took over their properties, including San Ildefonso. Within a year of the government takeover the workers staged a rebellion that sparked fears of a pan-indigenous uprising throughout the jurisdiction of Ambato. The focus of chapter 6 is the rebellion, the most overt and violent indigenous response to the conditions in the obraje. The violence was instigated by two mothers of obraje workers. Tensions spilling over from the obraje affected the social and ritual life of the town during preparations for the festival of Corpus Christi. The rebellion affected native Andean men in intermediary positions, and it revealed a growing mistrust between indios and mestizos.

Continuing from the mid to late eighteenth century, chapter 7 is based on an analysis of wills contained in land disputes to show how the Pilalata and Chumaquí reckoned kinship and inheritance. People maintained their families and their ties with one another through the cultural practices of ritual kinship, adoption, and bequeathing family property through wills. As the Pilalata and Chumaquí coped with the challenges of colonial society, they sold some of their family lands. Selling land was one response to colonial pressures, and transformations in landownership shaped the ethnic composition of Pelileo. People sold plots of land in order to pay for funerals and Masses for the souls of their deceased kin, to meet tribute requirements, or, occasionally, to liberate a family member from the obraje. Some of these lands were purchased by the Sigchos Collanas migrants, and in chapter 8 I show how these migrants consolidated those lands to create an ethnic territory and re-create themselves, through ethnogenesis, as indigenous Salasacas. The final chapter addresses the current cultural identity of the Salasacas. Together, the chapters provide a cultural history of the indigenous people of Pelileo and their varied responses to their historical circumstances.

Throughout the book, I use individual people's stories to flesh out the general historical patterns. Telling the stories of individuals serves several purposes. First, it humanizes the anonymous mass of the indigenous labor pool that supported the textile industry. I also provide the names of African slaves whenever possible, to humanize the black people of San Ildefonso, even though we have limited information on them.

Second, individual stories of compassion or close relationships between Spaniards, natives, and blacks are revealing for the case of Pelileo, which, in the first half of the twentieth century, was characterized by tension and social distance between indigenous people and nonindigenous people. Contrary to the assumption that since pre-Columbian times the Salasacas remained hostile to the growing mestizo population around them, the stories presented here show not only that Pelileo was a diverse economic hub but that there were various types of interactions among the different peoples, some of them amicable. I present stories of social intimacy as well as social tension in order to provide a more accurate portrayal of the complex dynamics of the history of race relations in the region, as well as to glean instances of empathy and compassion within structures of inequality and contexts of violence and mutual antagonism.[36] In the archival sources on which this book is based, conflict is overrepresented because the records are often based on disputes. The focus on individual people's stories gives us a better sense of the lived experiences within colonial structures of inequality, and some of those experiences include acts of compassion between people who were divided by colonial racial categories.

Finally, the strategies of cultural reproduction that indigenous people used in Pelileo were likely used by indigenous people throughout the Audiencia. Therefore, the study of how the natives of Pelileo coped with the pressures of the obraje and economienda also shed light on the larger history of native lives in colonial Quito and how indigenous people struggled to maintain their families and re-create their communities.

CHAPTER 1

FROM COCA TO CAÑA

The Rise of Sugar and Sheep in Seventeenth-Century
Pelileo (1605–1650)

THIS CHAPTER provides a brief description of the geographic setting of
Pelileo and the factors that led to its ethnic diversity in the early seventeenth century. After discussing the transition from native elite–owned
coca fields to Spanish sugar estates, I focus on the growing textile industry in the
early seventeenth century and the conversion of high grasslands around Pelileo
into sheep pastures to produce wool. The chapter concludes with the establish-
ment of San Ildefonso and the passing of its ownership to the heiress María de
Vera Mendoza, whose second husband controlled the labor of Pelileo's indigenous people through his encomienda. The purpose of this chapter is to provide
the setting for the historical narratives that follow in subsequent chapters.

GEOGRAPHIC SETTING

Andean food production has long been characterized by the exploitation of a
series of vertical ecological niches that allow for production of a variety of foods
at different altitudes. In the northern Andes, these ecological zones are closer
together than in the central and southern Andes, some within a day's walking
distance.[1] The central sierra of Ecuador, which includes the regions of Latacunga (colonial Tacunga), Ambato (where Pelileo is located), and Riobamba

FIGURE 9. The Central Sierra of Ecuador. Based on the Eighteenth-Century Map by Pedro Vicente Maldonado. Modified by Alejandro González.

(figure 9) is characterized by high-altitude (3,300 meters and above), cool, damp grasslands called páramos, and lower, warm valleys. Ecuador's páramos differ from the high-elevation puna of Peru and Bolivia in that the páramos are more humid and covered by permanent, dense, vegetation. The Pelileo-Patate region contains valleys and mountains ranging from 2,000 to 3,700 meters, and in

1986 Christoph Stadel identified five different altitudinal zones of agricultural activity for the region.[2]

In pre-Columbian times Pelileo was a center of coca production, and indigenous people came from different regions to work the coca fields for native elites. Before discussing the significance of coca, it is necessary to discuss different types of indigenous migration in the Andes. In the early seventeenth century, Pelileo was an ethnically diverse town inhabited by various different ayllus of indigenous people. Three different types of migration account for this diversity. Two began in the preconquest period, during the reign of the Incas, which in Ecuador lasted from around 1500 to 1534. The third type of indigenous migration was a response to Spanish colonialism. The three types of migrants were mitimaes, *camayos*, and forasteros.

Mitimaes were populations that were uprooted and moved to a new location by the Incas. The Incas moved rebellious populations to more pacified zones and loyal populations to unruly zones of the empire in order to better control the population. Some groups were moved because they had special skills and could teach those skills to the local population. The Inca mitimae policy led to the movement and resettlement of people among the modern-day countries of Peru, Ecuador, and Bolivia. One example of a mitimae group in colonial Pelileo is the ayllu of Carpinteros.

Camayos were people who were sent from their communities of origin to other ecological zones in order to specialize in the production of some product for the benefit of the home community. They would be sent there by their ethnic lords, called curacas or caciques, and they maintained their identity with their community of origin. The camayo system was implemented by the Inca. Prior to Inca imperial expansion in Quito, north Andean ethnic lords managed to procure a variety of products for the home community by managing exchange relations through trade specialists called *mindalas*.[3] After the Incas introduced the camayo system, caciques continued to send camayos to live and work in other zones during the Spanish colonial period.

After the Spanish conquest, colonial laws forced native men between the ages of eighteen and fifty to pay tribute and to do labor on a rotating basis, and these burdens sparked another type of migration. Those who ran away from their communities of origin to "hide out" in distant communities and avoid the labor and tribute requirements were called forasteros (outsiders) or vagabonds. Mitimaes as Incaic transplants, camayos as economic colonists, and forasteros as runaways were a major influence in the transformation of the ethnic composition of Pelileo.

Colonial administrators resettled native populations into concentrated villages called *reducciones*, where the indigenous population could be more easily controlled to facilitate Christian indoctrination and labor and tribute obligations. Pelileo was "reduced" by the Spaniard Antonio de Clavijo in 1584.[4] The Crown awarded Spanish conquistadors for their service with land and indigenous labor. An encomienda was a grant of indigenous labor to a Spaniard, called an encomendero, who was responsible for making sure the indigenous people received proper religious instruction. Encomiendas referred to labor, not land, and that labor could be sent to different regions. Nevertheless, the crown had a prohibition on establishing obrajes in the place where one had an encomienda, which referred to the area where the indigenous people of one's encomienda reside. Encomiendas were granted for a limited period (*vida*) after which they reverted to the Crown.

In 1588 the Crown awarded lands in Pelileo and Ambato to Pedro de la Parra, the son of Hernando de la Parra, "one of the first conquistadors and settlers in this city and the provinces of this kingdom [Quito]."[5] The legal ritual that marked possession of the lands was witnessed by the leaders of the Chumaquí. This award of land is key to understanding the indigenous history of Pelileo and ethnogenesis of the Salasacas. De la Parra's heirs would later inherit different tracts of land, but by the eighteenth century, his descendants had to sell the land to indigenous people, who transformed the plots into an indigenous ethnic territory. Hernando de la Parra was also awarded an encomienda granting him rights to the labor of the Chumaquí.[6]

An anonymous report from 1605 describes the indigenous population of Pelileo as being divided into three parcialidades, each with its own cacique: the Guambaló, with 768 people, the Chumaquí, with 530 people, and the camayos "who belong to diverse encomiendas and caciques of other provinces; because since the time of the Inga they are designated as camayos and hortelanos [gardeners] of the caciques for the cultivation of coca."[7] The writer reported the camayos to be one thousand people, under the native governor Don Cristobal Alomaliza, who, he said, was very poor. The report went on to describe the obraje of San Ildefonso in the "valley of Pilato," where up to sixty black men and women worked as well as some native volunteer workers. The fulling mill was next to the obraje. In the jurisdiction of Ambato there were also four centers for processing century plant fibers. The report does not specify where these centers were located, but one may have been in Pelileo. In chapter 8 I suggest that this was an activity in which the Sigchos Collanas were engaged.

ENCOMIENDAS

By the mid-seventeenth century, the encomendero of the Chumaquí was Antonio Lopez de Galarza, who also held the encomienda of the Pilalata. It is not clear how the encomienda went from de la Parra to Galarza. It might have reverted to the Crown after de la Parra's tenure and then later been granted to Galarza. The Guambaló belonged to a Crown encomienda. The Sigchos Collanas originally belonged to an encomienda of the duke of Uceda, who granted the encomienda to an order of Spanish nuns based in Madrid, the Monjas (or Madres) Bernardas del Santisimo Sacramento de Madrid. Administrators were appointed in the Audiencia of Quito to manage the Bernardas' encomiendas. The caciques of the Sigchos Collanas sent camayos out from their homeland in the *corregimiento* (jurisdiction) of Latacunga to various parts of the Audiencia, including the Chota Valley in northern Ecuador, and Pelileo. The encomienda to which indigenous people belonged shaped their experience of Quito's textile economy. The Pilalata, Chumaquí, and Guambaló belonged to encomiendas that were required to work in the obraje. The Sigchos Collanas did not, so they had a different historical experience. In chapter 8 I address the question of the economic activities of the Sigchos Collanas.

MITIMAES AND FORASTEROS

Since indigenous tribute was collected through the caciques of each parcialidad, runaways had no parcialidad or cacique in their new places of residence, and the Crown was losing tribute. Therefore, officials grouped them into "Crown parcialidades" under a cacique of forasteros in order to collect some tribute, although at a lower rate than what local natives paid, since forasteros lacked rights to communal lands. These aggregrates of forasteros were then referred to as "Crown forasteros" or "Indians of the Royal Crown." Some of these may have been descendants of earlier migrants from Peru. A census of Ambato from 1641 of the *vagamundos* (vagabonds) or forasteros states: "An Indian who said his name is don Fernando Cuxigualpa, principal tribute collector of the vagabond Indians of the Royal Crown of the Asiento of Ambato of the cacicazgo [chiefdom] and government of don Agustin Ullanaboa . . . declared some vagabond Indians who have neither caciques nor encomenderos nor do they pay tribute and have not been registered [*visitados*] because they belong to the Royal Crown and their parents were as well because they were forastero Indians, migrants from the province of Cusco to the town of Patate."[8] One of these Indian "vagabonds" was Joan Coro, whose cacique was Don Agustin de la Nasca. He worked in the obraje of San Ildefonso (which was already owned by María de Vera) and had been raised there, even though he had never been included in the census for tribute purposes. This 1641 census coincides with the Crown's attempt to aggregate forasteros.[9]

Other evidence of migration from the central Andes to the jurisdiction of Ambato is the last name Anasca, which historian Pedro Reino Garcés traces to migrants from Nasca, Peru, who went to Chillogallo in the city of Quito first and later settled in the jurisdiction of Ambato and other places.[10] In 1641 the cacique Augustin de la Nasca governed Indians in Ambato who had not yet been incorporated into tribute rolls. This included men whose parents were forasteros as well as men who had been abandoned as babies, left at the doorsteps of indigenous people or Spaniards, or found "on the road" and raised by single native women. They didn't know their ethnic groups or parcialidad, nor where their parents were from (except for the one who said his parents were from Cuzco), and therefore were not paying tribute. Two of these unincorporated men, possibly from Peru, had the last name Caxamarca. In the 1630s and '40s they were grouped, for tribute purposes, under the native governor de la Nasca.

De la Nasca said he was a descendant of natives of the "city of Cusco." If Reino Garcés is correct that the surname Nasca or Anasca indicates ancestry from Nasca, Peru, then perhaps the cacique's ancestors had migrated to Cuzco, and later they or their descendants migrated to Quito. Either way, de la Nasca claimed origins in Peru. He said that he inherited lands in the region (in Riobamba and Ambato) from his grandmother, whose last name was Culqui Guarmi. Culqui remained a feminine surname in Pelileo throughout the colonial period, and it indicates central or southern Andean origins (from modern-day Peru or Bolivia). Don Augustin, the son of the cacique Don Jorge de la Nasca, was able to hold an elite position by finding the "hidden Indians" and incorporating them into a Crown parcialidad as forasteros. In doing so, he secured a place for himself and his descendants,[11] and also protected unincorporated natives from being poached by local caciques who were pressured to send indigenous laborers into the service of Spaniards.

Individual claims of origins in Cuzco or other parts of the central Andes must be taken with a grain of salt, because there was an incentive to be incorporated into a Crown parcialidad of forasteros rather than a private encomienda:

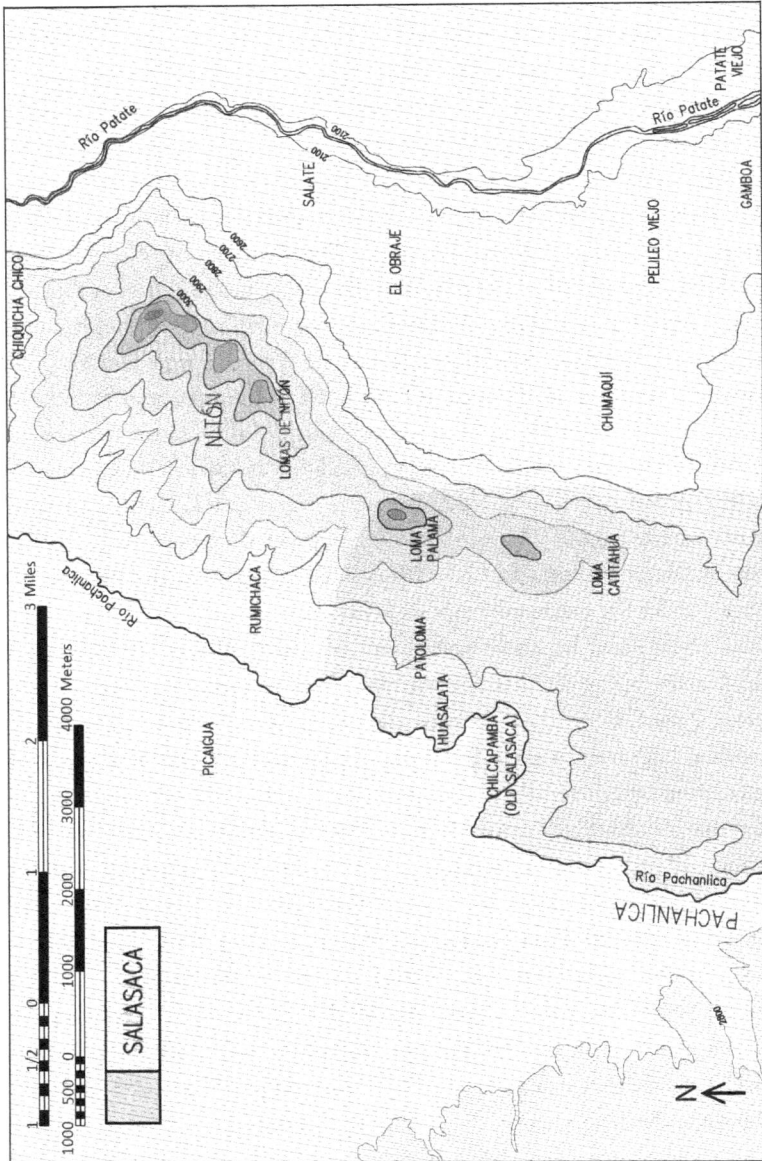

FIGURE 10. Topographic Map of Pelileo, Including Salasaca. Map by Alejandro González.

"[I]n 1626 one encomendero charged bitterly that any Indian who wished to be exempt from normal tribute and mita obligations had only to say that he was from Cuzco or some other distant province; he would then be summarily attached to the crown at the expense of his encomendero."[12] Indigneous individuals used a strategy of exploiting colonial administrative categories of indigenous parcialidades, taking advantage of the legal code that relieved forasteros of the pressures of the tribute and mita. Nevertheless, if the evidence of individual claims is taken together with evidence of mitimae and camayo populations from Peru who were sent to Pelileo, there is no doubt that some indigenous people of Pelileo were descendants of migrants from Peru.

COCA AND CAMAYOS

The presence of coca fields in Pelileo was one factor that contributed to the diversity of the indigenous population at the time of the Spanish conquest. Coca was a luxury good that was controlled by indigenous elites in the early colonial period. The Inca even brought people from Peru to work coca fields in Ecuador. The Inca emperor Atahualpa and his heir, the "Auqui," owned coca fields in Pelileo, and the cultivators and supervisors of the harvest were relatives of the Inca from Cuzco.[13] In 1597, the widow of the Auqui claimed rights over the camayos working the royal Inca coca fields in the region where Pelileo is located. Native lords from other regions of the Audiencia of Quito also owned coca fields that were granted to them by the Inca; in 1601 the cacique of Chambo (Riobamba) owned three coca fields in Pelileo.[14] One known location of the Inca's coca fields was in Guambaló. Another coca-producing site was Camboa, probably modern-day Gamboa located in old Pelileo (figure 10). Early seventeenth-century documents locate Camboa in the Valley of Pingue, near the Patate River.

By the early seventeenth century, both native caciques and Spaniards owned lands in Camboa and sold lands to each other. In 1607 Alonso Sanches de Ana, a Spanish resident in the "Valley of Coca," sold two plots of land in Camboa to another Spaniard. Sanches de Ana had previously purchased the land from a cacique of Pelileo, Don Francisco Chango, probably the common ancestor to the caciques of the Guambaló and Pilalata of Pelileo.[15] In 1610, a coca field (with all the coca) was used as restitution in a court case between an indigenous couple from Pelileo and their *principal* (secondary chief).[16] The cacique of the town of Quero also had an orchard of some unkown product in Camboa, but since he had other lands to tend to, he could not take advantage of the property.

In 1607 he wanted to sell the lands so that he could use the money. According to one witness, the cacique was thinking of using the money to invest in sheep, which makes sense given the growing demand for wool textiles in South America at the time.[17] In fact, the cacique's request to sell the land coincides with the increase of the Crown's granting obraje licenses in Quito. According to Ortiz de la Tabla, for the entire seventeenth century the majority of obraje licenses were granted between the years 1606 and 1610.[18] Other caciques, including the cacique of the camayos who cultivated coca, owned lands in Pingue and Guambaló.[19] In 1641, the cacica of Guambaló, Doña Francisca Alomaliza, declared a piece of land in Pingue called "Coca Angelis-lica" in her will. She also reported owning lands in Pachanlica (modern-day Benitez and Totoras) and three hundred head of sheep.[20] Wills show that caciques and cacicas were leaving lands in the coca-producing region to their heirs (daughters as well as sons), selling some to Spaniards or exchanging with each other, and leaving some to be sold to pay for Masses for their souls. They were also investing in the sheep that produced the raw material for Quito's textile economy. Soon, coca would cease to be a luxury item in the northern Andes,[21] and Spaniards would invest in growing sugarcane in the warm valleys.

SUGARCANE

In the seventeenth century, Spaniards started converting lands of Patate into sugarcane fields and sugar mills. For the indigenous peoples of Patate, this meant that they were displaced from their lands and cut off from their main source of water for irrigation. Some of their lands were sold to Spaniards by native elites. Don Joan Chipantiza, a cacique and governor of Patate, founded his own sugar mill on lands belonging to his indigenous subjects. He used the profits for the benefit of his own soul: in his will the cacique ordered that profits from the mill pay for a chaplaincy and Catholic Masses. Around 1631, the sugar mill was rented out to a member of one of the most powerful indigenous cacical (chiefly) dynasties of colonial Quito, Don Francisco Hati, the cacique of San Miguel (Latacunga).[22] The returns from renting out the sugar mill supported the cacique's elite daughters, Doñas Paula, Cecilia, Marta, and María Chipantiza, and his son, Don Joan Chipantiza, in addition to the chaplaincy for the late cacique's soul. The cacique's son sold the lands and sugar mill to the encomendero Galarza, claiming that the friar assigned to Pelileo convinced him to sell it. Chipantiza decided this was a good idea, because he had heard at the time that the land judge Antonio de Melgar was *taking* Indians' lands from them. He decided it was better to be compensated something for his lands by selling them, rather than get nothing. This came at a great cost to the indigenous commoners from the parcialidad of Yamate, who lost access to the water that they had always used to irrigate their orchards.

The buyer, Galarza, had another sugar mill called Santo Thomas near his (wife's) obraje of San Ildefonso. Spaniards, in particular Galarza and Francisco de Villagomez, used their mayordomos (estate managers) to violently keep indigenous people from getting access to water, making it impossible for the local indigenous people to grow their food. The mayordomos were armed with daggers and sticks and would beat the natives if they tried to irrigate their fields as their ancestors had. At one of his mills Galarza placed two African slaves to keep the local indigenous people from channeling water. According to one cacique, the lands were sterile, and indigenous people were leaving, until the Dominican friar Alonso de Aponte intervened.[23] Friar Alonso intervened on behalf of indigenous people on more than one occasion, which put him in conflict with Galarza.

In sum, in the early seventeenth century, local caciques as well as caciques from other towns owned lands in Pelileo, including coca fields. Some caciques began to invest in the growing economic enterprises of colonial Quito by focusing on sheep and sugarcane. The caciques sold some of these native lands to Spaniards. Spanish elite families owned ranches and sugarcane fields, and Galarza and his wife María de Vera owned the large obraje of San Ildefonso with its surrounding ranches, cane fields, and sugar mills.

OBRAJES IN SEVENTEENTH-CENTURY QUITO

The labor draft (mita) required indigenous males between the ages of eighteen and fifty to serve as workers on a rotating basis, and the Indian tribute forced men to work as "volunteers" in the obrajes in order to meet their obligations. Reports to the Crown expressed the rampant abuse of indigenous people in Quito's textile sweatshops, including debt servitude, forced labor, exploitation of workers' wives and children, starvation, beatings, and whippings. Workers were paid in cloth or food rather than money, if they were paid at all. Goods (maize, barley, cloth, hats, and wax candles) were always advanced at highly inflated prices, so that the artificial debt that workers incurred could never be paid off with their labor, and they became debt slaves. If they tried to sell these goods at the market, they were paid much lower prices than what the mill owner claimed that the goods were worth. Obraje owners were not fulfilling their obligations to allow the indigenous people time off on Sundays or Catholic feast days, and they were not allowing them enough time to sow crops on their own fields in order to feed themselves and their families as the Crown had ordered. Some concerned Spaniards wanted the obrajes to be demolished. However, officials also recognized Quito's economic dependence on the obrajes. In 1621, the *oidor* (magistrate) Matias de Peralta tried to strike a balance between the desire to end the brutal oppression of indigenous people with the economic need to keep the obrajes going. In the *Ordenanzas de obrajes*, Peralta established specific regulations for Quito's obrajes.

According to the *Ordenanzas*, each obraje was to have three indigenous officials: the alcalde, the alguacil, and the indigenous record keeper called *quipocama*. The alcalde was responsible for making the natives attend Catholic religious lessons, called the *doctrina*, in the morning prior to entering the mill. Obrajes in which two indigenous sectors or parcialidades served would have two alcaldes. The workers would be instructed in the Catholic prayers and other teachings, either in Spanish or Quechua, by a blind catechist.[24] The indigenous alguacil (constable), would assist the alcalde in gathering the Indians for work and had the right to go into the towns to round up those who were not attending.

Peralta stated that a *quipo* (or *khipu*) master should be present in every obraje to ensure that the natives were not cheated out of their work. The *khipu* was a pre-Columbian accounting device consisting of a cord from which several knotted strings were hung. The knots of different styles and colors represented numbers of specific kinds of goods, people, or units of time.[25] The Inca accountants were called *quipocamayuj* (quipo masters), and in Quito these were called quipocamas. Peralta not only encouraged this system of native record keeping but ordered it. In doing so, he created another official position for an indigenous specialist, along with the alcalde and alguacil. The quipo master was supposed to be present when the maestro (foreman) of the obrjae recorded the tasks completed by each worker, how much cloth was produced, and the number of days worked by each native. According to Peralta's guidelines, the quipocama should make his knots, and the maestro note in his book, the days worked while in the presence of the Indians, and the book and quipo could be cross-checked to prevent fraud.[26] In this way, Peralta said, the maestro could not put fewer days than what the natives actually worked, and the quipocama could not add days. It is one of Peralta's many recommendations for reducing the fraud that was taking place in the obrajes; since the workers didn't trust the maestro (with good reason), why not have one of their own record keepers present? It may seem strange that a Spanish official insisted on this pre-Columbian technique of native record keeping, but the order is an example of what Salomon calls the "khipu-paper colonial interface,"[27] in which Spaniards relied on native record keepers for producing their own legal documents, or in this case, for cross-checking account books.

However, official orders were often ignored, and it is not clear how many obrjae owners actually employed a quipo master as they were supposed to. The only reference I have found to an actual quipocama was from a 1604 report from the community obraje of Latacunga, in which an indigenous accountant kept track of the clothing made there and earned a salary of forty pesos per year.[28] In contrast, indigenous workers from San Ildefonso repeatedly complained that they were cheated because no indigenous person was ever present when the account books were made, so the order to have a quipocama present in the mill was not followed in mid-seventeenth-century Pelileo. However, the indigenous labor bosses on the haciendas that were part of San Ildefonso were called quipocamas. I will discuss this indigenous social position in chapter 3.

CONCLUSION

In the first part of the seventeenth century, there were several indigenous groups living in Pelileo, each with their own caciques: the Pilalata, the Chumaquí, the Guambaló, and the migrant colonies of camayos, among others. There were forasteros of unknown origin, as well as descendants of mitimaes from Peru. Spaniards, who had African slaves as their personal servants, controlled land and indigeous labor. Spaniards and caciques bought and sold lands to each other. Coca production faded, and sugarcane (in warm valleys) and sheep herding (in the páramos) became the new economic activities. Textile production became the mainstay of Quito's economy as elites obtained Crown licenses to erect obrajes. The merchant Alonso Guadalupe Espinsoa was granted a license to found the obraje of San Ildefonso, to be worked by his African slaves and also "volunteer" natives. In 1594 a wealthy citizen of Quito, Juan de Vera Mendoza, purchased the obraje, and from there it passed to his grandaughter María de Vera Mendoza. When Antonio Lopez de Galarza married María de Vera, they pooled their resources to create a mill-ranch complex with ninety African slaves and hundreds of indigenous laborers. The next chapter provides an analysis of indigenous experiences with the slaves of San Ildefonso.

CHAPTER 2

AFRICANS AND ANDEANS IN PELILEO
(1630–1666)

A
LONSO DE la Peña Montenegro, who served as archbishop of Quito from 1653 to 1687, described the natives of the Audiencia of Quito as "slaves of the slaves," who were the targets at whom the blacks (negros) aimed their anger.[1] While the report was not representative of black-indigenous relations everywhere, it did fit the case of Pelileo. The labor hierarchy at San Ildefonso created tensions between Africans and Andeans, not only in the obraje but even across the bridge, over the Patate River, and into the town of Patate. Here I analyze specific stories of individual interactions between black and indigenous people, based on indigenous testimonies from the 1661 investigation against Galarza by the oidor (judge) Don Luis Joseph Merlo de la Fuente and his commission from Quito (herein referred to as the Quito commission), which included a Quichua interpreter and an alternate interpreter as a substitute, as well as scribes. Some of the testimonies are written in the first-person voice, while others are written in the third-person voice ("this witness"), perhaps based on the style of the particular scribe. The stories uncover the little-known history of the African presence in Pelileo, and they contradict popular beliefs about the isolation of the indigenous population. After describing the situation of San Ildefonso in the mid-seventeenth century, I divide the chapter into types of interactions between Africans and Andeans: the presence of blacks when Andean obraje workers died, the effects of an impoverished slave force on

the indigenous people of the towns, and the indigenous wet nurses to African babies. While the obraje labor structure created hostilities between black and indigenous people, I pay attention to rare expressions of empathy that can be teased out from the indigenous testimonies. The stories told here are part of the indigenous history of Pelileo and show the type of contact Andeans had with Africans in the seventeenth century.

THE QUITO COMMISSION

In his 1666 conclusion to the investigation of abuses at the obraje of San Ilde-fonso,[2] Merlo de la Fuente said that Galarza had made "free Indians into slaves, and his blacks, being slaves, were freer, at least he lets them sleep and gives them relief."[3] Slaves were expensive, so the loss of a slave was a loss of an investment for the owner. On the other hand, if a native worker died, the administrators could send the mill authorities into the countryside to get another one. These authorities included the indigenous watchman, called "alcalde," and the white *recogedor*, who would round up indigenous people and bring them to the obraje. Not only were indigenous people considered expendable, but the cost of feeding those locked in the obraje was passed on to the indigenous family members. Although the Crown offered special legal protections to indigenous people, these were often ignored in practice.

Some indigenous people had tried to file legal complaints prior to the 1661 investigation. Not only were they ignored, but when they returned to Pelileo they were whipped for complaining. Unfortunately, when Merlo de la Fuente finally led the investigation, he only took the testimonies of the indigenous people, thereby silencing the voices of the Africans themselves. The idea was to build a case against the Spanish encomendero who ran his wife's obraje, so the testimonies about black abuse of indigenous people were meant as an indictment of the Spaniard who owned them, not the slaves themselves. The document provides the slave names, which give clues to their ethnic origins, and I attempt to recover whatever information I can about them. During his investigation of the case, Merlo de la Fuente went from Quito to Pelileo, where he lived in a small hut for five months while he recorded the testimonies of local natives. He documented the crimes against them, including twenty-two deaths, personally inspected the mill and its dungeon, and interrogated the owner and administrators.[4]

SAN ILDEFONSO IN THE 1660S

There were slaves in the jurisdiction of Ambato since at least 1604, and records show that Spanish families sold individual slaves, mostly personal servants, to one another throughout the colonial period.[5] In both the textile and sugar mills, African slaves were given the job of guarding and punishing indigenous workers. The anonymous report from 1605 stated that the obraje of San Ildefonso existed in the "Pilato valley" and that it had sixty black male and female slaves and volunteer (as opposed to labor-draft) Indians who received a salary and who wanted to work there due to "good treatment" and a favorable climate.[6] By the 1660s San Ildefonso "had 130–200 African slaves" working there, and an even larger number of Indians: "Between 1619 and 1665 over 2,000 different Indians had accounts with this obraje."[7] To expand his textile-sugar mill enterprise, Galarza built another sugar mill, Santo Thomas, near the obraje, and this mill was worked by local indigenous people from Pelileo. The mill went from Galarza's son, Don Joseph Lopez de Galarza, to María de Vera's grandson, Francisco de Borja, and was worked by seven Chumaquí, ten Pilalata, and nineteen Guambaló,[8] along with African slaves. Galarza also used a Chumaquí man's debt to force him to "sell" his lands, which then became part of Galarza's estate.

In his study of San Ildefonso, Jaime Costales accurately describes it as a "torture chamber."[9] The abuse is well documented. Indigenous men, women, children, and elderly people were beaten, mercilessly whipped, starved, shackled, sleep-deprived, and locked in a dungeon. People were locked in the obraje for debt or if it was suspected that they would run away. Elderly natives were abused, and children were kidnapped and beaten. One man said he was only eight years old when he was captured while walking to his family's field. There were many deaths from injuries, beatings, hunger, and illness contracted in the dungeon. Two common illnesses were called *sarna* and *pasmo* in the testimonies. While sarna is defined today as "scabies," it could refer to other parasitic or nonparisitic skin diseases, but witnesses related it to the open wounds in people's skin and the general unsanitary conditions of the dungeon. Pasmo could refer to the muscle spasms caused by tetanus, or to a host of other illnesses from respiratory problems to nausea and weakness. Whatever disease people referred to as pasmo, they attributed it to sleeping on the ground in the cold, humid dungeon. Indigenous witnesses who had spent time in the dungeon said that some prisoners slept directly on the ground, others on animal skins that their wives brought to them, and some sat up all night, away from the others, fearful of being contaminated by lice and fleas from the other prisoners. Merlo de la Fuente personally inspected the dungeon as part of his investigation. He described it as dark, with a stench, and crawling with fleas.

Andean workers, who were locked in the mill at night and guarded by the owners' African slaves so that they couldn't escape, were given high daily quotas for each task in the process of cloth production. When they did not meet these quotas on time, or if there was a flaw in the spun wool or the finished cloth, they were whipped. One man who worked in the mill testified that his son-in-law was whipped so badly that he was incapable of sitting down. Terrified of being whipped again, he worked all night by candlelight to finish his assigned task. A teenager who had not yet reached eighteen was forced into the obraje, where the foreman beat him in the small of the back with a weight. He returned home injured, emaciated, and weak, with puss coming out of the wound, and walked bent over with a cane, "like an old man." His parents said that he suffered like that for a year, and then died. One of the caciques of Guambaló, Don Gonzalo Puzia, was ordered to punish a subject who didn't finish his job on time by putting a rope around the man's neck and ordering two other indigenous men to hold his feet. If the men had grown tired and let go of his feet, the victim would have died from hanging. These are just a few of the many sufferings inflicted on the indigenous people. Knowing of the risk of harsh punishments, family members responded. They would bring products to the obraje, either as bond or to pay off a debt, to try to ransom their loved ones, but the bookkeepers made sure that the workers remained in perpetual debt that could not easily be paid off. So people came to the mill to help their family members meet their quotas. Parents whose children were taken and assigned impossible tasks would show up to help them complete the tasks, so that their children wouldn't be beaten. According to indigenous witnesses, women who were fearful that their husbands would run away from the obraje and abandon their families (as many men did) would enter the mill to help their husbands meet their quotas. In this way, the owners got free labor from family members.[10] If a worker did run away, the administrators would take his spouse or another family member to replace him. If a shackled worker managed to escape, the bookkeepers added the cost of the leg shackles to the debt.[11]

Black slaves in the position of *caporales* (labor bosses) were ordered to hold the natives down and whip them with hard, twisted leather, covered in hot ashes. The maestro Alonso Infante, whom the native workers referred to as "the bull," was so sadistic toward the workers that he gave names to the instruments of torture. The three different whips of hard, twisted leather were called "el barroso, el vermejo, and el valiente."[12] Some indigenous victims were whipped by two blacks at the same time, one on each side. The administrators wanted the slaves to whip the natives because, they said, one indio whipping another would be too compassionate, as "they didn't do it well."[13] Although Tyrer reported that there were 130–200 slaves at San Ildefonso in the 1660s, there were about 90 slaves (and a two-month-old baby girl named Gerónima) at the end of the criminal investigation in 1666. It is likely that this only referred to the slaves owned by Galarza, since he was the target of the investigation. María de Vera was deceased by 1666, but her heirs would have had slaves in the obraje, sugar mills, and associated estates. Among Galarza's ninety slaves that were confiscated as a result of the investigation, there was a roughly equal number of men and women. Some slaves lived in huts close to the mill. On their days "off" from the mill work (Sundays and fiestas), the native workers had to clean out the slaves' work quarters, and the slaves threatened to beat them if they didn't clean well.

Augustín Yumiquínga testified that when the indigenous wool carders worked together with the blacks, and the blacks saw them exchanging wool and food among themselves, some taking a bit of wool that they needed for their supply (perhaps after making a mistake in working the wool that they were allotted to be processed), the blacks would beat the native workers and scold them for taking from the "master's hacienda."[14] Natives of Pelileo also worked among slaves at Galarza's sugar mills. At the time of grinding sugar, they were sent to help with the process. One indigenous man, overworked and exhausted one night, started to fall asleep while working. Galarza's blacks whipped him, and when the man's mother tried to stop them, they punched her and called her a whore.[15]

Many of the local indigenous people did not know the names of the blacks who guarded them. Joan Yancha was one of the few who did. In his testimony he mentioned Diaguillo, the *capitan* (boss) who would beat the native workers with a stick; Chinchico and Carabalin, the *semaneros*, who also supervised the native workers; and Caten, the guard who made sure the indigenous prisoners did not escape at night. There were others, he said, whose names he didn't remember but who would sometimes steal the food that native Andean family members brought to the obraje for the workers. Africans also witnessed the deaths of Andeans in the mill.

INDIGNEOUS OBRAJE DEATHS

The deaths of workers due to torture and illnesses contracted in the mill and its dungeon are too numerous to discuss here. In his 1666 summary Merlo de la Fuente documented the deaths of twenty-two indigenous people from abuses in the obraje, and these were just the locals that were from Pelileo and known to the witnesses. There were other deaths of forasteros—indigenous people from other towns—whose names and families were unknown. Some had been sent there as prisoners for debt or petty crimes such as stealing. I selected a few cases of indigenous deaths for the details they provide about the presence of blacks when indigenous people died. Blacks' abuse of natives is well documented, but since the testimonies of the slaves themselves were never taken, we don't know their perspectives. Did they feel any compassion for the indigenous people, or did they see them as less than human? Or were they, as slaves, just trying to survive? Even the indigenous victims suggest that the latter was true, stating that "it was understood" (*se ha entendido*) that black slaves would steal from indios because the slaves were not properly fed and clothed, thereby placing the blame with Galarza.[16] One witness said that he noticed that on some days the administrators would give the slaves their rations of food, but on other days they did not.

In the immediate vicinity of the obraje, both indigenous people and slaves had their huts (*chozas*), while Spaniards had ranches in the area. When indigenous debt peons were finally sent out of the obraje "to be cured," some were already dying. Some of them couldn't make it home and died in the homes of blacks, native Andeans, or Spaniards. The following cases of the presence of blacks at the deaths of indigenous workers are taken from the testimonies of different indigenous witnesses who told their stories to the Quito commission.

CHRISTOBAL ALOPINTO

The witness Francisco Corcha, a middle-aged Guambaló man, declared in 1661 that he was forced to work in the obraje for more than thirty years, until the Dominican friar Alonso de Aponte released him along with the others, just a couple of months before he gave his testimony. Corcha served in the obraje along with his *compadre* (ritual kin), an indigenous man from Patate. When a worker named Christobal Alopinto was sent out of the obraje, he said, Alopinto was so sick that he only made it as far as the home of one of the slaves, where he died. Corcha was one of the men who had to carry the body from the slave's home to the church of Pelileo. He described the death as follows:

> [T]he maestros would place shackles on those who had run away and put them in the jail for one or two years, as [the maestros] saw fit, and the same with those who were there for debt. This witness knows it because he has seen it on many occasions and experienced the whippings himself, for which reason people die emaciated and consumed by hunger, as happened with an Indian named Christoval Alopinto about three years ago. Having been imprisoned in the dungeon with shackles for over a year, and only allowed out during the day so that he could work, as he was a rompedor [wool beater], he was consumed with hunger and walked around asking the other Indians who were eating lunch or eating parched corn [*tostado*] or greens [*yerbas*] brought from their homes, asking that they give him some for the love of God, and on the last day he was in such a state that he couldn't even move, they took him out [of the mill] and brought him to this town [Pelileo], carrying him, and in this state they said that they carried him to the home of a black man from the mill, whose name he doesn't know, where he died, and that the next day they made this witness and other Indians carry him, and bring him to this town where they left the body at the house of some relatives, he doesn't remember where it was nor who they were, nor their names, only that they buried him in the church of this town and that Father Vallejo had taken his confession, having been in the mill.[17]

The priest took confessions of workers who died from hunger, illness, and beatings. While some, like Fr. Vallejo, perfunctorily performed their religious duties and buried the bodies of native victims of the obraje, the Dominican friar Aponte repeatedly defended the natives and took legal action against Galarza. Aponte worked with the native alcalde de la doctrina (church assistant) Juan Machuca, who brought the fearful witnesses forward to give their testimonies.

This testimony shows the social distance between African slaves and natives, who worked together in the mill but didn't seem to know each other's names. Did the black man try to help save or cure Christobal Alopinto? Did he offer anything to eat or drink to those who were carrying the body? Or was he indifferent, too concerned with his own survival to worry about an unknown indio, and unable to do anything to help anyway? The lack of information on the black man in whose home Cristobal Alopinto died suggests social distance between blacks and indigenous people of the obraje. Likewise, in the next case, when Francisca Yansapanta was searching for her missing husband until it was dark, she spent the night in the home of "a black woman" (*una negra*) who lived close to the mill.

FRANCISCO QUISPE

The caciques of each parcialidad were responsible for assigning their subjects as workers in the Spanish sphere.[18] Francisco Quispe belonged to the parcialidad of Pilalata and was a subject of Don Andres Chango. He lived with his wife Francisca, a native of Machache "in Pansaleo," and his mother, a Guambaló woman, on the ranch of the Spaniard Don Pedro Flores. One night, two principales (secondary chiefs) came to the house to tell Francisco that his cacique had named him as *gañan* (worker). They deceived him, telling him that they were taking him to work on the ranch of another Spaniard named General Francisco de Villagomez, so Quispe went willingly. His wife, Francisca, followed, believing that she would accompany him. But after they passed the church of Patate, the principales informed him that he was really headed for the obraje, at which point Quispe became very upset and tried to get away. So the principales tied his hands and took him there by force.

At the mill, he spent the first couple of days in the dungeon. When he was let out, he saw a young man get whipped twice in the same day, and, fearful of suffering similar repeated punishments, Quispe decided to make a run for it that night. He jumped over the wall in the section of the mill where the black women worked, and the foreman and two black men were sent to chase after him. Rather than allow himself to be captured, Quispe threw himself into the Patate River and drowned. One witness said that she saw him in the river desperately hanging on to a branch.

Quispe's wife, Francisca, unaware of her husband's escape, had gone to the obraje, perhaps to bring him food. While waiting to see her husband, she heard some black men and the foreman say that an Indian had escaped and they were looking for him. It was the responsibility of the slaves to count how many indigenous workers were locked in at night, and then count them again in the morning. Francisca said that a black man, whom she "didn't recognize because it was dark," but identified by another witness as the guard Caten, came and told her that her husband had left and that she should leave too. By then the guard surely knew that Francisca's husband had drowned in the river. The foreman also lied to her, telling her that her husband had gone home. Since it was too dark for her to make it home, she had to stay at the first house available, which was the home of a black woman. The next morning she went to look for her husband at his mother's house, but, not finding him, she went back to the obraje. She saw her husband's white wool mantel hanging from a quishuar tree on the river bank near the obraje, at which point she suspected that her husband had fallen into the river. The next day, a Friday, Francisca and her mother-in-law, Angelina, went to look for the body downriver; and near the sugar mill of the Spaniard Francisco Ballesteros, down from the town of Patate, they saw the body half-buried in a sandbank in the river. Since the two women could not retrieve the body by themselves, they went to the priest of Patate to ask for assistance. On Sunday, the two women returned to the river, but the sandbar was flooded and the river swollen, and they never recovered the body.

The cacique, the priest, and Quispe's uncle continued the search for the body but never found it.[19] The mill alcalde Juan Challay declared that the foreman Christobal Lopez Noboa came to town for the priest to give a Mass for the soul of the drowned man, and they held the Mass in Patate (rather than Pelileo) "to cover up the death" (*por que callese la dicha muerte*).[20] From whom were they trying to keep the death quiet? The family and other obraje workers knew about it. Holding a Mass outside of Pelileo suggests that the foreman wanted to avoid dealing with the priest in Pelileo.[21] If he was trying to cover up the death, the indigenous witnesses who told the story of Francisco Quispe assured that the death would not be silenced.

Both blacks and natives talked about the incident in the obraje, and indigenous workers retold the story with morbid details. It became a haunting tale, since several witnesses said that they "heard" that the body *was* pulled out, and it was decomposed and eaten by buzzards and vultures. Although Quispe's wife and mother said that the body was never found, the tale seems to be a gruesome reminder of a grim fate that other runaways could suffer as well. When a worker did run away, the recogedor or alcalde would sometimes take a family member to replace him, as in the following case.

JUAN PIMBOMASA

Juan Pimbomasa was an elderly Guambaló man who was taken to the obraje to replace his son, who had run away. He wasn't in the obraje more than two weeks before he died there. Pimbomasa didn't know how to do the tasks well and was slow, and he was repeatedly whipped for that reason. The maestro Alonso

Infante took a six-pound iron and beat him in the ear. Pimbomasa passed out on the ground, and some black men sprayed water from their mouths into his ear until they revived him. Infante accused Pimbomasa of "faking it" and being lazy, and he sent him to do another task. The next day they brought Pimbomasa a load of wool to beat. Since he wasn't skilled in the job, he only finished two pounds of wool. Infante ordered two blacks, Alonso Cuzata (or Cussata) and Juan de Nicolas (both deceased by the time of the investigation), to whip Pimbomasa at the same time, one on each side. When they were too exhausted to continue, Infante ordered two native *alguaciles* (constables) to relieve them. One was Francisco Cuchitullo, who had long since fled town when the investigation took place, and the other was Andres Challuy, who described how Pimbomasa begged for mercy, but Infante ordered the lashings to continue. Pimbomasa was given 130 lashings, and between this and the blow he received the day before, he couldn't move and was nearly unconscious. Indigenous witnesses saw him lying on the ground. When he was finally able to move, he could only crawl. He was then locked in the dungeon.

Pimbomasa had two daughters, María and Lucía. María's husband, Ventura, was working in the obraje but in different quarters. When Ventura saw his father-in-law's injuries, he went to find his wife's sister to tell her that her father was not doing well. Since Ventura was allowed to leave the obraje, it is likely that he was considered a reliable worker who was not a flight risk. Lucía was living near Chumaquí on a ranch owned by Miguel de la Parra. She was staying there with her husband, who was in hiding after having fled out of fear of Alonso Infante. When Ventura told them the news, Lucía's husband told her that she should go to the mill to see her father. When she got there, she saw her father in a bad state. Weak and trembling, with pain throughout his body, he was desperately trying to finish his job of spinning wool so that he would not suffer further punishments. When he saw his daughter, he began to cry. He showed her the wounds on his back and buttocks from all the lashings. He begged his daughter to help with the job, since he was physically incapable. Lucía began to massage her father's back, but then Infante came in the room, accused Pimbomasa of faking it, and beat him with a cane. When Lucía protested, Infante punched her in the face. When Infante left, Lucía told her father to rest while she finished spinning the wool. Pimbomasa wandered to a room where the black women were cooking, perhaps to warm himself by the fire. He remained there until the next day, unable to move, while his daughter Lucía finished one job and started the next one that had been assigned to her father.

Pimbomasa's other daughter, María, was also in the mill, helping her husband, Ventura, spin wool. Pimbomasa sensed that he was dying, and so he sent for María and asked her to call for the chapel master (*maestro de capilla*), to make a will. Instead, she returned to help her husband with his task. Around lunch time, Pimbomasa began hemorrhaging from the mouth and nose. He was face down, near the fire. Others came and called María, who took her father in her arms until she felt him go cold, and he died there "without confessing or making a will."[22] At this time, Infante was in the mill with two slaves, who seemed to be father and son, perhaps belonging to María de Vera's son or grandson, Francisco de Borja. According to Pimbomasa's daughter María, when she saw Infante, "out of a daughter's love" she boldly told the maestro that her father did not die from illness, but because of the beatings he received, at which point Infante punched her in the face and accused her of lying. Then, grabbing his dagger, he was "about to kill her" when "Borja's blacks stepped in between them to defend her." In her declaration to the commission María said she didn't know the names of the blacks, and she had not seen them in the obraje since then.[23]

Lucía, Ventura, and one of Borja's slaves who was there with his son helped carry the body, wrapped in Ventura's poncho, out of the mill to Lucía's home on a nearby hill. When Maria "removed her father's shirt to wrap him for burial . . . she saw his back and buttocks, which were black and blue, injured from all the lashes they had given him, which caused her to feel compassion."[24] The daughters had no money for a funeral, and the body stayed there for three or four days. To get money for the funeral, Ventura went to see the lieutenant of Ambato and María de Vera, who was in Ambato at the time. María de Vera said she didn't know why Ventura was complaining about the death; didn't he know that everyone dies because it's God's will? If his father-in-law died, she added, it was because his time had come. Furthermore, she said that if the maestro did whip his father-in-law, it was due to the old man's laziness. She sent Ventura back to Pelileo and told him to bury his father-in-law, but she gave him a document for either Infante or for the priest, Fr. Vallejo (the testimonies say both), to hold a funeral and bury Pimbomasa. When Ventura returned to the mill, Infante was furious that he had gone to complain in Ambato. Ventura said in the investigation that he was there with Fr. Vallejo when Infante pulled out his dagger, but the priest and Borja's slaves stopped him. Infante gave María three *patacones* for her father's funeral and told her, and a nephew who had witnessed the punishment, to keep quiet. Pimbomasa was buried in the church of Pelileo.

Both María and her husband recall being protected from the maestro's dagger by slaves. The differences between María's recollection and that of her husband are probably due to the amount of time that had passed since the incident and the recording of the testimony. After ten years, it's natural that the witnesses might not remember all the details clearly. It is possible that María is confusing the exact day on which Infante became enraged and pulled out his dagger. She recalls telling Infante that her father *did not* die from natural causes, which seems a likely response to María de Vera's suggestion that Pimbomasa died a natural death because "his time had come." Perhaps María was with her husband, Ventura, when he returned to the obraje, when Infante became enraged at the suggestion that he was responsible for the elderly man's death. Then it would make sense that they both remember Infante pulling out his dagger, and two black men stepping in between them to prevent another killing. On the other hand, it is possible that Infante, "the bull," threatened both of them with his dagger on different occasions, and Borja's slaves happened to be there to stop him, especially if those slaves often accompanied Infante (perhaps as bodyguards). Given his sadism toward the Andeans, the presence of black slaves might have been what was preventing the indigenous people from rising up against the maestro.

What is common in all these cases is the presence of blacks at the moment of death of natives, and yet the natives involved, for the most part, didn't know the names of the blacks who were present. The black man and his son who defended María from being stabbed, and who helped carry her father's body to the house, were only known as "Borja's blacks." Francisco Quispe's wife did not know the name of the black woman in whose home she stayed the night that her husband drowned. Corcha did not know the name of the home of the black man where Christobal Alopinto died when he was carried out of the obraje "to be cured." It is understandable that indigenous workers would not form social ties with the black caporales or capitanes who were charged with whipping them. There was also a language barrier: few of the indigenous witnesses who gave their testimonies were said to be ladinos in the Spanish language, so they relied on a Quichua-speaking interpreter. It might have made communication difficult. But the social distance is still striking, given that blacks were there during intimate moments of death. Even the indigenous wet nurses (discussed below) didn't know the families of the babies they cared for, and they referred to the babies as "Galarza's black babies" (*una negrita de Galarza*; i.e., they were his slaves). One case of an indigenous death was especially used by the commission as an example of the owner's culpability in allowing blacks to take out the frustrations on indigenous workers: the case of Francisco Yunapanta.

FRANCISCO YUNAPANTA

Francisco Yunapanta, a young, single man of Guambaló, was considered a flight risk since he had no house, wife, or children to keep him from running away. Therefore, he was locked in a cell at night, which he shared with a black named Zaruma. The name Zaruma gives a clue to his origins as a worker in the gold mines of southern Ecuador. Tardieu suggests that Zaruma may have been sold because mine production was down at the time.[25] There are two versions about what happened between Zaruma and Yunapanta. One witness said that Zaruma, who had escaped, had been drinking in the home of an indigenous man when he was recaptured and brought back to the obraje. In the version of Joan Yancha, who said he was a relative of Yunapanta, he heard the two arguing in the dungeon at night. The incident occurred because Yunapanta was reprimanding Zaruma for "using" the wife of a native Puruguay man. Yancha heard Yunapanta saying it was wrong to do this to the wives of the compañeros, and that he was going to report it to the maestro. Zaruma responded that it was none of his business and stabbed Yunapanta in the stomach with an instrument.[26] Joan Yancha said that he found his relative on the floor groaning, and then he saw the wound, which Zaruma admitted to causing.

The more common version told by the native workers is that, one morning, Yunapanta woke up and prayed, saying, "Praised be the Holy Sacrament," which enraged the recaptured slave. Zaruma woke up, yelling loudly, "Why don't you let me sleep!" He took a spindle and stabbed Yunapanta in the stomach, killing him. According to Tardieu, this rage was not based on racial hatred but on the hypocrisy of a "Christian" society that held people in captivity. Zaruma did not accept his condition of captivity; perhaps he felt that the prayer suggested Indian submission and acceptance.[27] As punishment for killing Yunapanta, Zaruma was hanged, dismembered, and his head hung from a tree in front of the mill for all to see. Yunapanta was buried in the church of Pelileo. Although this was an isolated incident, the Quito commission used it as a prime example of Galarza's irresponsibility in allowing his slaves to attack indigenous people.

TOWN LIFE

The presence of a large number of slaves in and around the mill did not just affect the obraje workers and their families. Black men, women, and children stole from local natives' homes, fields, and market spaces. Slaves took advantage of the fact that the natives went to church on Sundays and holy days. Native Andeans were required to attend Mass and religious lessons. Witnesses saw blacks from the obraje in groups—and some reported groups of up to ten or twenty blacks—who were raiding indigenous-owned fields and homes. Some of the indigenous people of Patate said that groups of black men, women, and children were robbing them, suggesting that they were going as slave families trying to get food.

Blacks, especially the women but also some men, would also steal the products that the indigenous women were trying to sell at the market, beating them and kicking them when the vendors tried to defend themselves. Some forced the Andean vendors to accept unequal exchanges. Favian Picha said that about six months before he gave his declaration to the commission in 1661, his wife had gone to Patate to sell or barter maize and barley. Some black women of the obraje came and took an *almud* (variable unit of measurement of dry goods) of maize from her and gave her a little salt. Colonial law prohibited blacks from being at native markets,[28] but in Patate and Pelileo, nobody was enforcing that law. This was not the sly pilfering of slaves stealing from masters as an act of resistance. Rather, the slaves, who were said to carry sticks and clubs, violently and publicly robbed the market women in broad daylight, taking advantage of the weak social position of the indigenous population.

During home robberies, slaves stole clothing and spools of spun cotton and wool that the indigenous women were going to use to make clothing for themselves and their families. They stole food, chickens, and guinea pigs as well. Pablo Tipantasi, a native of Patate and a church cantor, said that one day when he went to Mass with his wife, he left a mute woman in his house. When he returned, she signed to him that a group of four to six black men and women had entered the house and stolen their goods. Sesilia Cazachini, a widow, was going around crying after she had been robbed twice in eight months. The first time, she went to irrigate her orchard when she found two slaves from the obraje there. They pulled her hair and told her that if they had a knife, they would have killed her, and then they pushed her to the ground, where she passed out. When she regained consciousness, she returned home to find that she was missing a shawl (*lliglla*), skirt (*anaco*), the wool she had spun to make clothing, the cotton she had spun, and two hams (*jamones*) from a pig she had slaughtered. Months later, upon returning from Mass, she caught two black men in her house, who looked to her like the previous attackers. They threw her to the ground, kicked her and punched her, and robbed her house of clothing, spun wool, plates, and clay pots, leaving her with nothing but "the clothes she was wearing."[29]

Another witness who was charged with guarding the sugarcane fields said that groups of black men, women, and children would come and cut the sugarcane and make off with bundles of it, as they had recently done on All Saints' Day. Since they were armed with clubs and knives, the guard said he didn't dare go after them. On one occasion, the caciques of Patate got together and did chase after the blacks, but they said that they couldn't catch up to them, and, being "feeble Indians" who can't fight, they were afraid. They said that the blacks from the obraje had been robbing them for thirty years, and it was a problem for many indigenous people.

Some indigenous people even stopped going to Mass. One victim, Thomas Culpa, knew the names of some of the blacks. He said that he saw a black man named Caranza and another named Carabalin with the clothing that had been stolen from his house. Carabalin was also named by another obraje worker as one of the cruelest semaneros, the blacks who made the natives clean out their work quarters on weekends. These black semaneros changed every eight days on a rotating basis, and as Andres Quilcacuri said, "some are crueler than others, and in his time the cruelest are two blacks named Thomasillo and Joan de Carabalin."[30] Other indigenous people also knew some of the blacks from the obraje, and specifically accused those named Lorenzo, Juan, and Lucas of stealing. Another said he "knew" that blacks had robbed him because he saw that the footprints were large and "tuertas [crooked], as those of the blacks are."[31] When Fray Aponte was the parish priest, he prevented the blacks from stealing, and all the witnesses said that during that time the robberies stopped. But when Aponte left the parish, the stealing continued once again. When the teniente of Patate, Juan de Villafuerte, and the alguacil went with the caciques to chase after some blacks who were stealing, the slaves ran across the bridge to go back to San Ildefonso, laughing. As one native witness put it, the indios were abused captives "among blacks, our enemies in our own land and country."[32]

Since some witnesses specified seeing black women steal from the indigenous market women, and since slaves were raiding the indigenous people as families, even with their children, it seems obvious that they were trying to supplement their food and clothing supply. This was Galarza's responsibility, and he and his administrators were interrogated by the Quito commission about it. Some native witnesses acknowledged that the blacks stole out of necessity. But this does not explain the violence against the local natives. A lone indigenous widow who came upon a group of black men was certainly not physically threatening to them, so it was not necessary to kick and punch her. When the various maestros of the mill were interrogated about the situation, they washed their hands of responsibility. They insisted that on Sundays they made the slaves go to Mass in the obraje chapel or the church of Pelileo, and whatever the slaves did after Mass was not their responsibility. One foreman said that he whipped the blacks for stealing from the indigenous people and put some of them in shackles. The testimonies suggest that blacks may have attended Mass in the obraje chapel first, and then gone to raid the indigenous people's homes. Sesilia Cazachini said that the slaves were all wearing *xerga*, a "Spanish-style twill-weave wool fabric,"[33] and Joan Yancha said that the slaves wore rags while working in the obraje but dressed better on Sundays and festival days.[34]

If black women were acting as mothers when they took advantage of native market women, who occupied a weaker social position, in order to get food for themselves and their families, we know of another practice that affected slave women as mothers. The owner of the mill, María de Vera, would take newborn babies from their slave mothers and give them over to indigenous wet nurses to raise for two to three years. The bodies of both African and Andean women were pressed into the service of cloth production: African women for their labor in the mill; Andean women for their breast milk, to nurse the babies who were forcibly separated from their mothers. I turn now to the testimonies of the wet nurses.

AMAS DE NEGRITOS: THE INDIGENOUS WET NURSES

In the colonial Americas, wet-nursing usually involved lower-status women nursing higher-status babies or foundlings. The existence of the *amas de negritos*, the indigenous wet nurses to black slave babies, was a unique aspect of race relations at San Ildefonso. Since the act often involves intimacy between people of different social status, it is worth considering the practice of wet-nursing before imagining what this meant in colonial Pelileo, where one subordinate group nursed the babies of another subordinate group. Having wet nurses for slave babies is rare but not unheard of in history. Ancient Greek and Roman slave owners would hire wet nurses for slave babies in order to make the slave women fertile again so that they would bear more slaves for the owner. At San Ildefonso, indigenous women served as wet nurses to African slaves, but the owner's motivation was to get the slave mother back into the obraje spinning wool as soon as possible.

In the Americas, indigenous or black women usually nursed the babies of whites. When Europeans visited the Americas, they were sometimes shocked at the custom of having women of different races nurse white children. A nursing relationship that lasted beyond the weaning period was believed to create bonds of affection. An Englishman visiting the American South in the late eighteenth, early nineteenth century wrote home about the common custom of having white children nursed by black women, stating: "It is not unusual to hear an elegant lady say, Richard always grieves when Quasheehaw is whipped, because she suckled him."[35]

In the seventeenth-century Audiencia of Quito, the European-born Juan de Mañozca held a general prejudice against American-born Europeans (creoles), stating, "Even though the creoles do not have Indian blood, they had been weaned on the milk of Indian women, and hence the creoles like the Indians are children of fear."[36] In eighteenth-century Pelileo, the idea that nursing creates an intimate bond was used by one Spaniard to justify a claim to an indigenous servant's land. Theresa Fiallo said that she inherited the lands, which once belonged to the Pilalata, from her uncle, a priest. The uncle, she said, bought the lands from a Pilalata woman, María Criollo, but Fiallos added that the lands passed on to her uncle because "he was raised on her [Criollo's] milk and she was his servant." This is a contradictory statement. First, if one has inheritance rights, he doesn't have to purchase the lands. Second, masters do not inherit land from their indigenous servants. Although Fiallo said that her uncle *bought* the lands (part of modern-day Salasaca), she reinforced his rightful ownership by bringing up the fact that he was nursed by the owner of those lands, as if it created some type of kinship.

In Latin America, the lower-status wet nurse, a woman from a stigmatized race, occupied "the most contradictory of roles."[37] If the role of the wet nurse was contradictory in that women nursed those who would grow up to be their oppressors, it was even more complicated by the racial division of labor in Pelileo. It is not clear how much choice the lactating indigenous women had; according to some witnesses, the women were forced to serve as wet nurses, while others said that the women agreed to the job because they wanted the money. The native alcalde Juan Challay said that it was María de Vera who would take the newborn babies from their slave mothers and bring them to lactating indigenous women from Pelileo, whether the women were from Galarza's encomienda or not. Some wet nurses said that it was Galarza who gave them the black babies, probably a continuation of his wife's practice after she passed away. A cacique of Guambaló, Don Gabriel Centeno, said that both María de Vera and her administrator Antonio Lopez would take the black babies to lactating indigenous women, promising to pay them: "He saw and knew that the Indian women of this town nursed, by order of the said Doña María de Bera [sic], the negritos and negritas that the black women of the obraxe [sic] bore, paying them only fifteen patacones for the two or three years that it lasted, and aside from nursing them at their breasts, the said Indian women also fed them whatever food they had."[38] The cacique's own niece, Yzabel Choazinguil, was nursing a one-year-old black baby at the time that he gave his testimony in 1665. The indigenous wet nurses were supposed to receive fifteen patacones for two years of nursing and caring for the child, but most said they were never paid but offered clothing instead. Their job of working as wet nurses was one role that they fulfilled in the obraje's labor force, but in addition to that job, the mill affected them in their roles as mothers and wives. Their experiences show how the demand for Quito's textiles, and the greed of the owner and encomendero, affected indigenous family and social life outside of the mill.

María Comasanta belonged to Galarza's encomienda. At the time of her declaration she was a widow. Aside from serving as a wet nurse, both she and her late husband had served Galarza. Her husband spent two years taking care of Galarza's two hundred chickens. Galarza would use older men who were *reservados* (retired) from the labor draft to tend to his animals, and he kept them in perpetual debt by counting "lost" animals against their accounts. María Comasanta was also made to spin wool and make trips to Patate to purchase firewood, eggs, and chickens. She had to cook for Galarza's greyhounds, a particularly onerous job for the hungry indigenous women, who were prohibited from taking a single piece of meat that was meant for the dogs. Comasanta and her late husband had worked in various tasks for Galarza without being paid, and along with those other jobs, she was given a black baby girl to nurse "so that the black mother could spin wool in the obraje."[39] She gave her declaration to the commission and asked that her encomendero be made to pay her for the work that she and her late husband had done.

Lorenza Santa was nursing a black baby girl at the beginning of the investigation in 1661. She complained that several years earlier her two small sons had been taken to the mill to work as spinners. Since they were too young to work well, she went the first few days to help them spin, so that the children wouldn't get whipped. After that, she sent their little sister into the mill to help them. She asked that she and her children be paid for their work in the mill, and that she be paid for the baby she was nursing at the time.

Luisa Umisinguil, of Guambaló, nursed seven different slave children in her lifetime, and she lost her own son to the mill during that time. She was probably the aunt of a cacique of the Guambaló (in 1661), Don Gonzalo Puzia y Alomaliza.[40] In 1665 Umisinguil said that her son had been taken about nine years earlier by their cacique, who delivered him to the maestro Alonso Infante. Infante placed shackles around her son's feet and made him work like that for a year. Due to the bad swelling of his feet, Infante replaced the shackles with a *corma* (wooden device around the feet), but her son's feet continued to swell. "As a mother," Umisinguil would bring food to her son while he was imprisoned in the obraje. Over the course of three years of visits, she saw how he languished: ill, beaten, whipped, not allowed to rest, and forced to sleep in the dungeon with the other imprisoned workers. Her son finally managed to escape, where he took refuge on the ranch of a Spaniard named Antonio Sanchez. Sanchez planned to allow Umisinguil's son to stay on the ranch as a worker, and he fed him and tried to cure him, but the son died on the ranch. Witnesses said that the swelling in the young man's feet never went down. Umisinguil declared that after the death, when she went to recover her son's salary, she was only given a hat, valued by the obraje at three patacones. When she tried to sell it, nobody would pay her more than two patacones, which she used to pay her son's debt to another native man for a white pair of pants.[41]

Prior to her testimony about her son's death, Umisinguil had given an earlier statement to the commission about her role as a wet nurse. When she went to give her declaration in 1661, Umisinguil had a black baby boy on her back, who looked to be about a year old, according to the Quito commission. After nursing seven black baby boys and girls over seven years, she had only been paid in clothing. She had been promised fifteen patacones a year, so they owed her 105 patacones. She added: "[A]nd they didn't give me anything with which to wrap the black babies [*negritos*], rather I had to look for something to keep them warm." She said that at the time of her declaration she had two black babies in her house, including the one she had on her back at the time. She told the commission: "I'm the one who feeds them and I am a poor Indian woman and I don't even have a way to support myself." She said that she had been so busy nursing black babies all those years that she had not been able to make a life for herself. In order to document all the evidence of her testimony, the commission asked her to pull her breast out from the left side and squeeze it to show that she had milk. They certified that at first two drops came out easily, and then "a subtle drip," and documented this as evidence of her truthfulness.[42]

The role of the indigenous wet nurse was used by both Merlo de la Fuente in the accusations against Galarza, and by Galarza in his own defense. Galarza's accusers cited the wet nurses as evidence of the mistreatment of the indigenous population. The commission charged that Galarza was not only ordering the black caporal to whip native workers, but he was requiring the women to nurse slave babies in order to "relieve" the African mothers so that they could spin wool in the obraje. In his defense, Galarza said it was not true that he allowed black abuse of natives in his obraje. Citing the same social position of the indigenous wet nurse, he said that blacks couldn't possibly be hostile toward the natives, because the native women were their affectionate nurses. Galarza claimed that the blacks knew their nurses as mothers and considered their own mothers to be godmothers. However, as Tardieu points out, any affection that may have been felt by a two-year-old child toward his Andean nurse does not rule out later violence against indigenous people.[43]

The fact that both the accusers and the accused used the indigenous wet nurse to make their case shows the ambiguity of this role: the wet nurse comes from a lower social position and must nurture the innocent children of her oppressors. Latin Americanist scholars have explored the role of black and indigenous wet nurses to white children.[44] In Brazil, black women belonged to the lowest-status, most stigmatized race and served as wet nurses to higher-status white children. According to one Brazilian black wet nurse whom John Burdick interviewed, no matter how racist the parents are, nursing a child is an intimate act of love. Burdick's informant had nursed two white children and firmly denied claims of the wet nurse's resentment toward the child, citing instead the warmth and love produced by the intimacy and closeness of the act itself.[45] Bianca Premo also uncovered stories of wet nurses in colonial Peru who developed strong emotional attachments to the children of other races (or castas) whom they nursed.[46]

The indigenous women from Pelileo who nursed slave babies did it for the money, or because they were pressured to by María de Vera. For them it was a job, and their testimonies focus on the lack of pay and the lack of resources they were given to care for the child. There are no expressions of affection in the testimonies.

Allowing a black mother to nurse her own baby would take time away from her assigned task of spinning for wool textile production. Throughout the Americas the slave system denied women the ability to fulfill their role as mothers. A commonly told story preserved by descendants of runaway slaves in Suriname tells of an overseer who drowned a slave woman's crying baby so that she would work continuously in the cane field without stopping to nurse her child. In this matrilineal society, the story was tragic, not only for the cruelty of killing the baby, but for the near extinction of the matriline.[47] Such stories exemplify the connections between the world economic system and local cultures. Whether the profits were from the market in sugar or wool textiles, the labor structure distorted African women's ability to fulfill their role as mothers. We can only imagine how the mothers felt as their babies were taken from them to be handed over to unknown indigenous women.

The witnesses don't say how many days old the children were when they were taken from their mothers. Perhaps the slave women were allowed a certain period of rest after giving birth, before being forced back into the obraje, or maybe slave women were not afforded the traditional resting period. What we do know is that the ama de negritos would be given the child for two years, and one witness said for three. Since María de Vera or her administrator were the ones to take the babies to the indigenous wet nurses, there is no evidence of any contact between the wet nurse and slave mother, or that they even knew of each other. When we think of wet-nursing, we must remember that the duty of caring for a child for two years involved much more than breastfeeding. For lack of information on what this involved in colonial Pelileo, we can only speculate about what it was like for the amas de negritos. In the absence of historical details, we can imagine possible scenarios to flesh out this interracial history and understand the day-to-day life of the black babies and indigenous wet nurses.[48]

Aside from getting up several times a night to nurse a crying baby, the job would involve caring for and cleaning the umbilical cord (with newborns), bathing the child, and washing her clothes. Indigenous women would have relied on home remedies for intestinal and respiratory infections. Since women carried the babies on their backs, a child with diarrhea would mean that the wet nurse was constantly washing not only the baby's clothes, but her own as well. They would have made infusions of herbs that they fed to babies to make them better, or applied the leaves of medicinal plants to rashes and bug bites. Perhaps they relied on folk remedies, such as applying milk from a black sheep to a cut or injury, and they would check the child's skin for parasites. Every culture has its beliefs about how babies and small children should be cared for. Andean women would have to rely on their own cultural knowledge and beliefs to properly care for black babies. Did they swaddle newborns tightly, to make them grow straight and strong? If the baby didn't sleep well, perhaps they did a spiritual "cleansing" with bundles of medicinal plants, to draw out the "bad aire" or fright sickness. If the wet nurse had the child for two years, she would teach the baby to urinate outdoors and to squat down outside to defecate. As the child cried from the pain of cutting her first teeth, the wet nurse would have to find a way to comfort her. And we can imagine the native Andean women mashing boiled potatoes or other soft foods and tenderly teaching the child to eat solid foods. Some probably became frustrated with constantly crying babies; maybe some even mistreated the two-year-old who got in the way or the child who bit his nurse while breastfeeding. Did the amas de negritos teach slave children to take their first steps? To stay away from the open fire over which they cooked? Perhaps the term *chuchu* (Quichua for breast/milk) and other Quichua words were among a black baby's first words, as he imitated the Quichua "baby talk" from his wet nurse (assuming that in the mid-seventeenth century they were speaking Quichua rather than another north Andean indigenous language). With two slave babies in her care at the same time, it is no wonder that Luisa Umisinguil could not "make a life for herself."

Given infant mortality rates in societies that did not have access to modern medicine, and that such rates must have been higher for oppressed populations (slaves and indigenous people), it is impressive that there are no reports of slave infants dying while in the care of indigenous wet nurses. If a child had died, at best the wet nurse would not have been paid (they complained that they weren't paid anyway), and perhaps they would have even been charged for the loss of "property" as an excuse to keep them in debt. None of the women reported having had a child die, and given that this was their chance to complain about their treatment, one would expect that if a child had died, the wet nurse would have said so in her testimony, perhaps even blaming María de Vera and the administrator for not providing enough food and clothing for the child. Of course, we only have the testimonies of the indigenous women who were brought forward by the alcalde de la doctrina, Juan Machuca. There may have been other amas de negritos, who did not come forward to give their declarations. It is possible that one of them may have cared for a baby who died. One man heard María de Vera complain to wet nurses on two occasions that a black baby was not growing well.

Relationships based on unequal status, and motivated by money and dependency, do not preclude genuine emotional attachments and affection. In Spanish America the "economic functioned as the cradle for the emotional."[49] Although the indigenous nurses were motivated by a need for money, they might have been tender and affectionate toward the innocent babies whom they nursed. But once the children were returned, they became, for indigenous people, "Galarza's blacks," and social distance between blacks and natives prevailed. The available evidence indicates that in spite of intimate, everyday acts, people labeled as *negros* and *indios* did not develop bonds of *familiaridad* (familiarity), which Bianca Premo uses to describe those nonbiological, family-like relations that develop among people from different class, race, and family backgrounds.[50]

The wet nurses of San Ildefonso confound the traditional social relations involved in nursing. The African babies were not from a higher social class; they were slaves. The indigenous people were "volunteers" who were really de facto slaves, stuck in debt peonage. If we think of the tripartite model (from the introduction) of the racial hierarchy in Ecuador, with whites at the top, black and indigenous people at the bottom, the whites in San Ildefonso forced one oppressed sector of society to nurse the other oppressed sector. In the same way, indigenous people labored on haciendas in order to produce the food supply to nourish the African slaves. In fact, not only did indigenous people work on Galarza's haciendas to produce the food with which he fed his African slaves, but Tardieu suggests that the slave raids on indigenous people's crops and market products were Galarza's way of allowing the system to work itself out.[51] In short, he did not provide sufficient food or clothing for his African slaves, knowing that they would figure out a way to make up the difference by stealing from local indigenous people.

THE NAMES OF THE SLAVES

Who were the blacks at San Ildefonso? In her will María de Vera freed three slaves that were inventoried as part of the obraje: Agustín Angola, age twenty-six; Mozambique Angola, thirty; and Francisco, twenty-four. She gave land in San Sebastián (Latacunga) to another mulatto slave and said that he should be freed upon her death but continue to serve her husband, Galarza. Freed slaves in colonial Quito were not necessarily free to leave.[52] María de Vera also "freed" three female slaves with the stipulation that they serve her husband until they married. One of these may have been a wet nurse or nanny (*Beatriz ama negra*). If any of these women should bear children during the time of their servitude, the will stated, the children were to be born free. She left two slave girls, Esperanza, ten, and Dorotea, four, to her granddaughter and namesake. To her grandson Francisco de Borja, she left a slave named Bernabé and a slave boy of her husband's choosing, of eleven or twelve years old.[53]

Among Galarza's slaves, there were a roughly equal number of men and women, seven children, and a two-month-old baby in 1666, when they were confiscated after the Quito commission's investigation. The only information we have in the record is of their names, which give a clue to their African ancestry. Most were American born (criollos). There were four named Mexicana and one named Latacunga, a slave who was sometimes charged with whipping the natives. In his sugar mill Galarza also had a slave named Francisco Latacunga who was about fifty-five years old in 1665. Several had names that indicated origins in Africa, including eight who were listed as Angola, one Malembe, and one named Marcos with the ethnic moniker Bañon.[54] There were two named "de Carabali": Lucrecia and Joan (most likely the above-mentioned Carabalin who supervised indigenous workers). The name Carabalí indicates origins in modern-day Nigeria. According to Rachel O'Toole, "[M]ost slave holders referred to enslaved men and women sold from today's eastern Nigeria along the Bight of Biafra as *carabalí*, a corruption for the name of the inland region (and origin for captives) Calabar, employed by Transatlantic slave traders."[55] Some had Spanish names, or names of professions such as sacristan, *chantre* (chanter), and *de boticario* (apothecary). At the time that they were confiscated, one was in Ambato with the Spanish landowner Ballesteros "because of a debt." Two had run away: a woman named Feliciana Criolla and a man named Balthazar Guasca, and some were sick in bed.[56] The low number of children is in accordance with low fertility or survival rates of African slaves in colonial Quito.[57] Out of the ninety slaves who were confiscated by the authorities, six of them were taken, to be used at the discretion of the oidor, and were probably sold to pay the debts that Galarza owed the workers.[58] Among those six was a twelve-year-old girl. The black caporales Diaguillo (who was married to a slave woman named Leonor) and Ignacio, who were specifically named by some as being brutal toward native workers, were arrested.

WHIPPING THEM SOFTLY: CLANDESTINE
COMPASSION AND RESISTANCE

Although indigenous alguaciles were sometimes orderd to whip native workers, blacks were often preferred to carry out punishments because of the assumption that people of different "races," if pitted against one another, would not be compassionate. Most of the testimonies of the indigenous victims indicate that this is true; there is no doubt that many blacks were cruel to the natives. Natives resented the blacks, not for whipping them, for they recognized that blacks only whipped them when ordered to do so by the foreman. Rather, indigenous people complained of other types of aggression that they suffered at the hands of blacks: stealing, sexual harassment of indigenous women, and coercing native workers to clean out the slaves' quarters and garbage (*porquerias*). But one middle-aged indigenous man, Joan Yancha, revealed an act of both compassion and resistance on the part of the slave named Chinchico. There was one whip made from a bull's penis, of dry leather split down the middle. Infante used this when he was especially angry, when the cloth was no good or for a recaptured indigenous runaway (*cimarrón*). Then he would order someone to be lashed with this particular whip, and "they would whip [the victim] from both sides, between a black and an Indian. The black Chinchico, many times out of compassion, when the maestro wasn't looking, would hit the lashes to the ground, or he would soften his hand a lot, and this witness got it three times, according to his memory, with the said whip."[59]

This is only one story of compassion out of a multitude of testimonies about black abuse of natives, but it is important nevertheless. First, the witness's entire testimony is based on what he himself observed during the nine years that he was locked in the mill, and on similar experiences that the workers told one another. Second, he said Chinchico did this "many times" "out of compassion." It is interesting that Chinchico did this while an indigenous person was participating in the whipping; Yancha doesn't say that the indigenous punisher was compassionate, perhaps because indigenous compassion was assumed and black compassion was not, or because the indigenous man was not resisting the order to whip the way the black was. Chinchico's story, like that of the other slaves, was never recorded.

The indigenous testimonies indicate that Chinchico's clandestine compassion and resistance to the maestro's orders were the exception, not the rule, in relations between indigenous people and Africans. Other witnesses testified to being whipped by Chinchico, but I did not find any others who sensed any compassion or softening of the hand. When witnesses complained that children were whipped as harshly as if they were adults, some specifically mentioned that the maestro would call Chinchico to whip the children if the native alguacil was not available. One would think that a compassionate slave would show some tenderness toward the children, yet there is no indication that this was the case. It's possible that nobody else noticed, or that Chinchico had few opportunities to resist orders—he could only do so when he was sure that the maestro wouldn't notice. The act of hitting the whip to the ground is the type of sly, individual act of resistance that rarely gets preserved in historical documents.

Everyday acts of resistance and hidden critiques of power reveal that subordinate peoples do not accept the conditions of their subordination. What may appear as the subordinate's acceptance of the ideology of the dominant might only be an act of survival, a "public transcript." If we are to understand whether hegemony is really at work, we must look for individual acts—sometimes private, anonymous acts—of resistance in the "hidden transcripts," the critique of power that is disguised, or in everyday individual acts of resistance.[60] In fact, Chinchico performed this act of resistance to Infante's authority at great risk to himself; had the maestro glanced over and seen Chinchico whip the ground instead of the indigenous worker, Chinchico surely would have been punished. His brave act of compassion and resistance stands out as a gesture of humanity toward a person from an oppressed race. Because everyday acts of compassion rarely make it into historical records,[61] and because the voices of the blacks were silenced and written out of the historical archive,[62] any possible compassion on the part of other blacks remains a hidden history.

Joan Yancha's testimony is also the only one in which an emotive ("compassion") is used regarding blacks. Native witnesses occasionally used emotives in their testimonies when discussing acts among themselves. For example, the act of one indigenous person giving food to another who had none was done "out of pity" (*lastima*) or out of compassion. Parents brought food to their children and took the whippings for their children "out of love." With the exception of this testimony that attributed "compassion" for the natives on the part of Chinchico, the indigenous witnesses did not use emotives when discussing blacks, not even the women who were caring for black babies. Yet, even in their complaints, the natives did express some empathy for the status of the slaves, acknowledging that slaves stole from natives because they were not properly fed and clothed by the owner, and that when they whipped natives it was because the foreman ordered them to do so.

CONCLUSION

During the second half of the seventeenth century, if not earlier, the social structure of Pelileo was one in which African slaves were used in controlling the indigenous population.[63] Slaves guarded indigenous mill workers, chased after them when they ran away, and punished them when ordered to do so. They guarded the door to the mill, where Andean women or children brought food to the workers. They also prevented an indigenous woman from being stabbed by the foreman, thereby, according to the witness's own testimony, saving her life.

Despite the presence of Africans at the moment of indigenous people's deaths, and, in at least a couple cases, despite Africans having indigenous people spend the night in their homes, there was great social distance and mistrust between Africans and Andeans. Even the amas de negritos, who nursed and cared for black babies, did not know who the parents of those babies were. It is unclear whether the babies even had names, or whether they were ever baptized. Although their bodies were linked through nursing, and black and indigenous people were side by side during intimate moments involving nursing, illness, and death, they did not develop familiaridad[64] as far as the evidence shows.

FIGURE 11. Woman Spinning. Nineteenth-Century Ecuador. From *Álbum de costumbres ecuatorianas* in Biblioteca Digital Hispánica.

This chapter showed the social positions of Africans and native Andeans in relation to each other in seventeenth-century Pelileo, how the underfed slave force at the obraje affected rural indigenous people, and the nature of interactions between Africans and Andeans. In the next chapter I continue analyzing testimonies from the investigation against Galarza, with a focus on the social positions within indigenous communities. The testimonies allow us to analyze the role of indigenous intermediaries, such as caciques and quipo masters, as well as relationships within the indigenous family, and how the obraje affected indigenous people's interactions with one another.

CHAPTER 3

VOICES AND SILENCES IN INDIGENOUS TESTIMONIES (1630–1666)

I N THIS chapter I look at how the mill affected people occupying different positions in indigenous society. The narratives presented here show how indigenous social life was affected by the textile economy, and they provide some of the clearest examples of the lived experience of the workers and their families. The Quito commission's investigation gave indigenous victims the opportunity to become "voices aware of their vocality,"[1] as they gave their testimonies and attempted to uncover the silenced deaths of indigenous people in the obraje. From their statements I selected those that reveal the positions of indigenous people as intermediaries, caciques, family members, or forasteros and how individual social actors experienced the obraje differently. The pressures were too much for some families, and some people ran away and abandoned their families, but there are also examples of efforts to keep families together, mutual support, and collaboration within and among indigenous families. The stories told by the indigenous people reveal everyday strategies for survival and for maintaining their familial, cultural, and social lives.

INDIGENOUS AUTHORITIES

Native intermediaries were indigenous people who occupied some position of authority in colonial society and mediated relations between common indigenous people and Spanish government or Church officials. Throughout Mesoamerica and the Andes, native intermediaries balanced their obligations to the colonial government with their obligations to their indigenous subjects. These intermediaries include caciques, Church assistants, indigenous constables, and other middlemen.[2] In seventeenth-century Pelileo, native intermediaries in the mill and on Galarza's ranches were tasked with strict supervision of laborers. It would have been difficult for workers to rebel, given the large number of middlemen charged with keeping the native workers, and one another, in line. The labor hierarchy went something like this: the owners who spent much of their time in Quito; the obraje administrator; the white foremen (maestros), of which there were several over the years; various white recogedores, who would round up indigenous people and bring them to the mill; the indigenous alguaciles and alcaldes, who would go after the caciques, who would then go after their subjects or have their principales go after the subjects, who were controlled inside the mill by African slaves and indigenous alguaciles. Both black and indigenous men were forced to guard the obraje "so that the prisoners wouldn't run away or burn down the obraje."[3] Indigenous middlemen enforced one another's behavior. If a cacique didn't force boys into the obraje, he would be punished. If the indigenous alguacil didn't bring the noncompliant cacique to be locked up, the alguacil would be whipped. The alcalde Juan Challay said that if he didn't provide indigenous workers, and punish them, he himself would be punished by the administrators. Challay said that in the past he had been whipped by the blacks and the indigenous *maestrillo* (native obraje labor supervisor). So he carried out his job of forcing other indigenous people into the mill. Challay was especially cruel in his punishment of recaptured indigenous runaways (cimarrónes). According to one witness, Challay was "crueler than the maestro."[4] On one occasion he was repeatedly lashing a native worker so brutally that even the white foreman said, "That's enough already." Challay defended his actions, saying that when Indians run away, *he's* the one who gets charged, and he continued with the lashings.

This hierarchy of middlemen stood as a buffer between the administrators and indigenous victims. The first part of this chapter shows how the labor structure of the obraje economy distorted the positions of these indigenous authorities in relation to other indigenous people, focusing on quipo masters, the alcalde de la doctrina (Church assistant), and caciques, and then turns focus to the obraje's effects on indigenous families. I begin with the quipocamas, whose titles would indicate that they were specialists in pre-Columbian accounting techniques or masters of the mnemonic record-keeping knotted strings called khipus.[5] However, in the context of seventeenth-century Pelileo, their roles were akin to thug-like labor bosses.

QUIPO MASTERS: FROM ACCOUNTANT TO LABOR BOSS

The obraje of San Ildefonso always had sheep ranches and grain-producing haciendas associated with it. Antonio Lopez de Galarza owned ranches and haciendas in Pelileo, Patate, and the town of Quero, and through intermediaries he was able to shift labor from these estates to the mill. One class of indigenous intermediaries were the labor bosses on the haciendas known as quipocamas (quipo masters, following the spelling in the documents for colonial Quito). Under the Incas, quipo masters were accountants who kept records with their cords of knotted strings. In the mid-colonial period, quipo masters were native record keepers who used their knotted cords to keep track of the number of animals and labor contributions on Andean haciendas. In Ecuador, the native administrators called quipocamas or quipos worked on Spanish-owned haciendas in the central sierra at least through the second half of the eighteenth century, but their roles changed and their positions evolved along different paths. For example, during the 1764 indigenous rebellion in Riobamba, it was the quipos of the haciendas who led native contingents against the Spaniards. In seventeenth-century Pelileo, by contrast, the quipos served the hacienda administrators to the detriment of the native workers. Indigenous men were punished "by the hand of the quipocama,"[6] who also moved indigenous workers from field to mill and forced them into the obraje.

Around the mill and in nearby towns, Galarza owned large ranches where workers were responsible for tending to hundreds of sheep to produce wool for the textile mill. Some of the shepherds and other ranch hands who complained of their conditions were native Chumaquí men who worked on the ranch of Chumaquí, while others were from the town of Quero and worked on the hacienda and ranch of Ipolongo. Their complaints indicate that the social position of the quipocama, which once involved knowledge and mastery of native accounting techniques, devolved from the role of keeping track of the number of days a native worked to the role of forcing indigenous people into service. Joan Poaquisa, a Guambaló man, complained that Joan Toasa, the quipocama of the ranch of Chumaquí, beat him up (*aporreo*), "as he is accustomed to do."[7] Poaquisa was coming back from Mass with other indigenous people, when he stopped to visit someone. Since he did not return right away, the quipocama beat him. According to Poaquisa, it was the (white) mayordomos who taught the quipocama to behave this way. Poaquisa complained against all the administrators but most of all against Galarza himself. He specifically wanted the quipocama to be punished. Toasa is the surname of a long line of caciques of the Chumaquí. It is possible that Joan Toasa gained the position of quipocama due to his ties to the caciques.

Diego Masaquisa (listed as a Guambaló) also served on Galarza's hacienda of Chumaquí. He complained that the quipocama, together with the mayordomo and administrator, took him by force to the obraje of San Ildefonso, where he saw others being whipped and beaten. They told him that if he did not submit to work on the ranch, he would be forced to work in the mill. Under that threat, he worked on the ranch against his will. At the time of his declaration, he had worked there for three years without pay. Furthermore, his wife was forced to cook and make maize beer for the mayordomo and to sell products at the market to benefit the mayordomo's extramarital mistress. Masaquisa complained that his wife was not even allowed to rest on Sundays or Catholic feast days. Diego Masaquisa had to stay up all night guarding the crops from the mayordomo's dogs, "and so that I don't suffer being whipped, I can't spend even one night with my wife and children, or know the warmth of the hearth during the time of the worst rains."[8] He complained that he was in a continuous state of sleep deprivation and that neither he nor his wife had been paid.

The reference to the warmth of the hearth brings to mind the concept of the home as a site of resistance in the sense that scholar bell hooks[9] describes: as a place where one's value is affirmed by family members, and as an escape from a hostile, racist, and violent world where one is valued as less. Writing of blacks in the United States, hooks says that homes were the domain of women, "not as property, but as places where all that truly mattered in life took place— the warmth and comfort of shelter, the feeding of our bodies, the nurturing of our souls."[10] By affirming one's human dignity, women made homes a place of resistance in a world that defined black people as objects, and hooks calls on people to recognize and honor this history of resistance that took place in slave huts and later African American homes.[11]

In the Andes, where indigenous people were devalued and treated as work objects, the sense of the indigenous *wasi*, the home—the location of the warm hearth, around which the family sits and eats together—is captured by Jorge Icaza in his novel *Huasipungo*. The protagonist of the novel, an indigenous worker living on an hacienda prior to the agrarian reform, longs to be home with his wife and baby, where they slept next to the hearth. "[A]nd feeling themselves, as usual in such moments while sheltering each other, far—stupefying forgetfulness—from all the injustice, from all the humiliation and sacrifice which existed outside the hut, they fell asleep, covered by the warmth of their own bodies, by the poncho still soaked from the páramo, by the fury of the lice."[12] Although Icaza was a twentieth-century novelist, he captured the sense of comfort of the indigenous home as a place of refuge from the harsh conditions of hacienda labor. Diego Masaquisa's expression of yearning to be home with his family and "know the warmth of the hearth" hints at the unofficial history of homeplace as site of resistance and restoration of human dignity. The hearth represents both physical and emotional comfort.[13]

At Ipolongo, another of Galarza's ranches, the quipocama Geronimo Cuxana was also abusive. Cuxana, a native of Tisaleo (but part of Galarza's encomienda), forced other indigenous people to work all week. Workers had to guard the sheep in the high, cold hills every night during the week, and on Saturdays they had to do agricultural tasks. One worker, Thomas Quilcatoma of Quero, said that if laborers didn't show up for work on Saturday, the mayordomo and quipo would add the same chore to their weekly jobs, saying, "This is what you should have done on Saturday."[14] Another worker from Quero, Mathias Gualpamullo, said that he was in debt for losing sheep, and the quipo put a shovel across his neck and tied his thumbs to it, tightened the rope, and led him to San Ildefonso. So after working for years on the ranch, he was forced into the obraje, where he was whipped for not meeting his quota and locked in a cell at night with the other indigenous prisoners, where they slept on the floor. His wife gave a pair of oxen to the mayordomo (Clemente de la Parra) to try to free her husband from the debt, but they didn't release him.[15] Several other shepherds working on the ranches complained that the administrators ordered them to be whipped by the quipo. When he was questioned by Merlo de la Fuente, the quipocama described his own position as foreman (*mayoral*) on the hacienda of Ipolongo. He served as a quipocama in the sense that when the administrator and mayordomo settled the accounts of the number of sheep lost, Cuxana was called to assist with the accounting.[16] Geronimo Cuxana's duties of keeping track of days worked by an individual and number of sheep lost from a particular flock reflect the role of quipo masters on colonial haciendas who kept track of the information on their khipus. In contrast, by the 1660s the shepherds of Quero had to show the skins of the sheep that had been killed by predators for accounting purposes, and the quipocama/labor boss was called to assist with this accounting.

For the most part, Cuxana confirmed the testimony of the witnesses against him, and, while he admitted that he would whip the workers, he said he did it lightly. He mentioned to the commission that he only had a few years left until he turned fifty, when he would be free from labor obligations, indicating that despite being classed with the other administrators, his position was obligatory and he looked forward to retirement.

The witnesses never made any mention of a khipu as a set of knotted cords but used the term *quipo* or *quipocama* to refer to the indigenous intermediary who assisted the administrators in keeping track of indigenous labor and debts from loss of sheep. The lack of reference to a khipu, even by the quipocama himself, suggests that khipus were no longer being used by these intermediaries. Taken together, the testimonies indicate that if the quipo masters of the ranches of Ipolongo and Chumaquí ever did have knotted cords, their role devolved into that of a thug-like labor boss: an indigenous person closer to the inner circle of administrators who could get some benefit for himself by keeping the other indios in line. It is easy to see how one might go from using knowledge and skills to keep track of work days to accepting the position of labor enforcer, especially if this meant that one was exempt from working in the obraje.[17]

ALACALDE DE LA DOCTRINA

The quipocamas were one type of indigenous intermediary known as bullies to the indigenous workers. Other indigenous intermediaries, such as Juan Obralay, the mill guard (*alcaide*), and Juan Challay, an alcalde charged with bringing workers to the obraje (as his father did before him), were also abusive to other indigenous people. But there was one indigenous intermediary, Juan Machuca, who voiced the complaints of the indigenous people of Pelileo and brought them forward to denounce the abuses. Machuca was a principal and alcalde de la doctrina (also called the *fiscal*), the indigenous official charged with ensuring that other indigenous people attend Mass and religious lessons. Records indicate that he was from the parcialidad of Camayos (Puruguayes) in Pelileo, but in his capacity as assistant to the Dominican friar he dealt with indigenous people from different sectors. When children failed to show up for their religious lessons, Machuca would go to their homes looking for them. He said that he would find their parents crying, saying that their children had been taken to the obraje by force. In fact, some men claimed that they had been taken to the obraje as children while they were on their way to their religious lessons. Machuca, perhaps emboldened by his relationship with Fray Alonso de Aponte, presented grievances to colonial authorities on behalf of the natives of Pelileo. Together with the caciques of the neighboring town of Patate, Machuca complained to the Crown of the abuses suffered by the indigenous people on the obraje-estate complex of San Ildefonso. He specifically criticized the indigenous mill guard for forcing children into the mill and for keeping people imprisoned. The natives were missing their religious lessons because they were not allowed to attend, Machuca said.

Fray Alonso was having his own problems with the encomendero. Galarza was trying to "divide the parish" by having a different priest come to the mill chapel on holy days in order to celebrate Mass.[18] In order to keep the workers from leaving the obraje, he wanted to convert the obraje chapel into an annex of the church of Pelileo.[19] This way he could keep workers from going to their parish church in Pelileo. Fray Alonso also obtained an order from Quito to free the many indigenous boys who were locked in the mill. Together with the teniente of Ambato, he went to the obraje and released the boys who were working there.

Galarza, for his part, denied the accusations against him, and blamed Fray Alonso de Aponte for inciting the Indians, especially Juan Machuca. It wasn't true that he was forcing his encomienda Indians into the obraje, Galarza said. He claimed that the majority of the workers were blacks, and there were only a few natives who freely chose to work there for a daily wage, for which they were "punctually" paid. Galarza said the accusations against him were false and that it wasn't even his obraje but his wife's. If the obraje were demolished, he argued, it would leave them in ruin.[20] Actually, in addition to his wife's obraje of San Ildefonso, Galarza had his own obraje in Riobamba. But Galarza was echoing an economic argument that was used by colonial officials of Quito: if the obrajes were demolished as the Crown had ordered, Indians would not be able to pay tribute, and Quito's economy could not be sustained.

During the investigation of the crimes against the natives of Pelileo, Juan Machuca was instrumental in getting fearful indigenous witnesses to come forward and give their testimonies. According to witnesses, the administrators had spies who would watch as people left their homes to report whether they were going to speak to the Qutio commission. One witness refused to testify because he said they would kill him.[21] Machuca reported that the Indians were afraid to talk, so Merlo de la Fuente had Galarza removed from Pelileo during the investigation. Juan Machuca, together with the protector of natives, then brought witnesses forward to give their statements. Some witnesses were summoned to the home of the cacique of Chumaquí the night before giving their testimony. There, they said, one of the administrators bribed them to keep quiet. Fortunately, after taking the two patacones of hush money, they gave their testimonies anyway. The caciques of Chumaquí and Pilalata must have been working together with the administrator, since even the Pilalata were brought to the home of the cacique of Chumaquí and bribed prior to giving their testimonies. One Pilalata man said that his wife was taken, by their principal, to the home of the cacique of Chumaquí (Toasa), where the administrator gave her ten patacones. The man added that the administrator was "trying to keep me quiet with ten patacones when they owe me eighteen patacones and six reales."[22]

While most indigenous intermediaries served the obraje administrators, Juan Machuca mobilized people against Galarza. He complained to the Crown (with the caciques of Patate) and encouraged the native of people of Pelileo to give their testimonies to the Quito commission.

CACIQUES

Several scholars have analyzed the role of Andean caciques as intermediaries. On the north coast of Peru, Susan Ramírez found that since the onset of Spanish colonialism, Andean caciques who did not serve the best interests of Spaniards were removed, and others, even commoners, took over the position with all the symbolic accoutrements of their status; the *duho* (ceremonial stool), staff, and insignias.[23] Similarly, for the Audiencia of Quito, Powers found evidence of usurper caciques who made up claims to elite status after the Spanish conquest.[24] Caciques were indigenous elites exempt from the labor draft and tribute obligations to which commoner indigenous people were subject. In addition to the above-mentioned symbols of authority and prestige, they were entitled to wear certain clothing that was reserved for high-status members of society.[25] They were responsible for sending their subjects into the service of Spaniards on a rotating basis and for collecting tribute. In Andean history, some caciques were attacked by their own subjects for occupying this middle position and enabling the oppression of the natives. Others got in trouble with colonial officials for protecting their subjects, enabling the continuation of native religious practices, or inciting rebellions.

In San Ildefonso, the caciques of Pelileo had to provide laborers for the mill. If they didn't, they themselves would be locked up in the mill, although caciques were not forced to do manual labor. During the second half of the seventeenth century onward, the hereditary caciques of the Chumaquí were the Toasas, and those of the Pilalata were the Changos. Several witnesses complained that they were tied up and taken to the obraje by their caciques, although it seems that the caciques sent principales or alcaldes to carry out the orders, as the following case shows.

The case of Marta Pancha shows the effect of the mill complex on indigenous people occupying two different social positions: a cacique as intermediary and an indigenous mother. Pancha, a widow, complained that Don Andres Chango, the cacique of the Pilalata, entered her house and took three of her sons and a young daughter named Francisca. Seven years prior to the 1661 investigation, her children were taken to the obraje to spin wool, working "among the blacks," and she hadn't seen them since. She didn't know whether they had been murdered, drowned, or if they had run away or were locked up in a jail cell. She asked Merlo de la Fuente to order her cacique to appear before the commission and explain where the children were and, if they were alive, to bring them back. If they were dead, she wanted those responsible to be punished.

When the cacique was brought forward, he said that when he assumed the *cacicazgo* (hereditary chiefdom) upon the death of his brother, it was already the custom to bring ten boys from his sector of Pilalata to the obraje to serve for one year. His position required that he continue with this obligation, so he sent his principal, Garcia Tintin, to bring ten boys, among them the ten-year-old son of Marta Pancha. The boy's little sister, described as *tierna*, or very young, was taken along to "take care" of her brother by cooking for him. But Chango said that he never went to Marta Pancha's house himself, so they would have to ask the principal the whereabouts of the children.

When the principal was brought forward to the commission, he acknowledged that he took the boy and his sister to the obraje. There they worked spinning wool until suddenly one day they fled the obraje. Tintin said that he searched all over for the children, but couldn't find them. One day, he saw their mother crying to Fray Alonso de Aponte, telling him that she heard that her children had drowned in the Pachanlica River trying to reach the family's fields. As for Marta Pancha's other children, he said, they ran away from home out of fear of being taken to the obraje. According to the principal, rumor had it that they were seen at a dock where people get salt, dressed as Spaniards.[26]

Like Marta Pancha, many people testified against their caciques, but the caciques had also been imprisoned in the obraje when they didn't have enough indigenous workers to spare. As Merlo de la Fuente said, "[T]hey do not respect the privileges of caciques and curacas, since the power of the encomendero prevails."[27] An imprisoned cacique's status was only respected in that he was not forced to work while locked up in the obraje, while secondary chiefs (the principales) were forced to work like ordinary tributary Indians. A cacique would then have to leave his wife in the obraje as a "pawn" until he came back with a supply of boys to meet the labor demands. One Chumaquí man said that the late cacique Ventura Toasa had informed him that Galarza said the cacique "owed" twenty indigenous boys to the obraje to compensate for loss of tribute from those who had fled. His successor said that the "custom" was to send thirteen indigenous laborers each year from his parcialidad to serve Galarza's enterprises: two to the ranch of Chumaquí, two to the sugar mill of San Antonio, three to the sugar mill of Santo Thomas, and six to the obraje. The principal Garcia Tintin testified that he himself had been imprisoned three times in the obraje for not providing enough laborers.

Although the Guambaló were not part of Galarza's encomienda, they were also pressed into serving against their will. Don Esteban Uyalloa, cacique of the Guambaló, said that when he did not have enough laborers to send, the administrator of the obraje imprisoned him, along with the cacique of the Pilalata, for two weeks.[28] Uyalloa testified that he saw various men from his sector as well as those of Galarza's encomienda (Pilalata and Chumaquí) shackled in the obraje as punishment for missing work on days when they had to tend to their own crops. For this reason, and the frequent lashings, workers were fleeing their communities, he said, sometimes taking their wives and children with them. Uyalloa also confirmed the deaths of several men from his parcialidad in the obraje.

In the town of Quero, on Galarza's hacienda of Ipolongo (which was next to the ranch), a cacique and his wife did stand up to the mayordomo Clemente de la Parra. Don Favian Cabuco, the cacique of the Collanas Chumbivilca Indians of Quero,[29] and his wife went to the hacienda to see some of the indigenous workers. There they saw Geronimo, the quipocama, whipping Mathias Gualpamullo, under the orders of de la Parra. The mayordomo and quipocama were yelling at him for the loss of sheep. Gualpamullo spoke up, saying, "How is it my fault that recently sheared sheep died from the cold of the páramo and the water?" The cacique and his wife interfered, telling de la Parra to stop and criticizing him for being so abusive. The wife, Doña María Mulmuquis, told the mayordomo that it wasn't necessary to whip the shepherd. It would be better to take him to the authorities, she insisted. De la Parra told them to get out and mind their own business, at which point Doña María threatened to report the mayordomo to the authorities. Grasping his dagger, de la Parra threatened the cacica and told her he would "show her justice" and that they and the authorities could all "kiss his ass" (*le bezase el culo*).[30] The cacique and his wife retreated, fearful of the "crazy" mayordomo.

Others had tried to use legal channels to get relief prior to the Quito commission's investigation in 1661. Women reported abuses against their husbands and sons to authorities in Riobamba. Not only were the reports ineffective, but when they returned to Pelileo, the administrators whipped them for filing complaints. A group of indigenous people went directly to Galarza when he was living in Quito and reported the illegal abuses, but they returned feeling hopeless. Galarza blamed the punishments on Indian "laziness" and tendency to flee. Likewise, during the criminal investigation Galarza tried to use stereotypes of Indian drunkenness to discredit the testimonies. Psychologically, the victims had little hope prior to the 1661 investigation. Administrators would tell people that while any priest, *corregidor* (colonial administrator), or judge that had supported the Indians was long gone, Galarza was the eternal encomendero.[31] Some indigenous workers were told that Galarza would kill them and feed them to the dogs. During the investigation, when indigenous victims were going to the commission to give their statements, administrators warned them to think about what would happen to them after the commission left and went back to Quito.

The testimonies about indigenous intermediaries show how this position was skewed by the demand for labor in the obraje. The quipo masters of the ranches became the hand that moved labor from the ranch to the mill by force, justifying it by claiming that workers were in debt for lost sheep. The alcalde de la doctrina, by contrast, became the voice of the people who denounced Galarza, probably with the protection of the friar. The caciques occupied an elite status within indigenous communities, but they were still locked up in the obraje when they did not meet the demand supplying labor to the obraje. Most people were not elites and intermediaries but ordinary people trying to make a living and provide for their families. Many of these individuals took the opportunity to tell the Quito commission how the obraje work affected their families.

EFFECTS ON THE INDIGENOUS FAMILY

For a person who was locked in the obraje, having family members who lived within walking distance, who were willing to offer help or at least some comfort, could make a difference in the worker's experience. It meant being able to sleep on animal skins brought by one's parent, rather than on the cold dungeon floor, or having home-cooked food brought by one's wife or mother, rather than having to rely on obraje advances and getting further into debt. A worker's situation could also put a great strain on family members' relationships to one another. Mothers complained that their children were punished because, due to their young age, the children were incapable of meeting the work standards set by the administrators. In his scathing denunciation of Galarza, Merlo de la Fuente reported that not only did parents go to help their children complete the tasks, but, moved by a natural parental love for their children, they would take the whippings in place of their children. They were concerned for their children's suffering, and that their children would run away, as Marta Pancha's children did. One man said that he was eight years old when he was taken by force while walking from his family's fields. He served twenty-four years in the obraje and told the commission, "Even though it's true that I had many opportunities to run away I didn't because one time that I ran away they took my mother who gave birth to me and they had her imprisoned making her spin [wool] as they are accustomed to do . . . whenever some imprisoned Indian or youth flees, they bring entire generations making them work, imprisoned, until the person shows up."[32]

We have already seen in the last chapter how the obraje affected Lucía, one of the daughters of Juan Pimbomasa. Her husband ran away and hid on the ranch of Miguel de la Parra. At least she knew where her husband was hiding and was able to stay with him on the ranch. But when her brother ran away, Lucía's elderly father was taken to replace him, and her father was beaten to death in the obraje. Runaways were often caught and brought back, and they would be locked up and placed in shackles after their punishment. Local men were caught easily if they went back to work their fields, in order to grow the crops that sustained their families. The obraje made it nearly impossible for some indigenous men to fulfill their roles in ploughing fields and performing other agricultural tasks that were necessary for survival, forcing their wives to rely on relatives. Although the Crown mandated that workers be given time off during the agricultural cycle, to allow them to tend to their own crops, in practice the rule was ignored. If a man did leave to work his fields, a spouse or child was sometimes taken to the mill to replace him.

Not all workers suffered extreme punishments. Jacinto Curillo said that he was allowed to leave the obraje on Sundays and feast days to attend to his fields, because he was a skilled, fast worker. Furthermore, his wife would bring him food so that he didn't suffer as much as others, "and since this witness worked carefully day and night and was able to finish his tasks they didn't whip him as they did the others."[33] But his brother was not so lucky. Curillo said he used to go visit his brother, who was considered a flight risk and shackled in the obraje. When the brother managed to escape, the recogedor went to Curillo's home and accused him of hiding the brother. Curillo swore that he didn't know where his brother was, and ran away to avoid being attacked by the recogedor, who then attacked Curillo's wife. Later, Curillo's father was taken and forced to work in the obraje until the brother returned. Curillo also told the commission about his sister's son, who worked in the obraje for some time. After his nephew was whipped, he showed Curillo the scars on his back, and Curillo said he was "moved by compassion." But he convinced his nephew not to run away, telling him to have hope, and that God would help him get through his year of service. The youth's father would bring him food, but sometimes he was unable to see his son, so Curillo would take the food to his nephew. Unfortuantely, the nephew died shortly after being released from the obraje.

Some families relied on the Andean practice of reciprocal exchange of labor. Geronimo Moposita reported that when men needed to leave the obraje to work the fields, those who had wives who knew how to spin wool would send their wives in their place "while they tended to their fields so that the husbands wouldn't fall behind [their daily quotas] and even if it was a different task [such as carding, fulling, or beating the wool] that [the husbands] had they would exchange it during those days for spinning wool, and if not, the wives would have to take advantage of *mingas* [collective labor] with their relatives to work the fields."[34] Those who could not choose either option would leave the obraje for three or four days, but the maestro would send the recogedor and alcalde to get them, even if they were in the middle of ploughing, leaving the yoke of oxen in the field.

On the other hand, when Favian Picha asked other men to help weed his field, he compensated them with *chicha* (maize beer) that he obtained from the obraje. Since pre-Columbian times, maize beer has been an important ritual and social symbol in the Andes. Aside from its use in sacred rituals, caciques would distribute chicha to their subjects on certain feast days, and ordinary Andeans who got help from friends, neighbors, and relatives in agricultural and other tasks would provide chicha for the helpers. When Favian Picha wanted to provide chicha for the workers who helped him, he requested it from the obraje owner, María de Vera, who gave him a slip of paper and told him to go to any of the native women who made chicha for the obraje. He gave the paper to the administrator, who gave him two jugs of chicha against his work account. In this way, Picha got help working his field. The workers were forced to depend on the obraje for advances in order to properly observe Andean customs. During the interrogation of Galarza, when he was questioned about advancing food (including rotten meat) to the indigenous people at inflated prices, he denied all the accusations against him, but he admitted that it was common to give "lambs for those who were sick, which [the Indians] ask for, or for their weddings, or mingas for their houses or fields, which is very common, and without meat and maize beer they cannot perform these tasks."[35]

When the wives of the workers stayed in the obraje helping them, María de Vera would give them half a *fanega* (about a bushel) of maize and promised to pay them for making chicha. However, men complained that the women had to use their own jugs, their own firewood, and sometimes had to supplement the maize from their own supply. Favian Picha also said that when María de Vera lived on the estate, she would take two widows from each sector of the encomienda to spin wool in her home. The women would only be allowed to go home at night to sleep if they finished their daily quotas, which Picha said were two spindles full of wool. If possible, the widows would bring their sisters or daughters to help them meet the quota so that they could go home to sleep at night. So, not only were Andean men working in the mill, but some of the women were forced to work for María de Vera in her home. One indigenous woman, a servant of María de Vera, ran away. The woman's husband was then made to work in the obraje to make up for the cost de Vera had incurred by clothing and feeding the woman. After the husband worked in the obraje for a year and seven months, they deducted the cost of his wife's anaco (indigenous woman's skirt) from his salary.[36]

THE SHEPHERDS AND THEIR WIVES

A common complaint among the men who worked on Galarza's ranches was how their wives were treated. This complaint was expressed especially by the indigenous shepherds of the mill-ranch complex. Pedro Toctaquisa was a Chumaquí man who worked on the ranch of Chumaquí and in the mill. When he was a child, his cacique, Ventura Toasa (deceased by the time of his declaration), delivered him to the obraje, where he worked as a spinner and carder. He was imprisoned there for twenty years. When he was whipped, if he cried out from the pain, the indigenous alguaciles would punch him in the face, telling him to keep quiet. According to his testimony: "I was living with this oppression, as if I were a captive in the land of the Moors," adding that his own captivity was even worse. They gave him seven tasks to complete each day, and since it was impossible to reach the quotas, he was forced to pay other indigenous workers to help him. When he complained, Galarza sent him to the hacienda of Chumaquí, where he had worked for six or seven years without the rest that "His Majesty has ordered." When he had to attend to his own fields to grow food for himself and his family, the administrators took his wife, forcing her "to work among black men" spinning wool. Toctaquisa, like other witnesses, complained that the mayordomo Francisco Oñate kept a mistress on the hacienda of Chumaquí, even though he was married and had a wife in the town of Quero, "setting a bad example for the Indians."[37] In this last statement he might have been echoing a complaint made by a priest. The mayordomos' maintenance of mistresses, as well as their demand that indigenous women sell products in the town of Patate for the benefit of those mistresses, was a complaint voiced by several indigenous workers.

On Galarza's hacienda of Ipolongo, in the town of Quero, the mayordomo Clemente de la Parra was cruel toward the shepherds and their wives. The men could not sleep; they had to stay up all night protecting the sheep that grazed in the high hills, in the cold and the rain. De la Parra ordered that corrals be removed, because he said the wool of the sheep would get caught on the wood and damaged. High-quality wool was the basis for the success of Quito's famous cloth called paño, so quality assurance was important. But taking out the corral made it harder for the shepherds to keep track of the huge flocks for which they were responsible. Claiming that a shepherd owed the encomendero for lost sheep allowed Galarza and his administrators to keep the workers in perpetual debt. Those who owed were then forced into the obraje. The obraje account records list numerous native men who were sent to the obraje "for sheep." Several shepherds complained of the conditions under which they worked: staying up all night in the cold, fearful of wild predators that attack the sheep, being held accountable for sheep that died from the cold after being sheared or for miscarriages of pregnant sheep, which were counted against the shepherd. The shepherds were forced to go hunting as well, and their wives would have to look after the large flocks while the men were gone. When sheep were lost or killed, the shepherds and their wives would be whipped by the quipo. The mayordomo also kept the men from attending religious services during Holy Week and stopped them from going to confession before Easter, as they were supposed to. He only allowed the workers to attend Mass after the priest of the town of Quero yelled at him for keeping the native workers from fulfilling their religious obligations. The testimony of some shepherds appeals to Spanish efforts to create good, Christian Indians, as in the following case.

Pedro Condori was a native of Quero who worked on Galarza's hacienda of Ipolongo. Condori's cacique, Don Lorenzo Mollocana, appointed him to take care of Galarza's sheep, but they also had him busy hunting deer and rabbits. He had to stay up all night protecting the sheep from mountain lions and foxes, or he would be whipped for losing them. After years of serving by pasturing sheep in the mountains, hunting, and doing agricultural tasks, not only was he not paid, but he was told that he *owed* money for lost sheep. He was imprisoned in the mill, where, in order not to go hungry, he had to accept advances of corn and barley at high prices. The town of Quero was probably too far away from the mill for a wife or children to bring food on a daily basis; one worker said that the shepherds had it the worst because their wives didn't bring them food.[38] Condori was in perpetual debt and routinely whipped. His wife went to Riobamba seeking justice from the corregidor, but de la Parra found out and whipped her. "If a Spaniard hadn't been present [de la Parra] would have slit her throat," Condori said.[39] The men were in an impossible situation, so their wives had to watch the sheep while the husbands were occupied with other tasks.

After telling this to the Quito commission, Condori then shifted his testimony from telling his personal experience to speaking for the group of indigenous shepherds: "But the women are afraid of the [mountain] lion that comes from the *monte*, so they flee, leaving the sheep unattended. They treat us so badly, worse than if we were slaves, or Christian captives under Xivaros or Turks, being that we are free, and before such Christian judges as Yourself, protected by his majesty in our land." After comparing their own form of captivity to a historical example of Christian captivity, Condori went on to mock the name of the cruel mayordomo: "He is no Clemente [compassionate one], he is more of a cómitre [abusive overseer] of Christians," who would curse at them.[40] He continued complaining of how the wives of the shepherds were treated: when the wives would lose sheep to predators, Clemente would whip them with a saddle strap on their naked buttocks,

> allowing others who are not their husbands to see. When he finished he would tell them "now go run and tell the Corregidor, the teniente, the priest and the governor, they will kiss my . . ." well, You understand, modesty prevents me from saying where. He has no respect for justice, not on earth nor heaven. During Holy Week, when the shepherds want to go to their towns for confession, as God's law commands, because the indigenous fiscal of the parish has called them [to confess], [de la Parra] detained them, saying "you drunks! I'm not even going to confess and yet you all want to go. You will work and whoever doesn't show up will be whipped."[41]

Despite the threats, several indigenous men did sneak away to go to their towns to confess during Holy Week. Of course, in addition to fulfilling their religious obligations, they would have been able to celebrate with their families. When they returned on Holy Friday, they were whipped for leaving the hacienda without permission.

While most of the testimonies seem to be glosses of the native plaintiff's words, this testimony raises questions about the extent to which the words are a legal ventriloquy[42] by the Quichua interpreter or the scribe, especially in their references to old-world Christian history at the hands of Turks and Moors. But it is possible that the witnesses were coming up with these critiques on their own, using the language of Christian morality to expose white Christian hypocrisy, just as several of the witnesses complained that the mayordomos had mistresses even though they were married. Even illiterate native people were aware of Spanish Catholic moral codes and willing to expose Spaniards who violated them, especially when trying to get justice for themselves. It is possible that both Condori and Toctaquisa (in his reference to the "land of the Moors") were repeating references to Christian captivity in the Old World that they had learned from priests' sermons or dramatic reenactments. If this is the case, then the two shepherds were appealing to a Christian sense of oppression and injustice.

Although it is unclear how much these particular testimonies are mediated by the voices of the interpreter and scribe, Pedro Condori was telling his own story, if not in his own words,[43] and he made it clear that he was speaking of not only his own suffering, but that of other shepherds, such as Marcos Maqui and

Lucas Puma and others who had served seven or eight years only to end up in debt. In doing so, he transformed his declaration into something similar to the genre of the Latin American *testimonio*: "a form of collective autobiographical witnessing that gives voice to oppressed peoples."[44] Other male and female witnesses also added that the testimony they gave was of their own experience but that the same sufferings were experienced by others. We see similar examples of the collective voice in the testimony about blacks robbing the natives when one witness stated that "it is understood" that the blacks rob the Indians due to their hunger and lack of clothing (see chapter 2).[45] As Tardieu says, by prefacing the statement with "it is understood" (*se ha entendido*), witnesses made it clear that this was not a subjective opinion but a view that is shared by other indigenous people.[46] These are a few among several of the declarations that became seventeenth-century testimonios as individual stories gave voice to an oppressed group, and as indigenous men and women linked the personal to the political.[47] The testimonies of the workers did lead to some relief for the natives of San Ildefonso, who got their salaries and whose maestros were sent to jail. The commission's report also exposed the brutality of the system and surely contributed to later calls for reform. Unfortunately, calls for reform were undermined by Quito's economic needs.

The shepherds, and other ranch hands like Diego Masaquisa, used their declarations to express how the labor system affected them as husbands: they were prevented from spending the night by the warm hearth of their homes, with their wives and children; their wives had to herd sheep when the men were required to go hunting and to defend the sheep from wolves and mountain lions; and their wives were punished in a way that exposed their nakedness in front of other men. In their criticisms, they drew on concepts of Christian morality, including the obligation to go to confession during Holy Week. Condori's testimony mocked the name of the cruel mayordomo and appealed to the king's compassion and mercy, as protector of the Indians. Like Toctaquisa, he compared the indigenous people's oppression to the captivity of Christians under Muslims or "Xivaros," the Shuar people of the Ecuadorian Amazon.[48] While these seventeenth-century indigenous men were probably not familiar with early colonial writings that compared indigenous people to Moors, they both used the analogy of Christian captivity in which *they* were the Christians, turning the earlier comparison on its head. The testimonies of these ranch hands show how colonized, subordinate people in the colonial Americas "actively engaged with the rhetoric and rituals of Christianity to create alliances that might help them in their search for justice and opportunity."[49] They also made it clear that their experiences were the experiences of an oppressed class of people, indigenous people who were also husbands, wives, and family providers. In focusing on their family relations, the natives of Pelileo used the legal commission's recording of their declarations to express their humanity in a system that defined them as laborers.

"WERE IT NOT FOR HIS WIFE HE WOULD PERISH": FOOD, FORASTEROS, AND SILENCES

A common feature of the testimonio genre is to make one's personal experience political. In their references to food in the declarations, indigenous people linked the intimate domestic act of feeding to the labor system of the textile industry to show how they experienced and responded to the oppressive conditions. For example, the widow Marta Pancha, whose children were taken to the obraje and disappeared (mentioned above), described the hunger she experienced while she was made to cook meat for the encomendero's greyhounds. Galarza placed a black man to guard her while she was cooking to make sure she didn't take a single piece of meat: "valuing *us* as less worthy than the greyhounds and dogs; upon seeing that the dogs got meat and bread I cried, dying of hunger in the house of my encomendero who didn't give me a kernel of corn to sustain myself" (my emphasis).[50] Notice that she didn't say "me," but rather "us," which could include other indigenous female cooks, or other indigenous women, or indigenous people in general. She switched back and forth between "I" and "we" in her declaration. Pancha said that many of the wives of the workers were made to cook for Galarza's greyhounds. Like those other women, she expressed the difficulty of cooking meat for the dogs while she went hungry.

A focus on food stories in testimonios, according to Carole Counihan, can reveal information about women's "nutritional status, economic realities, psycho-emotional states, social networks, family concerns and even spouse abuse,"[51] thereby highlighting information that might be otherwise inaccessible. Like bell hooks's call to honor the histories that took place within slave huts, Counihan uses food-centered testimonies to counteract the erasure and silencing of women's contributions to their families and communities. By highlighting statements about women's "food work"[52] in the testimonies of those who worked in San Ildefonso, we get a better sense of how indigenous women shaped their families' historical experience of the textile economy.

Food served as payment among the workers who helped one another. If a man didn't know the techniques of his assigned task, he would have to ask for help from a more skilled worker and share his food in return; or, in some cases, the wife of the worker would bring seasoned guinea-pig meat and corn tortillas for the helper. When an indigenous man was locked in the mill for months or even years at a time, he depended on his women folk to bring him food; workers specifically mentioned *tostado* (probably parched corn, or *sara cancha* in Quichua), corn tortillas, and greens (*yerbas*). The procurement, preparation, cooking, and serving of food is an everyday activity for Andean women. Food carries meanings; aside from the biological necessity of eating, food carries symbolic meaning, and the act of preparing and eating food is entangled with larger cultural and social meanings. While toasted corn and greens were probably basic daily foods, guinea-pig meat was usually reserved for festive occasions.[53] Therefore, it was probably an especially valued food to offer the more skilled worker who helped the less experienced worker. In such cases, the wife of the unskilled worker, among her other tasks, would have to prepare the seasoned guinea-pig meat. For roasted guinea pig, this meant removing the hair and entrails and slowly roasting it over the fire, before taking it to the obraje as compensation to the more skilled worker, so that her husband would not suffer being whipped.

In indigenous men's testimonies, they frequently cite the lack of food as evidence of their suffering in the obraje. In some testimonies, indigenous men who had wives in Pelileo emphasized the important role that their wives played in bringing them food. Those who had wives and children who knew how to spin wool could get some help completing their quotas, as their family members would bring them food and then stay to help them spin wool.

Sometimes fathers would be the ones to bring the food to their children who were working in the obraje. There was a policy of allowing boys' parents and siblings into the obraje when they brought food, because the administrators knew they might stay and help. But other relatives who brought food were sometimes barred from entry, out of fear that they would steal spun wool. The worker would have to take his food and say goodbye at the door. When people did stay to help, the guards would check their clothing at the door when they left, to make sure they were not pilfering wool or other supplies.

Four different Guambaló men gave their testimonies about having their wives bring them food.[54] Melchor Guachambala told the commission of his reliance on his wife: "[A]nd if it weren't for the wife of this witness who brings him food from the town of Pelileo, where she lives with their children, he would perish, and many days when his wife doesn't bring him something to eat he goes hungry." The scribes emphasized this by summarizing and repeating the statement "and if it weren't for his wife, he would perish" in the margins. Similarly, Francisco Aguacunsi, who had been locked in the mill for a year at the time of his declaration, gave his testimony:

> [A]nd he hasn't received one *real* for his food, nor any maize to sustain himself, for which his wife brings him food from the town of Pelileo where he has his house, and his wife lives there, and if his wife on a given day doesn't bring him something to eat, either because she can't or because she doesn't have anything, being that this mill is more than half a league from his said town, then on that day and others that she doesn't come to bring him food [*socorro de comida*], he goes hungry, which wouldn't happen if they would let him work freely without being held as a prisoner.

Sebastian Pubanda had worked in the mill as a weaver since he was a boy. During the years that he was not allowed out to sow his fields, he would be given three and a half fanegas of maize in the obraje. He had a house in the obraje complex, where his children lived with his wife, "who brings him food from outside." But when he would leave to go sow his fields, he would get punished with twenty to thirty lashes in the mill. By stating this, he showed the parallel contributions of his own sacrifice (to fulfill his familial role as one who ploughs and sows the family's crops to produce the food) and his wife's provision of prepared foods in order to support him while he was working in the mill.

Another man told the commission how the difficulties of the mill took a toll on his marriage:

> [A]nd his wife, upon seeing the poverty and hard work they endured, he could not provide for her, nor she for him, with support and food, and she fled, leaving him seven years ago, and in those years he suffered great hardship and hunger, and lost the house that he had in Pelileo, and about two years ago his wife came back, and she helps him as best she can, with a morsel [*bocado*] of food, and if it weren't for her he would perish once and for all in this mill, where his life is at risk, fearful of the whippings and the heavy workload, tormented with fear that he will die there because he is an elderly Indian.

Another worker expressed the importance of having a wife. Miguel Caiza-tassi worked in the obraje as a boy, and he married young, before reaching tributary age (eighteen). He was a wool spinner who had trouble meeting the high quotas that were assigned. He seems to have met his wife in the obraje, and he expressed the importance of having a wife when he said, "I had no one to turn to nor anyone to give me food until I married my wife, who was also working in the obraje spinning [wool] for Doña María de Vera, to make native women's skirts and shawls [*anacos y lligllas*] and after getting married my wife would help me complete my quota." However, the owners also used his marriage as an excuse not to pay him his full salary, claiming that once he got married, they had to pay his tribute.[55]

Through their testimonios, these men transformed the everyday domestic act of feeding into a heroic act. In doing so, they made private acts public and highlighted the value of their wives' roles in bringing them food. Jon Holtzman states that food's symbolic power to move between domestic and public spheres (through open sharing) makes it an especially important focus of collective memory.[56] The men and women who spoke to the commission expressed their memories of hunger, charity through the sharing of food, and the importance of having a wife to bring food on a regular basis.

With no local support network to bring food to an imprisoned obraje worker, that worker could starve. A Chumaquí man, Jacinto Quibisa, was imprisoned in the mill for tribute owed.[57] He had been sent there as a very young man by his cacique and spent thirty-five years imprisoned there, in perpetual debt. Despite having a sister who was married to a cacique, he had nobody to bring him food on a regular basis. María de Vera gave him some food for his work, but it was not enough. Witnesses described him as gaunt and emaciated, full of lice, and so threadbare that his private parts were exposed. He would beg the other workers for food and pick up the scraps from the ground to eat them. Witnesses said that after eating the indigestible stalks of the corn that the other workers discarded, Quibisa's stomach swelled up, and he died several days later. One witness, Don Diego Tubón, a cacique of Guambaló and distant relative of Quibisa, said that once when he was imprisoned in the obraje for about a month for *enteros* (that is, not sending enough workers), he saw Jacinto Quibisa there, who complained of his hunger. "Out of pity," Tubón would share some of his food with Quibisa while they were locked in the mill together, and after his release, the cacique would sometimes send him a *xigrilla* (little shigra—a mesh bag woven from cabuya fibers) of toasted corn or hominy, "whenever he could."[58] Tubón said that he did so with fear, because the maestros didn't like outsiders talking to the prisoners; they would accuse those who brought aid to the prisoners of advising the prisoners to run away. At some point Tubón was reassigned to the position of alcalde in another town and worked there for a year. When Tubón returned, he learned of Jacinto Quibisa's death.

Others told of bringing aid to Quibisa. Luisa Sinaylin, a Chumaquí woman, was the mother-in-law of Jacinto Quibisa's brother (the brother was deceased by the time of the 1661 investigation). Sinaylin also had occasionally provided charity for Quibisa, sending him not only food but old tattered shirts that had belonged to her husband and son. There was a week or two when she didn't send him anything (she didn't say why), and it was during that time that she got word that Quibisa had died. While indigenous people were sending food to Quibisa, each was doing so on an occasional basis, and the diffusion of responsibility left him stranded. The most shocking part of his story is that he had a sister, Doña Potenciana Malqui, who was married to an indigenous elite man, Don Joan Almagro, probably of the Camayos Puruguayes.[59] Like the cacique Don Diego Tubón, Doña Potenciana had to send her brother food in secret: "[S]he would go to see him often and if she went with some type of [food] aid of toasted maize to give him to eat and relieve the great hunger that he said he was experiencing she did it secretly and she found him so consumed, full of lice, and naked that it caused her to feel compassion."[60] When she learned from Luisa Sinaylin that her brother had died, the two women started heading for the mill. Along the way, they met up with an indigenous man who informed them that Quibisa had already been buried in the obraje chapel. Other witnesses said that Quibisa was buried secretly, in the middle of the night, in the obraje chapel, without telling his relatives. Since most natives who died in the mill were buried at the church in Pelileo, some workers interpreted this as an attempt by the foreman to hide the death from the relatives and the priest.[61] The fact that a cacique's wife could not get her own brother out of the mill shows the weakness of the position of the caciques at this time.

If a boy or adult missed one day of work, he would be locked in the obraje for up to a month. The family would have to bring chickens, eggs, or fruit to the maestros as bond. The situation was so bad that some people in Pelileo stopped visiting their family members who were imprisoned in the obraje because they didn't want the administrators to know who they were. They feared that if their family members fled, they would then be recognized as a relative and taken to replace them. As one witness said, some lamented that "even their relatives denied them."[62] The fact that some broke the relations shows that the fear reached extreme levels.

As Andean men considered whether to run away from the obraje, they had to think about their families. Augustín Hambacho had run away many times, but he didn't abandon his family, and the alcaldes and alguaciles always brought him back. Once he was caught ploughing his fields with his wife; the alcalde Juan Challay took him from there back to the obraje. As punishment for running away, Infante ordered four blacks to whip him, taking turns in pairs. They placed him in a leg iron (*toba*), "used for blacks," and bathed his wounds in old urine (*orinas podridas*; urine was mixed with water as part of the solution for cleaning the wool), and they never returned his pants. Hambacho told the commission that his most recent attempt to escape was just the week before. He tried to escape from the dungeon with a rope, but the rope broke, and he fell to the ground and split his chest open. The administrator Lopez Noboa would not allow him to leave to be cured, unless someone came and posted bond to ensure his return. But everybody was afraid to come to the obraje, so nobody would bail him out.[63]

Just as indigenous people from Pelileo were fleeing to other towns, even as far away as Cuenca to the south and Otavalo to the north, others were migrating to Pelileo. But many of the forasteros serving in San Ildefonso were not runaways but debt prisoners or petty thieves sent from other towns by the authorities. They were called forasteros because they were outsiders, not known to the indigenous people of Pelileo. Several witnesses testified that the forasteros had it the worst, because they lacked a kin support network in the town. Some outsiders also suffered because, unlike those who grew up in the shadow of the obraje, they lacked the skills of carding, spinning, beating the wool, weaving, and dyeing that were expected of them. As one person put it, local indigenous children in Pelileo were acculturated (*conaturalizados*) in the tasks of the textile mill. Even some of the local people were not skilled in cloth production, since many of them grew up learning only agriculture and animal husbandry. When a person was inexperienced in his assigned task, he would be beaten for any little imperfection. Furthermore, the local Pilalata, Chumaquí, and Guambaló workers had spouses, children, siblings, parents, and ritual kin (their children's godparents) in Pelileo. People knew one another. The forasteros, by contrast, were alone and didn't know anybody in Pelileo. People didn't even know their names.

Estevan Vasquez was a Crown forastero (that is, he had been aggregated with other forasteros for the purpose of paying tribute) living in Ambato, a subject of the cacique Lorenzo Zuniga. He was accused of stealing maize and sentenced to the mill of San Ildefonso along with other prisoners. Upon entering the obraje, he was given one hundred lashes, and from there on he was forced to work spinning wool by day and locked in the dungeon at night. During the year and a half that he worked in the mill, he was given nothing more than three fanegas of maize and one patacón worth of silver for food. He said that he was perishing because he didn't have a wife to bring him food. He appeared to be young; the scribes estimated his age around eighteen. Fortunately for Vasquez, the Quito commission ordered his release.

Gabriel Centeno, an elderly cacique of Guambaló, gave statements about what he had witnessed for twenty years prior to the investigation. When asked if he knew "the Indian who died from hunger," Centeno replied that he wasn't sure, because during the time that Alonso Infante was maestro

> there were many forasteros in the obraje who died from hunger, skin infections, and melancholy from finding themselves imprisoned, the skin infections [*sarnas*] from the lashes that they gave them in the buttocks and backs, and the hunger because they didn't have anyone to give them food because they were forasteros. Those from *la tierra* [local people] have wives, sisters, or children who sustain them. This witness doesn't remember their [the forasteros'] names, he doesn't even know them, he can't say who they were, only that many of the said forastero Indians were not known. They sent them to the said obraje because of debts and other things from different lands, even from the Puruguayes and from San Andres, which, since there are so many obrajes there [i.e., in Riobamba] this witness doesn't know why they sent them to this one of San Ildefonso. He has heard that in that time the said General Don Antonio Lopez de Galarza rented the obraje of San Andres to Joseph de Villaviancio and that's why he stopped sending them [debtors] to that obraje.[64]

The forasteros of which Centeno speaks were indigenous people whom Galarza had ensnared in debt, and he used his wife's obraje as a debtor's prison. Augustín Hambacho also declared that in his thirty years of being stuck in the obraje, many outsiders from other parts of the jurisdiction of Ambato (Tisaleo, Píllaro, and Quero) died from whippings ordered by Infante, but he didn't know their names. The testimony of Centeno and others highlights the importance of having family members to bring food to the obraje. Other witnesses testified that the forasteros were the ones who were forever trapped in debt because with no family they had to rely on the obraje *socorros*—advances of food and goods against one's work account—in order to eat. Since the food and clothing was always valued at inflated prices by María de Vera, the forastero worker could never get out of debt.

Men relied on their mothers and wives for food, but women helped their husbands and sons in other ways besides bringing their meals to the obraje. The wife of Pedro Tasiquiña helped him by begging a Spaniard to pay off his debt (from sheep) and free him from the obraje. That Spaniard, Andres de Miranda, "felt compassion" for Tasiquiña, so he paid off the debt and took Tasiquiña to work on his ranch.[65] But many indigenous men came out of the obraje very ill with sickness and injuries contracted in the mill or its dungeon, and Tasiquiña died about a year after his release. Augustín Ullalloa's wife had run away, so he had nobody to bring him food. He had been sent to the mill as punishment for assault and robbery. There, he was shackled, hungry, lonely, and depressed. He began defecating blood, and when they sent him out of the obraje, he only made it as far as the nearby home of an indigenous widow. Ullalloa's mother turned to her cousin, a cacique of Guambaló, for help in paying for the funeral and recovering the money he was owed. Proper funeral rites were a concern for the workers and their families: some reported that their husbands or fathers requested on their deathbeds that their salaries be recovered to pay for their funerals.[66]

Men related to each other through marriage helped each other, but the suffering endured in the obraje could lead to guilt and resentment among men who substituted for one another. Augustín Yumiquínga said that when he became ill in the obraje, his son-in-law agreed to substitute for him working as a wool beater. Because the son-in-law didn't do the job well, he was given one hundred lashes. When Yumiquínga came forward to give his statement to the commission, he took the opportunity to tell not only his own story but also the story of his loyal son-in-law who substituted for him. He declared that the injuries were so bad that it looked like his son-in-law had been skinned alive.[67] Favian Picha went in to the obraje as a guarantor for his wife's brother. Picha's brother-in-law, Don Damian Alomaliza, was not allowed out of the mill to attend his own wife's funeral, without a guarantor. Picha entered temporarily, but his brother-in-law did not return right away from the funeral. Picha was put to work in the batan (fulling mill), but since he didn't know the technique well, the maestro Alonso

Infante found a flaw in the cloth. Infante beat him and ordered four indigenous men to hold him down while the slave Chinchico whipped him. When Picha's wife came to bring him food, he scolded her, telling her that it was because of her brother that he was in that situation, and that if she didn't bring her brother back, he would kill her. She went, along with her husband's brothers, to bring her brother back to the obraje.

For indigenous wives and mothers, the reality of the obraje must have been a dark cloud that was constantly hanging over them. Given the stories of children being captured for labor while walking to do chores, such as tending the fields or moving animals, mothers must have worried about the risk of sending their children to the fields. Stories portray the alcalde of the obraje and recogedores as going out late at night, when the priest couldn't interfere, to take boys from their homes. Witnesses told the commission that women also feared that their husbands would join the many forasteros who ran away from the mill and abandoned their families to seek a new life in another town or in the city. If that happened, the women or their children would be taken by force to replace the husband. Ventura Cunamasi said he could not risk having his wife or children forced into the obraje to replace him, so when he ran away, he took his family with him. But he was recaptured, and eventually he gave up any hope of escaping. Instead, he built a house near the obraje chapel so that they could live closer.[68] Indeed, so many local natives, as well as men who married the daughters of those locals, built their houses close to the obraje, so that one witness said it looked like a populated town around the mill.[69]

One strategy of mothers whose sons were taken was to try to keep siblings together. Although Marta Pancha said that the cacique took her daughter along with her son, other testimonies indicate that parents would send a sibling, even a younger sibling, along with a child who was taken to the obraje. The wet nurse Lorenza Santa (mentioned in chapter 2) sent a sister along to help the two brothers who were taken to the mill. The alcalde, she said, "with a staff of authority entered my home and took two of my sons and delivered them [to the obraje] on the encomienda's account, and they have served as spinners in the obraje in the company of a sister of theirs, my daughter, which, so that they wouldn't whip [the boys] for [not meeting] the quotas, and because they couldn't [complete the tasks] due to their young age, the first few days I worked at the spinning wheel helping them, and after that my daughter went to help."[70] Clara Chunchu, a widow of the encomienda whose husband was a pig caretaker for Galarza, was also made to spin wool and cook for Galarza's greyhounds. Her very young son was sent to the obraje to work as a spinner and could only reach his quota with the help of his young sister. None had been paid for their work. When Merlo de la Fuente went to inspect the mill himself, he found "a little Indian girl" (*una indiazuela*) spinning wool, working there in place of her father, who had to tend to the family's crops. Her brother, who looked to be about ten years old, accompanied her.[71] At least a child wouldn't be completely alone if he or she had a sibling to help in the mill and, if anything happened, would possibly have a witness. Unfortunately for Marta Pancha, both of her children disappeared after going to the mill, and the others ran away to avoid a similar fate.

SPANISH LANDOWNERS

As mentioned above in the story of the wife of Pedro Tasquiña, there were landowning Spaniards who allowed workers who escaped from the obraje to stay on their ranches and haciendas as workers. A cacique confirmed that many indigenous men were running away and volunteering to work for Spanish hacendados in order to avoid the obraje. When Andres de Miranda, who had a ranch in Mocha (near Quero), paid off the debt of Pedro Tasiquiña to take him as a laborer, the indigenous witnesses interpreted this as an act of compassion. Although Miranda may have hoped to benefit from having another indigenous laborer, he did not take Pedro Tasquiña out of the obraje on his own initiative, but only after Tasquiña's wife begged him to do so. Another Spanish landowner, Antonio Sanchez, took in Estevan Ayuquina, hoping to cure him and get his labor, but the swelling in Ayuquina's feet from the shackles never went down, and he died. When the principales came for Francisco Quispe, the man who drowned in the Patate River (see chapter 2), he was living with his wife and mother on the ranch of Don Pedro Flores. The principales tricked him into going with them by telling Quispe that they were taking him to the ranch of another Spaniard, General Don Francisco de Villagomez, and he was happy to go (according to his wife). That natives hoped to work on the ranch of a Spaniard as a way out to escape the obraje is best summed up by the testimony of Augustín Yumiquínga. He described the vicious circle of debt peonage: those who were locked in the mill and didn't have family had to get into further debt by accepting advances of food at inflated prices, which only increased the amount of time that they had to serve, "and some were there until they were old, unless there was some Spaniard who got them out so that they would serve him, or if their caciques got them out."[72] Men and their wives sought refuge from the mill on these estates.

INDIGENOUS CULTURE AND THE OBRAJE

Merlo de la Fuente's careful recording of the testimonies of indigenous people in Pelileo allowed indigenous people to voice their experiences in the textile economy. They related their personal experiences to the experiences of other indigenous people, even indigenous people whom they didn't know. The workers were not just telling their personal stories but, knowing that their statements were being written down, made sure that the story of the deceased Jacinto Quibisa and the stories of the unknown forasteros would not die. In doing so, they were, as Nancy Saporta Sternbach says, "creating a consciousness of what has been silenced or what could be forgotten—the dead."[73]

The testimonies reveal how the textile economy affected indigenous culture. It did not determine indigenous culture, much of which would have taken place within indigenous homes, in private, away from the eyes of priests and administrators. Practices such as healing, story telling, family interactions, performing domestic ceremonies, praying, and sharing jokes would have constituted aspects of indigenous culture that are rarely accessible from the record. However, the testimonies show that the textile economy had a major impact on Andean cultural and social life.

Local children were socialized into the tasks of wool-cloth production from the time they were young. Caciques spoke of the customs of the land and the traditions, which they inherited, of sending laborers to Galarza's mill and associated estates. Indigenous elders who were reserved from the labor draft were made to work taking care of Galarza's chickens, guinea pigs, and pigs. The indigenous middleman position of maestro de capilla involved being present when someone made out his will, sometimes dying from illnesses and injuries suffered in the obraje. The priests would come to the obraje to take confessions from the dying indigenous workers and would bury their bodies at the church in Pelileo. People relied on Andean institutions of kinship, marriage, reciprocal help, and mingas as cultural resources on which they could draw in order to survive in the textile economy.

They also relied on obraje advances (against their work accounts) for the ritual paraphernalia that they needed to properly celebrate feast days. Among the goods paid to indigenous workers as salary were ritual objects, including candles for Holy Week and feathers, ankle bells, special clothing, and silk ribbons—items which constitute part of the Corpus Christi dancers' costumes to this day. Galarza told the Quito commission that the Indians themselves asked for advances against their work accounts in order to obtain these items to dance in the festivals of Corpus Christi and San Pedro, as well as meat and chicha for occasions such as weddings, mingas, and house-raising work parties. He said that the Indians had their religious confraternities (*cofradías*) and that since the time the obraje was founded, there were always proper religious services during Holy Week (such as confession). Throughout the seventeenth and eighteenth centuries, different obraje owners would advance bread (or wheat flour for baking bread) to the native workers for the Day of the Dead, November 2, a time when modern indigenous people of Pelileo bake bread to take to the cemetery and to exchange with one another and, symbolically, with the souls of their deceased ancestors. Therefore, they were dependent on the obraje for the symbolic foods necessary for observing the collective memory of their families. During the festival of Saint Thomas (the saint for whom the sugar mill was named), María de Vera would give maize to the wives of the workers and ask them to make chicha for the workers; but if their husbands drank some of that maize beer, it was charged against their accounts.

Occasionally, the owners would give money to pay for the burial of a native worker who died in the obraje, while at the same time denying any responsibility for the death. Several men, on their deathbeds, asked their families to recover their wages from the obraje, and families would attempt to recover unpaid wages in order to pay for the funeral. The shepherds who had to sneak away to go to their towns for confession around Easter time were not only fulfilling their Catholic obligations, but possibly spending holiday time with their wives and children. The warmth of the household hearth must have been a welcome comfort from the lonely, damp, cold pastures where they spent most of their nights. Indigenous family life and culture were pervaded by the culture of the obraje in Pelileo, and the children of the Pilalata and Chumaquí were enculturated to obraje life from the time they were young. From the testimonies we can see the intense pressure that was put on families, the guilt and resentment generated by having one relative or in-law substitute for another, and occasionally the acts of compassion among indigenous people and between people occupying different colonial racial categories. Several witnesses said that there was one compassionate maestro named Pedro Nuñez, who was deceased at the time of the investigation. One indigenous witness even made a policy suggestion, recommending to the commission that the cruel maestros be replaced with someone good like Nuñez; then, he said, the king would get his tribute because Indians would work there voluntarily, rather than running away.

CONCLUSION

The testimonies I presented in this chapter tell the cultural history of the indigenous people of Pelileo when San Ildefonso was owned by María de Vera Mendoza and labor was controlled by Antonio Lopez de Galarza. The stories told reveal how the labor structure in the textile economy affected people's relations with their caciques and other indigenous intermediaries, how it affected indigenous families, and the strategies people used to survive and maintain their families and cultural lives. Andeans relied on their kin as a resource, and they relied on the obraje for maintaining certain cultural, religious, and social practices, although accepting advances kept them indebted to the obraje.

Although Galarza was temporarily detained during the investigation, he kept his encomienda, and María de Vera's obraje stayed in the family. Alonso Infante (who had been fired prior to the investigation) and the mill guard "were convicted of crimes against the Indians and were sent to prison. Their moveable property was confiscated by the crown; their homes were razed, and salt was spread on the empty sites of their houses, symbolizing sterility and complete disgrace."[74] The criminal case against Galarza, and criminal sentences for the administrators, may have curbed some of the worst abuses, and native workers were paid money that was owed to them. Accounts were settled with more than 1,518 indigenous people who had worked for Galarza between 1619 and 1665.[75] The obraje passed on to the heirs of María de Vera Mendoza. The Pilalata, Chumaquí, Guambaló, and other indigenous people continued to work in the obraje as it changed ownership. It is not clear whether, or how much, working conditions improved at San Ildefonso, since we do not have detailed investigations of the obraje after 1666. The level of violence against workers depended on the individual foreman, but unfortunately the abuses reported at San Ildefonso were widespread throughout obrajes of the Audiencia of Quito. As Nicholas Cushner said of the 1661 investigation of San Ildefonso, "similar conditions existed in other mills and no government inspections were made."[76]

While many natives of Pelileo fled to avoid the obraje, indigenous peoples from other towns migrated from their home communities and came to Pelileo. The labor grab continued, and caciques often complained that Spaniards were pressuring them to send more and more indigenous workers into their service. Under such pressure, and perhaps hiding their own private workforces,[77] caciques engaged in disputes with one another over succession to the cacicazgo and rights to govern indigenous subjects. The next chapter examines these disputes in multiethnic Pelileo during the first decades of the eighteenth century, with special attention to native elite women. While the testimonies presented in this chapter reveal how the obraje affected indigenous society, the analysis of gender and native governance in the next chapter reveals information about indigenous society outside of the obraje, to give us a better understanding of the social organization of the ayllus of Pelileo.

FIGURE 12. Prayers for the Deceased. Nineteenth-Century Ecuador. From *Álbum de costumbres ecuatorianas* in Biblioteca Digital Hispánica.

CHAPTER 4

CACIQUES AND CACICAS

Gender and Native Governance among the Ayllus of Pelileo
(1675–1728)

B Y THE late seventeenth century, the obraje had passed on to Don Fernando Dávalos, an heir of María de Vera. Dávalos was married to María Villagomez de Larraspuru, a niece of Galarza's son, in a union that was typical of marriages between elite families.[1] Dávalos owned four obrajes in the central sierra and rented another, and these passed to his widow after his death (sometime between 1697 and 1707).[2] Galarza's son became the new encomendero of the Pilalata and Chumaquí.

The records from this time period reveal information on the cultural history of Pelileo's indigenous peoples and the strategies they used to improve their circumstances and that of their descendants. Through an analysis of three legal dramas involving the daughters of caciques, I show how both native elite women and commoners manipulated colonial laws and exploited ambiguities in colonial administrative practices in order to improve their status. Since all three cases involve female chiefs, a discussion of Andean concepts of gender, descent, inheritance, and succession is necessary. The first part of the chapter provides a sketch of the ethnic and racial diversity of Pelileo in the late seventeenth century, followed by a discussion of gender parallelism as practiced by the indigenous families at the time. The rest of the chapter examines the three disputes involving cacicas, and each case tells something about the ayllus of Pelileo and the people who governed them. The first case, of Sebastiana Chango, cacica of the Pilalata, includes descriptions of her two investiture ceremonies, revealing details of colonial indigenous political rituals. Shortly after Sebastiana's ordeal, a cacica of the Chumaquí had her own dispute with a male relative over succession to the cacicazgo, and both sides debated the rules of female succession. In both cases, these daughters of the caciques of the Pilalata and Chumaquí grew up to challenge male relatives who had been placed as interim caciques.

The final case involves not the obraje Indians but the Sigchos Collanas, who used a strategy of manipulating the competition between a cacica and cacique in an effort to get the best treatment for themselves. While native elite men and women used legal maneuvers and exploited ambiguities in colonial laws of succession, the commoner Sigchos Collanas played caciques against one another and changed their ayllu affiliation back and forth. While all three cases provide information about indigenous social and cultural life during the transition period between Galarza's ownership of the obraje and the Jesuit purchase in 1724, it is the final case that reveals information about the ethnic transformation from Sigchos Collanas to Salasacas. I begin with a description of Pelileo's diversity in the post-Galarza years.

AYLLUS AND THEIR CACIQUES

We have some clues as to the ethnic composition of Pelileo toward the end of the seventeenth century, although the parcialidades were not pure ethnic groups, since they intermarried. By 1675 there were many indigenous migrants who had fled their home communities and settled as forasteros in Pelileo, who remained free from the labor obligations imposed on the local indigenous people.[3] By 1693 a Dominican friar said that thirty forastero families were present in the obraje complex but were not listed in tribute rolls. In the 1693 report the friar also said that Pelileo contained eighty-three black male and female slaves belonging to Galarza's son.[4] In addition to a few Cañaris from southern Ecuador, the friar said there were 628 families divided into Pelileo's different parcialidades, which correspond to the ayllus around which eighteenth-century baptismal records were organized: Guambaló, Chumaquí, Pilalata, Camayos Puruguayes, Carpinteros, Salasacas (Sigchos Collanas) and forasteros, Tacungas (or Latacungas), and the Royal Crown (Corona Real). Each of these had their own caciques. Although the Guambaló, Pilalata, and Chumaquí might be considered the same ethnic group, because their caciques shared a common ancestor, other ayllus

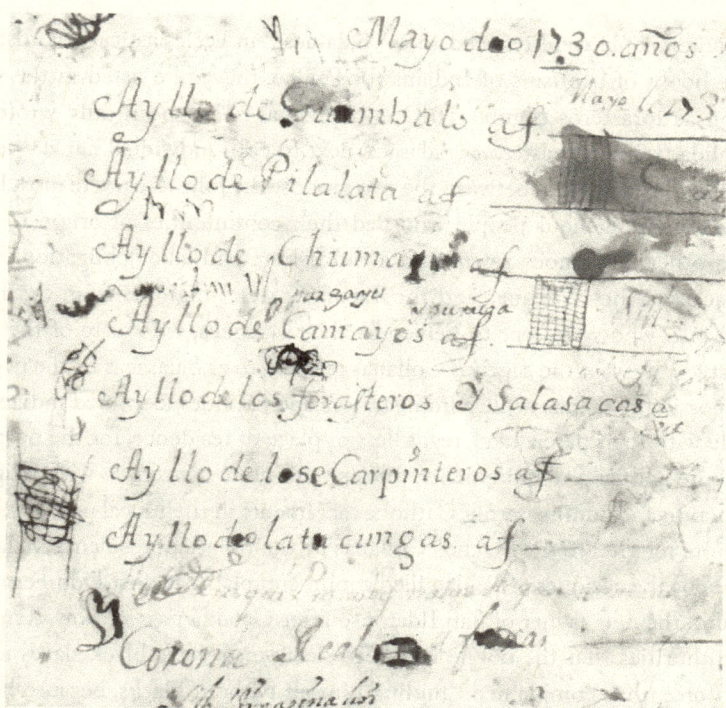

FIGURE 13. "Book of Baptisms (Indians)." Pelileo, 1730.

probably constituted different ethnic groups. For example, the Carpinteros were not the same ethnic group as the Tacungas or Sigchos Collanas. I will briefly describe some of these ayllus.

The Camayos Puruguayes may have been descendants of earlier settlers sent to work the native elites' coca fields in Pelileo; later they served Spaniards on their ranches as part of the labor draft. The Carpinteros, sometimes referred to as Incas Carpinteros, were one of three mitimae populations brought to the town of Quero by the Incas. They were renowned for their wood furniture craftsmanship[5] and exempt from the labor draft.[6] Some of the Royal Crown natives must have been descendants of the earlier "Royal Crown" forasteros who were aggregated by Agustin de la Nasca in 1641 (chapter 1). These included descendants of people from Peru as well as abandoned babies whose ethnic groups were unknown.

The Salasacas were usually listed as "Sigchos Collanas" in court records and often identified themselves this way (for example, *dijo ser de los Sigchos Collanas*).

The same people were referred to as "Salasacas" in ecclesiastical records; and in the books of baptisms of Indians for Pelileo, they were listed in the same section as forasteros (figure 13). One baptismal book specifically wrote the parcialidad, either forastero *or* Salasaca, next to each individual name, thereby showing the distinction between the two groups. The forasteros were most likely runaways—indigenous people who fled their communities of origin to hide out in other indigenous towns and avoid tribute and labor obligations.[7] The Salasacas/Sigchos Collanas and the Tacungas were migrants from the Latacunga area who were sent to Pelileo by their caciques, who were of the Hati dynasty. Why were the Sigchos Collanas referred to as Salasacas by the priests? One possibility is that while administrators and caciques identified indigenous people with their parcialidad, regardless of place of residence, for the purposes of tribute and labor requirements, priests were more concerned with religious instruction and administering Catholic sacraments in their local parishes. They therefore referred to the Sigchos Collanas by their place of residence, Salasaca.

In 1695 the caciques of Pelileo filed a joint complaint against Don Fernando Dávalos, the new owner of San Ildefonso after Galarza passed away. Reminding authorities that the obraje had been licensed to have black slaves as the labor force, they complained: "finding himself without blacks, because he has distributed them, [Dávalos] is making use of the Indians of the town, at the expense of the hacendados," who were harassing the caciques for laborers.[8] Later documents do not mention blacks at the obraje, indicating that some time after 1695 obraje owners stopped using slave labor. Competition for indigenous labor between the obraje and haciendas continued, and it was compounded by late seventeenth-century epidemics and out-migration that led to a decrease in available indigenous workers. Additionally, an earthquake in 1698 caused flooding that killed hundreds, including many workers of San Ildefonso,[9] and Spanish and indigenous survivors had their lands destroyed. The caciques faced mounting pressures from Spaniards to provide workers from a dwindling indigenous labor force.

Despite the difficulty of ruling in this intermediary position, being a cacique had its benefits. Aside from status symbols and prestige, for men it meant that they were exempt from tribute and labor requirements, and for women it could serve as a seat that their sons could inherit. Therefore, the death of a cacique left a power vacuum in which different relatives competed for the right to take over the position. Before discussing the role of the cacicas of Pelileo, a discussion of gender in the colonial Andes is necessary.

GENDER PARALLELISM

In the colonial Andes, the rules and ceremonies of succession to the political administrative position of cacique were based on a combination of indigenous and Spanish customs. The process of succession was complicated by different Andean and Spanish ideas about gender and kinship. Irene Silverblatt's work on gender parallelism provides evidence for a pre-Columbian tradition of complementary male and female powers. Gender parallelism included the idea that men descend from a line of men, and women from a line of women. Prior to the implementation of Spanish-style patriarchy, Andean women would inherit property, and even religious offices, from their mothers, and men would inherit from their fathers. Women would ask their mothers for permission to marry, and men would ask their fathers.[10] When a parent died, sons were sent with their father's family, while daughters went with their mother's relatives.[11] There are some ethnographic examples that suggest a continuation of gender parallelism in the modern Andes. The Saraguro of the southern Ecuadorian Andes show gender parallelism in the area of festival sponsorship, in which women can be sponsors in their own right, not just as the wives of male sponsors.[12]

In colonial Pelileo, and some other parts of the Andes,[13] gender parallelism is most clearly seen in the parallel transmission of last names. Most indigenous families in Pelileo assigned the mother's last name to daughters and the father's last name to sons. Although this seems to be a clear example of pre-Columbian parallel descent, the practice was also mandated by ecclesiastical authorities in the Third Council of Lima in 1583. After it was noted that some natives were repeating baptisms and marriages, and as a measure to get them away from using pagan names, it was stated that natives should be given Christian names at baptism, and that men should be given their father's surnames and women should be given their mother's surnames.[14] If pre-Columbian Andeans of Quito had surnames, then the Council's mandate could be a continuation of a pre-Columbian pattern. However, it seems that very few native Andeans used surnames prior to Christianization.[15] Whether the mandate was continuing an older pattern or establishing a new one, parallel transmission of surnames fits very well with the Andean concept of parallel descent and was the dominant pattern among indigenous people in Pelileo up to the nineteenth century. Wills typically group sons together under one last name and daughters under another. A typical will, say from a man named José Masaquiza, might state his declaration that he was married to María Comasanta, and during the time of their marriage they had as their legitimate children sons Manuel, Pedro, and Juan Masaquiza and daughters Magdalena, Angelina, and Teresa Comasanta. The testator would then divide up property among both daughters and sons.

There are some last names that were feminine surnames in the colonial period, including Sinalin (and its variations Sinailin or Sinaylin, one of the most common), Comasanta, and Culqui. While the parallel transmission of last names seems to be a clear example of a "continuation" of gender parallelism, the question of female leadership as a pre-Columbian institution is debated by scholars.

There were many female chiefs and governors in the colonial Andes, but it is not clear how widespread female leadership was before the colonial era. Karen Graubart cautions that colonial cacicas were more likely the result of a colonial reworking of indigenous "custom" than the continuation of a preconquest tradition,[16] but other ethnohistorians provide some evidence for a tradition of female leadership. For the northern Andes (Quito), Powers cites evidence of female rulers and matrilineal succession at the time of conquest and argues that it was Spanish officials who stripped cacicas of their power and administrative duties.[17] Lane found a case from colonial Quito that suggests a tradition of female leadership. In that case, a cacica from the northern Pasto region chose her nephew to succeed her to the cacicazgo, with the stipulation that *he* was to choose a female successor. According to Lane, "The immediate naming of a male successor satisfied Spanish expectations in lieu of primogeniture, but the call for future reversion to female leadership was a bold challenge, perhaps even a blast from Pasto's prehispanic past."[18] David Garrett assesses arguments about the tradition of female succession and examines cases of female cacicas in eighteenth-century Peru. According to Garrett, the existence of cacicas allowed indigenous people to have a leader who also conformed to Spanish ideas about descent and inheritance of office.[19] There were probably regional variations in the pre-Hispanic traditions of female succession. By the colonial period cacicas could be found throughout the Andes. When a new cacica or cacique took over, colonial administrators performed a public investiture ceremony in which all the subjects were required to recognize the new leader, as described in the following case.

PILALATA: THE CASE OF SEBASTIANA CHANGO

In 1709 Sebastiana Chango claimed to be the legitimate successor to the cacicazgo of the Pilalata. Sebastiana was challenged by a male relative, Bernardo

Chango Toassa, who claimed that he inherited the cacicazgo from his mother, who he claimed was the "cacica principal" (supreme leader or paramount lord) and "cacica y governadora" (governor) of the Pilalata, although she does not appear as cacica in any records that I have found. Sebastiana had an official grant giving her the right to the cacicazgo, and since she was a woman, her minor-aged son would carry out the administrative duties of tribute collection. Her brother had been carrying out the administrative duties, "with her permission." This is a case of being cacica in name only and not actually performing administrative duties.[20] Several elderly indigenous men, including those from the Sigchos Collanas, gave statements about Bernardo's genealogy that supported his succession.

Bernardo was not Sebastiana's first challenger to the cacicazgo. Sebastiana had previously been challenged by Bernardo's grandfather in 1700. Bernardo's grandfather, she said, was a foster child raised by her uncle, the cacique Don Francisco Chango. At that time the colonial authority (corregidor) gave Sebastiana possession of the cacicazgo in the "ancient custom" (*al usansa del tiempo jentelisimo*), and Sebastiana, recalling that investiture ceremony, stated, "[T]he Indian men and women of the parcialidad (of Pilalata) and said caciacasgo recognized me as the cacica, and even though Don Gegorio Toasa, cacique of another parcialidad called Chumaquí and governor of the said town of Pelileo, objected to the possession without having the right, he later dropped his objection, recognizing that I am the legitimate cacica."[21]

Investiture ceremonies were the same for men and women, although Paula Daza found a case in which there was a "certain feminization" of the ceremony for the seating of a cacica in Ambato in 1720. In that case, the colonial official crowned the cacica with a flower wreath.[22] Although I have found slight variations in the details that were recorded for investiture ceremonies in Ambato at different times, the general aspects of the legal ritual were the same throughout the Andes.[23] The common elements of Andean investiture ceremonies include Spanish officials seating the new cacique on a ceremonial stool, traditionally called a duho or *tiana*, but in eighteenth-century cases from this region it was simply referred to as a *silla*. The ceremonial stool was an indigenous symbol of authority.[24] Another part of investiture ceremonies commonly recorded in official documentation is that the subjects publicly recognize the new cacique through acts of deference such as kissing the hand and, in Sebastiana's case, kneeling before her. Although not mentioned here, some documents explicitly describe the distribution of maize beer as part of the ceremony. Another investiture ceremony from Ambato during this time period mentions the cacique resting his feet on top of a strongbox or community chest.[25]

Sebastiana Chango's first investiture ceremony took place on Sunday, August 15, 1700, when all the indigenous people were gathered together for religious instructions (*doctrina general*). In the middle of the doctrina, a seat (silla) was placed with a rug stretched out and straw and branches placed on top. Sebastiana, wearing "an insignia of the Inca on her head," was taken by the corregidor and "he made her sit, giving her possession of the said cacicazgo, and as a sign of such possession he ordered that the secondary chiefs [*pricipales*] and Indians, her subjects, come forth and kiss her hand, which many Indian men and women did, giving signs of their happiness to receive her as their cacica during which time Don Gregorio Toasa, governor and cacique of this said town [of the sector of Chumaquí], said two times 'I object, I object.'"[26]

Despite the objection, the corregidor granted possession to Sebastiana. The details of Sebastiana's ceremony—the Inca insignia worn on the head, or the rug and straw placed on the ceremonial stool—are not mentioned in other descriptions of ceremonies that I have seen for the region, but the continuation of a ceremony despite a challenger's objection three times (usually) does seem typical. The authorities would record the objection as part of the record, but proceed anyway.

Although Sebastiana claimed that the ceremony legitimized her as cacica "according to the ancient custom," claims to Inca or pre-Columbian customs were thrown around in the colonial period as rhetorical devices rather than accurate descriptions of pre-Columbian traditions.[27] The investiture ceremony itself, according to Thomas Cummins, "created the ritual nexus between Spanish and native authority and hierarchy," and the ceremony combined Andean and Spanish symbols of prestige. While the cacique would shed native ethnic attire for Spanish clothing, the seat or stool remained as an indigenous symbol of authority. The symbols and ritual of the possession ceremony, says Cummins, linked the curaca (cacique), and by extension the entire ayllu "in a subordinate relation to Spanish rule and culture."[28] The ceremony was a formality. As Sinclair Thomson points out, the community members are called to give their approval after the fact—that is, after the cacique or cacica has been ritually seated and given power by the Spanish official.[29]

Although colonial authorities legally granted possession of the cacicazgo to Sebastiana, it was taken from her by her male relative. In a complaint she filed, Sebastiana said that after about a year and a half of possessing the cacicazgo, Bernardo took it from her. She stated: "[A]nd I as a lone woman, and without any recourse, allowed him to take it from me, for lack of means" to resist. Sebastiana was a widow from her first marriage, but her second husband, the cacique of camayos (most likely Puruguayes from Riobamba) living in Pelileo, also asked that the court restore his wife as cacica, on behalf of her son. Indeed, this seemed to be what was at issue for Sebastiana and her husband: keeping the cacicazgo in Sebastiana's name so that Sebastiana's son could inherit the position. Becoming cacique would mean that her son was exempt from tribute and labor requirements.

Sebastiana's petition to restore her as the cacica was granted on November 6, 1709. Her challengers, Gregorio Toasa (cacique of the Chumaquí) and Bernardo Chango, were legally notified of the decision, and on November 24, 1709, Sebastiana was given another investiture ceremony. In the central plaza during the doctrina general, among many native men and women, caciques, subchiefs, and leaders, the chief constable (*alguacil mayor*) of Ambato restored Sebastiana's right to the cacicazgo. Sebastiana sat on a seat or stool "where there was much straw and branches in the custom of the Indians and some Indian men and women from the sector of Pilalatas gave her obedience, bending their knees to the ground and kissing her hand."[30] At this time, Don Bernardo Chango, who had been governing the Pilalata after Sebastiana had been deposed, stated his objection three times, but the alguacil mayor continued with the legal recognition of Sebastiana as cacica. That concluded the documentation of Sebastiana's case. Common Pilalata were called and gathered to participate in the ceremony by promising obedience to the new cacica, who would be the one to designate them as laborers in the obraje or on Spanish ranches and estates. Legal disputes between two contenders for the cacicazgo often involve older indigenous men as witnesses, some in favor of one contender, others in favor of another. One question raised by this case is why Gregorio Toasa, the cacique of the Chumaquí, meddled in the investiture ceremony for the Pilalata. It seems that he preferred to deal with Sebastiana's male relative as his fellow cacique. Shortly after this incident, Gregorio would have his own battle with a female relative over the cacicazgo of the Chumaquí.

CHUMAQUÍ: MARÍA TOASA

In 1712 Gregorio Toasa was competing with his "niece," the daughter of his cousin, over the right to govern the Chumaquí. Although Gregorio had been the "acting cacique" of the Chumaquí, María Toasa argued that since she was the legitimate daughter, and therefore a "first-degree" relative of the previous cacique, she was next in line for succession. Her case was represented by the protector of natives. According to the protector, María's father died leaving no male heirs, and since she was a minor at the time, her uncle (Gregorio) took over as interim cacique to perform the administrative duties. Now that she was of legal age to govern, and married, she argued that she should take over as cacica. In this case, both María and Gregorio claimed the cacicazgo based on descent from a common cacique ancestor, Ventura Toasa. However, María was in the direct line of descent, tracing her line to the elder son of Ventura, while Gregorio was descended from the younger son, making him a "second-degree" relation. Gregorio's legal representative admitted that the common ancestor, Ventura, had two sons, and María was a descendant of the elder son, but "being that she is female and my client male, she is excluded," and this, he said, is according to both legal doctrine and the custom of the province, adding that "males, even if they are of the second degree relations, exclude females even of the first degree," and he requested that the court nullify María's possession of the cacicazgo. Furthermore, he challenged the legitimacy of María's investiture ceremony since, as acting cacique, Gregorio was not notified and did not have the opportunity to object one, two, and three times.[31]

Each party in the dispute had indigenous, mestizo, and Spanish witnesses, mostly older men, who gave statements about the elite contenders' descent and history. Part of the diversity of Pelileo's past was the involvement of Spaniards, Indians, and mestizos in each other's legal dramas. In 1713 Doña María Toasa's witnesses included a cacique of Ambato and Doña María Villagomez de Larraspuru, the widow of Don Fernando Dávalos and the owner of San Ildefonso at the time. The heiress to the obraje testified as to the geneaology of the cacica and her legitimacy as successor. Perhaps the obraje owner had her own motivations for preferring María Toasa as cacica.

The protector, representing María, argued that until the direct line of primogeniture is extinguished, second-degree relatives are excluded from the cacicazgo. He accused the other party of trying to confuse Spanish officials about the law. Since Gregorio descended from the younger son (Antonio), he was a "mere administrator" and an interim administrator, who was placed to administer until María was of legal age or married. She was now of legal age to govern, and she was married to Don Marcos Quinabanda with whom she had three legitimate sons, so she should immediately succeed to the cacicazgo, he argued.

Like Sebastiana Chango, María Toasa had sons, and retaining the title of cacica was a way of protecting a son's future inheritance.

While María's legal representative accused Gregorio's counsel of trying to confuse officials about the law, Gregorio's counsel asked the court notaries (*escribanos de camara*) to certify the custom of giving preference to males. It backfired. The court notary, who was young and new to the office, asked his father, who had served in the position for more than forty years. His father confirmed that, in the absence of males in the direct line, women inherited the cacicazgo by right of succession, and there were countless examples from the Audiencia of Quito. To name only a few that he could remember, he cited the example of cacicas from the towns of Otavalo, Saquisilli, and Pujilli, and he said it was known that in the five leagues (of Quito) "there are many females in the cacicazgos with whom tribute collection is regulated and set during the visitas."[32] While this court notary's father remembered the cacicas actually performing administrative duties, another court official mentioned other cacicas whose husbands fulfilled those functions. The fact that the notary had to draw on his father's past experience indicates the ambiguity in the law. A second notary (the escribano de Cabildo y Real Hacienda de Quito) also certified that in his thirty-two years of serving it had been the custom that in the absence of a male heir in the direct line, females had a right to succession to the cacicazgo. He also cited four examples of women who were in possession of cacicazgos at the time, and "other cacicas who have succeeded in the cacicazgos in the towns of [Quito's] five leagues of this jurisdiction, who, being married, their husbands administered the parcialidades, which I have seen practiced in this city and its jurisdiction in the time I referred to." He added that when he served previously as protector of natives, he remembered three different cacicas who inherited the position from their fathers in the absence of male heirs, and he certified the custom of female succession.[33]

Both of these cases from early eighteenth-century Pelileo involve the daughters of caciques who challenged male relatives. In both cases, Spanish legal authorities upheld the women's rights to the position of cacica, and in both cases, their success was short-lived. In the years following the women's victories, court cases involving indigenous people from Pelileo list the person's sector (Pilalata or Chumaquí) and cacique, always male. By 1718, the tribute records for the Chumaquí listed Gregorio Toasa as the cacique because María had died. Although Sebastiana Chango was granted a second investiture ceremony in 1709, restoring her to the cacicazgo of the Pilalata, three years later it was her challenger, Bernardo Chango, who was listed as cacique of the Pilalata. Future caciques of the Chumaquí were also male.[34]

The final case of an early eighteenth-century dispute between a cacica and cacique involves the cacica of forasteros of Ambato, Doña Getrudis Vivanco, and her coopting of the Sigchos Collanas of Salasaca.

SIGCHOS COLLANAS: GETRUDIS VIVANCO

Doña Getrudis Vivanco's case shows the transfer of a cazicazgo among women in the family. Vivanco inherited the right to govern the forasteros of the jurisdiction of Ambato from her father in 1715, and when she got too old to govern, she passed it on to her oldest granddaughter and *primogénita*, Faustina Amanta. Faustina had too many other responsibilities, for she also inherited the cacicazgo of Pasa from her paternal grandfather, and she was married to the cacique of Chumaquí. So in 1749, Faustina passed the cacicazgo of forasteros on to her younger sister.

Getrudis Vivanco's tenure as cacica of the forasteros likely lasted from about 1715 to the 1740s. During the time that she governed, she managed to temporarily coopt some of the Sigchos Collanas. Prior to this, in 1710, the Sigchos Collanas colony had been governed in Salasaca by a secondary chief from the corregimiento of Latacunga, Don Francisco Masaquiza, who was himself a subject of the paramount lord of Latacunga, Don Francisco Hati Haja (also written Hatiaja or just Hati). Although the Sigchos Collanas did not work in the obraje, the secondary chief was under considerable pressure from Spaniards to send laborers to their estates and ranches, prompting him to request an official exemption from sending more laborers because, he said, he didn't have any more Indians to send.[35] The out-migration and natural disasters of the late seventeenth century would have caused a drop in the indigenous population and increased the labor burden on the surviving indigenous men.

Some of these Sigchos Collanas attempted to change their status in order to avoid colonial labor and tribute requirements. By 1727, a group of men living in Salasaca, all with the last name Masaquiza, were at the center of a dispute between Doña Getrudis Vivanco and Don Francisco Hati. Hati claimed that the Masaquizas were "his Indians," and that they belonged to the encomienda of the Monjas Bernardas del Santisimo Sacramento of Madrid.[36] Hati charged that the cacica of forasteros had "tricked" the Masaquizas, who were designated as camayos, into incorporating themselves into her Crown parcialidad, as if they were forasteros.[37] The Masaquizas supported this argument, stating that they were promised good treatment by the cacica, but then she forced them into the labor draft. The eighteen Masaquiza men at the center of the dispute claimed descent from a woman of the Sigchos Collanas region in the western portion of the corregimiento of Latacunga (some specifically said the place called Colaquilad). According to indigenous witnesses, a woman named María Asuchimbo migrated to Salasaca and had many children. In accordance with gender parallelism, the sons all had the last name Masaquiza, and her daughter was Pascuala Laynchimbo,[38] whose own daughter was named Ana Asuchimbo. María Asuchimbo, who would have migrated some time in the mid to late seventeenth century, was only one of several migrants from the Sigchos Collanas to the camayo colony in Salasaca.

On behalf of Don Francisco Hati (the original cacique), the protector of natives stated that "the mothers and grandmothers of these Indians [the Masaquizas living in Salasaca] were always from the community of Sigchos Collanas, whose *naturaleza* [original status] they should continue because they are out of wedlock and have not been of legitimate matrimony, even though at some time they have recognized themselves as intruders in the community" of Getrudis Vivanco, because she and her husband "seduced these with flattery and promises of better treatment."[39] While Don Francisco Hati lay claim to the Masaquizas, he simply said that their grandmother went to Salasaca from his jurisdiction of Sigchos Collanas, and that the cacica Doña Getrudis Vivanco had been governing them illegitimately as vagabonds. However, two other indigenous witnesses confirmed that the Masaquizas were camayos. Camayos lived outside of their home communities but were supposed to maintain membership in their home communities and paid tribute to their home caciques.

In his attempts to have the Masaquizas reregistered as his subjects, Don Francisco Hati stated that the ancestors of "his Indians" were listed in the record as his subjects. Hati listed the names of the eighteen "brothers and cousins" living in Salasaca with the last name Masaquiza. Several Masaquizas themselves testified that they were "all Indians from Sigchos Collanas who reside in the site of Salasaca . . ." and that "we are all legitimately . . . subjects of Don Francisco Hati." They spoke of the "good treatment" that the old caciques had shown toward their parents and other Indians, as opposed to the injustices they were suffering at the hands of Spanish landowners and the cacica who possessed them at the time, stating: "[T]hey have us tied up, as prisoners, with chains in a private jail such that without the slightest recourse we are obligated to do the so called *mita* [labor draft] without the enjoyment of rest." They asked that they be removed from the registry of forasteros and matriculated in that of Sigchos, the original territory (of their mother and grandmother).[40] The indigenous witnesses used knowledge of the genealogical succession of caciques as proof of the origins of the Masaquizas. By naming the relationships between the Hatis going back three generations, witnesses used memory of the successions of caciques of Latacunga to strengthen the case that they were legitimately subjects of Don Francisco Hati and *not* the cacica of Forasteros.

A statement made by one of the witnesses provides a crucial piece of information for understanding the role of place, as ethnic territory, in the process of ethnogenesis. Speaking as a group, the Masaquizas complained: "[W]e are poor ones who don't even have a plot of land on which to live or lands on which to support ourselves independently."[41] This is significant because it shows that at the time, the Sigchos Collanas still identified with their original community in Latacunga, and they lacked lands in Salasaca, even though they resided there. They would later purchase these lands (see chapter 8). This 1727 case shows part of their transition away from their community of origin, as they attempted to become "free agents," and as some of them attempted to change their status (and ayllu affiliation) from camayos to forasteros. Once they realized that Doña Getrudis Vivanco had made false promises, they wanted to return to being subjects of Don Francisco Hati of Latacunga. Vivanco not only tried to force the Sigchos Collanas into labor, but at one point she even put her own nephews in jail when they resisted the labor draft.[42]

CONCLUSION

To summarize, in the first half of the eighteenth century, there were several indigenous parcialidades in Pelileo, and some constituted different ethnic groups. Culturally, the families not only practiced gender parallelism, but elite female descendants fought to take over their ayllus as governing cacicas. The investiture ceremony combined pre-Columbian Andean ritual and symbols with Spanish colonial ceremonies for the granting of power, and indigenous men and women were required to recognize and promise obedience to their hereditary cacicas after the leader was confirmed by Spanish colonial officials. The cacicas and caciques of the parcialidades of the Pilalata and Chumaquí governed their indigenous subjects, and their parcialidades existed side by side with the subjects of Don Francisco Masaquiza, a secondary chief of Latacunga who was governing the Sigchos Collana camayo population in Salasaca. While so much of the indigenous history of Pelileo is characterized by the shadow of San Ildefonso, the Sigchos Collanas, who belonged to the encomienda of the Monjas Bernardas, did not have to serve in the obraje. Nevertheless, they were pressured into serving on local haciendas and ranches.

The stories presented here show how Andeans in different social positions coped with colonial pressures. While the daughters of the caciques of Pelileo tried to claim their rights to succession, perhaps to guarantee a spot for their

FIGURE 14. Indigenous Woman Governor of Ambato. Nineteenth Century. From *Álbum de costumbres ecuatorianas* in Biblioteca Digital Hispánica.

sons, and Getrudis Vivanco attempted to increase her number of subjects by tricking the Sigchos Collanas into joining her parcialidad, the Sigchos Collanas attempted to improve their lot by taking advantage of the competition between caciques. When they found themselves forced into the labor draft by their new cacica, they sided with their original cacique in his case against the cacica of forasteros. In 1743 another cacique of Pelileo tried to force a Sigchos Collanas man and his father into the obraje. That man, Carlos Masaquiza, used the legal system to resist forced labor in the obraje and negotiate for access to lands in the community. I discuss this case in the next chapter, which focuses on Pelileo during the time that the Jesuits owned San Ildefonso.

CHAPTER 5

VAGABONDS, INFIDELS, AND JESUITS

Quito's Textile Industry (1724–1767)

THE EIGHTEENTH century was marked by a decline in the textile industry in colonial Quito due to falling prices of cloth and competition with European cloth imported to South America, and some obrajes closed down.[1] However, large rural obrajes survived and adapted to the economic changes. San Ildefonso was one of the obrajes to survive the economic downturn, and production actually increased under Jesuit ownership, starting in 1724 when the order purchased it from Nicholas Dávalos. By the mid-eighteenth century, the wool cloth from San Ildefonso was famous for its quality. Throughout Peru and Chile it was known for its softness and beautiful color; and, according to the Italian Jesuit writer Mario Cicala, it was superior, in terms of durability, to cloth from France, London, or Spain. According to Cicala, one only had to hear that it was cloth from San Ildefonso, and he would be willing to pay more than he would for other cloth.[2]

Despite the slow decline in the textile industry, in the 1730s indigenous people in the northern and central sierra of Ecuador were still being forced to work in obrajes, where they labored under inhumane conditions. This chapter begins with a general description of the situation, based on colonial reports on indigenous responses to the textile industry in the Audiencia of Quito in the mid-eighteenth century. Then I focus specifically on Pelileo during the time that the Jesuits owned San Ildefonso and acquired many lands to expand their ranches and sugar estates. Through the story of Carlos Masaquiza, we see how one indigenous man took legal action to resist being forced into the obraje. The chapter ends with the expulsion of the Jesuits in 1767, when the government took over their properties.

TEXTILE PRODUCTION AND FORASTERISMO IN THE AUDIENCIA OF QUITO IN THE 1730S

Some Spanish colonial officials in Quito reported extreme responses of indigenous families to forced labor in obrajes, as in the following description of the situation in Otavalo, in the northern Ecuadorian province of Imbabura:

> The witness observed that in the Asiento de Otavalo there were groups of blind Indians, which he attributed to the night mist from the local lakes, and when he asked the cause he was told that it wasn't from the lakes but rather that the Mothers who are from Indian sectors that are subject to labor requirements, upon seeing that they were born males, the most compassionate ones blinded them, others killed them, so that they wouldn't be subjected to the obraje. And in the same way he saw that some Indian women would carry loads of roots, which they said are from totoras [reeds], to aid the hunger of those imprisoned in the said obraje, for which the witness was moved by great compassion.[3]

This testimony of Capitan Don Antonio de Vera Pizarro, executor of Quito in 1737, describes the continuing pressure that was placed on indigenous families who lived in towns that were dominated by obrajes. Whether reports of mothers blinding their male babies to spare them from the obraje were exaggerated or not, similar stories circulated into the nineteenth century. The nineteenth-century Ecuadorian painter Juan Agustín Guerrero painted a picture (figure 15) of a blind Indian of Cotacachi (also in the province of Imbabura), and his book of art includes the description that "when they are children, their parents take their eyes out so that they don't have to pay tribute."[4]

Blinding one's children seems extreme, and it is not clear how common the practice actually was. Records indicate that a much more common response to avoid labor was for indigenous people to run away. Despite the Crown's attempt to protect natives from abuse, royal orders regarding the treatment of indigenous workers in obrajes were still ignored at some obrajes, as they were

FIGURE 15. "Blind Indian of Cotacachi." From Juan Agustín Guerrero, *Imágenes del Ecudor del siglo XIX*.

in the seventeenth century. The orders that were violated in the eighteenth century include prohibitions on child labor, obraje jails, and debt prisoners. Most of these Crown protections were never enforced in Quito, because improved working conditions for the natives were seen as detrimental to the economy.

In 1732, the escribano de camara (court notary) of the Audiencia, Manuel Gregorio de la Zerda, wrote to the Crown arguing for the need for Indian labor to keep up cloth production. He stated that the Indians of Quito had the most idolatrous ancestors, were naturally lazy and indomitable, and were more unruly than Indians from other parts of America. De la Zerda emphasized the need to use the Indian tribute obligation to force laborers into the obrajes. *Forasterismo*, or out-migration, was still a continuing problem, as native Andeans fled their communities to avoid the tribute and labor-draft requirements. De la Zerda's solution was to charge the same tribute rate for "vagabonds," those living outside of their towns, as for *llactayos*, those living in their own towns. In this way, he said, there would be no incentive to run away. But aside from leaving their hometowns and living in other towns and cities, many Indians, de la Zerda complained, were fleeing to the mountains and living among infidels. Rather than working in the obrajes, the Indians would prefer to live off herbs and wild roots, raiding local haciendas at night by stealing the crop from the fields. He described populations of native people living like pagans in the Llanganates Mountains, Huamboya, and behind the *caldera* (volcanic crater) of Pimampiro, "and other unknown places which there are in both mountain ranges, of which we have knowledge because of some Indians who have a secret trade with them to supply some of their needs, and that these are lands from which they extract a lot of gold."[5]

Was there really a subaltern population of natives living in far-off places resisting both work and religious indoctrination, trading with other natives who were complicit in the resistance to colonial control and who supplied them with basic necessities? Probably not, but his naming of specific places where indigenous runaways were allegedly hiding out is worth examining. The Llanganates Mountains were rumored to be the place where the Inca general Rumiñahui hid the empire's gold after the Spanish conquest.[6] De la Zerda's mention of the Llanganates plays in to Spanish fantasies of Inca gold hidden in far-off places, accessible only to indigenous people with esoteric geographical knowledge.

It seems that the second place mentioned, the Amazonian site of Huamboya, *was* a destination for Andeans who were hiding out from the Spanish sphere. Indigenous people continued to migrate to Huamboya up through the 1760s. For example, after a rebellion in Riobamba in 1764, entire native families fled, and the leaders of the rebellion threatened a mass exodus to Huamboya. After the Riobamba rebellion, one priest warned of zones of paganism that safely continued and said that natives would take refuge there, while another warned that the whites would be sorry if all their Indian workers moved to Huamboya.[7] The threat was taken seriously enough that officials agreed not to punish the leaders of the rebellion. So it seems that Huamboya was a destination for indigenous people seeking to escape life in the Spanish colonial sphere.

Pimampiro, the third place mentioned by de la Zerda, had long been a center of exchange among natives from different ecological zones.[8] De la Zerda's statement about pagans living in far-off places is reminiscent of the early colonial "women of the puna" in Peru, a subaltern population of women, high in the mountains, who continued to practice their old religion.[9]

It is tempting to speculate that the forasteros who fled from Quito's obrajes led a similar subaltern life, supported by a secret commerce with other indigenous people, out of reach of colonial control and Christian religion, where they lived off wild foods, practiced a wild religion, and remained wild Indians (outside of Spanish control), with the clandestine support of their indigenous brethren who remained in the Spanish sphere. De la Zerda's mention of specific places, and his claim of knowledge from reliable native sources, lends a convincing credibility to the existence of such populations, but we must place de la Zerda's letter in context. De la Zerda's report is an attempt to convince the Crown of the need to force the natives into the obrajes, both for economic and religious reasons. He argued that it would benefit indigenous people to "civilize" them. His suggestion to remedy the situation was for the Crown to offer an incentive to any "persons or vecinos" who want to "reduce" a number of Indians (bringing them into towns).[10] So, whether or not there was any truth to the reports of subaltern populations living in far-off places, the reports were used as a persuasive device to bring more indigenous people into the obrajes.

The large numbers of people who ran away from the obrajes separated indigenous families and broke up communities, and some caciques sold off the lands of their subjects who ran away, leading to further disintegration of indigenous communities. While natives of the obrajes of other regions, such as Otavalo and Latacunga, were still suffering extremely harsh conditions, the situation of Pelileo's indigenous people in the 1730s is less clear.

JESUIT PURCHASE OF SAN ILDEFONSO

In 1724 the Jesuits purchased San Ildefonso and associated estates in order to support their seminary of San Luis in Quito, and they expanded production at the mill.[11] There are no documented complaints (from accessible documents) about the labor conditions during the Jesuit ownership, but Cushner found that the workers were still in debt from accepting advances of food in the obraje.[12] Payment records that I examined also list, in addition to men, a number of local indigenous women, both single and married, who worked in the obraje when it was owned by the Jesuits.[13] Although the Jesuits had black slaves on their other haciendas, there is no mention of blacks at San Ildefonso under the Jesuit ownership.[14] For this period there are account records of payments to workers, but no descriptions of labor conditions. If there were complaints about the treatment of workers at San Ildefonso during the Jesuit ownership, they were not preserved in the archive. In accordance with the Jesuit strategy of owning the farm-factory complex described by Cushner, the Jesuits purchased the haciendas associated with the obraje, and they purchased many other pieces of land in and around Pelileo. In their attempt to expand their sugarcane enterprise, the order found lands that were ideal for growing sugarcane. These lands were occupied by the Chumaquí and Pilalata, so they made a deal with the indigenous people, discussed below.

THE JESUIT LAND SWAP

The Jesuit investment in cane fields and sugar mills sometimes put them in conflict with indigenous people, but in 1727 the order came up with a solution that was favorable to both sides. The natives had a royal grant of land known as "the llano of Salate," but these lands were ideal for growing sugarcane. Cane fields required access to irrigation water, which the natives lacked. The Jesuit administrator of the hacienda of San Ildefonso, and procurator of the seminary of San Luis, offered to exchange the natives' lands for lands owned by the Jesuits in the sector called Chiquicha. The Jesuit hacienda of Chiquicha was for the benefit of their seminary, but these lands were good for growing food without the need for irrigation. The administrator offered the natives who had land in Salate to swap for twice as much land in Chiquicha, an offer which they "immediately embraced."[15] Indeed, many years later, in 1795, Antonio Masulli, a very elderly indigenous witness in another land dispute, recalled the Jesuit land swap and said that the Indians were happy with the deal: "[T]he one that had one unit [in Salate] was given two [in Chiquicha], and in this way they satisfied the Indians" (*al que tenia una cuadra se le daba dos y de este modo contentaron a los indios*).[16] The land judges carefully measured the size of each plot of native-owned land, and, in a collective possession ceremony in Chiquicha, gave each indigenous owner a plot that was twice as large (see Salate and Chiquicha Chico in figure 10).

The Jesuit barter with native landowners to exchange subsistence plots for cash-crop lands was a mutually beneficial compromise that satisfied all parties. Afterward, the Jesuits continued buying up property in Pelileo, especially in the 1740s, when the order made many deals to get land from both Spaniards

and natives in Patate and Pelileo.[17] This followed a decision in the 1730s to stop
purchasing wool for the obraje of San Ildefonso from the Jesuit ranch in Chil-
los.[18] Perhaps the aggressive Jesuit purchase of Pelileo lands in the 1740s was
to use the local ranches to supply the wool to San Ildefonso, in addition to the
Jesuit investment in sugarcane lands. Some purchases from Spaniards included,
along with the land, large flocks of sheep and an *indio del quinto*, an indigenous
labor-draft worker who would serve on a rotating basis. The list of receipts for
mid-eighteenth-century purchases includes more than thirty Jesuit purchases of
ranches and smaller plots of land around San Ildefonso and Pelileo. Most of the
sales (and some donations of water holes and sheep, with a shepherd included)
were from Spaniards, but there were a couple of sales from native Andeans to
the Jesuits. Sometimes natives sold lands because they needed the money to pay
tribute or wanted to buy different lands. The Jesuits, like other Spaniards, had
a variety of creative means for taking over indigenous lands. In other parts of
the central sierra, the Jesuits were known to use their native Andean employees
as middlemen to get indigenous lands. By having their estate workers acquire
the land from the indigenous owner first, and then transfer it to the Jesuits, the
order was able to circumvent colonial regulation of Spanish takeovers of native
lands.[19]

OBRAJE LABOR

Although there are no public records of indigenous complaints about the labor
conditions in the obraje under the Jesuits, there was still a demand to get more
indigenous workers. Someone, perhaps a lay administrator, must have been
pressuring caciques of Pelileo to send more workers to the obraje, because one
of those caciques tried to force a Sigchos Collanas man to work there. In 1743
Carlos Masaquiza, who was living in Salasaca, filed a complaint because the
cacique Manuel Ganan listed him as a subject and was trying to force him and
his father to work in the obraje of San Ildefonso. Manuel Ganan appears in
other records as a cacique of the Camayos Puruguayes of Pelileo.

Carlos Masaquiza said that his grandfather, Simon Masaquiza of the Collanas, went to Salasaca, where he married Marta Jerez, an indigenous woman
from the same "ayllu and parcialidad of Collanas." Carlos's father was born in
Salasaca, but he and his parents all remained subjects of Don Francisco Hati
Haja and paid the lower Latacunga tribute rate of three pesos and two and a

half *reales* each year. As proof, Carlos used the census (*visita*) of Latacunga from 1730 of "the Collana Indians of Isinlivi of Don Francisco Hatihaja [sic] and parcialidad of the Salasacas who reside in the Jurisdiction of the Asiento of Ambato." Carlos is listed there as someone who "resides in Salasaca with his parents." Carlos stated that "we have been in this region [Pelileo] many years in lands that, *although purchased*, belong to the town of Pelileo. [Ganan] could obligate us to serve the mita *giving us community lands* because in no way should he make us serve like census Indians [como de padron] in the obraje of San Ildefonso because we are not from this community" (my emphasis).[20] He said that they should be allowed to live freely in Salasaca, in lands that they purchased. "Freely" here is understood to mean exempt from obraje (or other) service. Carlos Masaquiza also wanted to assure that he and his children continue to pay the lower tribute rate, and not the six pesos and three reales a year that the Pelileo natives paid.

This case shows (1) that under Jesuit ownership there were local attempts to coerce indigenous workers into the service of the obraje, even those who were exempt; (2) that not only did María Asuchimbo's descendants (see chapter 4) identify as Sigchos Collanas, but other Collanas women, such as Marta Jerez, came to Salasaca from the greater Latacunga region (Isinlivi), and other men with the last name Masaquiza migrated directly; (3) that by 1743 these migrants and their children had already begun to purchase lands in Salasaca; and (4) that Carlos Masaquiza used the legal system to resist being forced into the obraje unless he was given access to local community lands, which are usually assigned by caciques to individuals who participated in the labor draft. Although the outcome of the case is not included the record, the fact that Carlos Masaquiza was willing to negotiate obraje work for land serves to indicate that conditions were not as deplorable under the Jesuits as they were when the obraje was owned by María de Vera in the mid-seventeenth century. Carlos Masaquiza was fighting for himself, his father, and his descendants.

CONCLUSION

In the mid-eighteenth century, indigenous people throughout the Audiencia of Quito were still suffering in the obrajes. Reports from the time period describe extreme measures that mothers took to prevent their male children from suffering in the obrajes, while Spanish officials were concerned with the large numbers of indigenous people who were running away from colonial control. In Pelileo, the Jesuits purchased San Ildefonso and expanded their mill-estate enterprise by purchasing many lands in Pelileo. Indigenous people took action to prevent the taking of their lands and to improve their cirucmstances. Local indigenous people from Pelileo made a deal with the Jesuits in which native landowners ended up with more land than they originally had. Carlos Masaquiza, an indigenous man of the Sigchos Collanas migrants living in Salasaca, took legal action, on behalf of himself and his father, to avoid being forced into San Ildefonso, but he also used the demand for obraje labor to try to negotiate for land in the area. Acquiring land meant that indigenous families would have something to pass on to their children, so land was crucial to maintaining families and communities.

When the Jesuits were expelled from the South American colonies in 1767, their property in Quito was taken over by the administrative branch of the government called Temporalidades. Geronimo Ruiz was appointed as the new administrator of San Ildefonso. When workers had a problem with the administrator, they responded, like Carlos Masaquiza, by going through proper legal channels available to indigenous people. When this failed, they violently rebelled. The next chapter analyzes the uprising of 1768 and its aftermath.

CHAPTER 6

REBELLION, RITUAL, AND RUMOR IN PELILEO (1768)

THE GOVERNMENT agency of Temporalidades took over San Ildefonso and other Jesuit properties in 1767 and appointed a new obraje administrator, Geronimo Ruiz. Shortly thereafter the native workers rebelled, killed the obraje administrator, and briefly held the town hostage. I show here how the tensions created by the obraje affected social and cultural life in the town. The labor conditions in the mill and the response to the uprising affected people's views and suspicions of one another as they prepared for the upcoming Corpus Christi festivities. Festivals, as a cultural space of interaction between people from different backgrounds, hold the potential to release underlying tensions. The fiesta served as a common spatiotemporal locus—a microcosm of life in the town, involving people of different ethnic backgrounds and specializations and guilds. In Pelileo, as in other parts of the Audiencia, the people who came together to celebrate festivals did so within the context of tensions created by labor relations in the mill. In my analysis of the rebellion and its aftermath, I continue to emphasize the actions of people in specific social positions: mothers of obraje workers, indigenous intermediaries, and mestizos. Each of these social actors responded to the pressures of the textile economy in their own ways: the mothers by instigating the killing of the administrator; a cacique by using a drinking festival as a context for denouncing mestizo occupation of indigenous lands; mestizos by choosing to side with Spaniards over natives, and spreading rumors of indigenous revenge when they feared the consequences of their actions.

THE REBELLION

When Ruiz took over as administrator, he increased the daily quotas for cloth manufacture required of the workers and reduced the advances of food and clothing, the socorros on which workers depended, causing a growing tension. The following account is based on my reading of the testimonies of multiple witnesses from the criminal trial and from the analysis by Segundo Moreno Yánez in his book *Sublevaciones indígenas en la Audiencia de Quito*.

In April 1768, during an argument between the foreman and two workers who were brothers, Phelipe and Romualdo Llagua, Romualdo threw a knife at the foreman, and both brothers were subsequently whipped and placed in shackles. Perhaps Phelipe intervened on behalf of his brother, and that's why he received the same punishment as Romualdo. Bárbula Sinailín, mother of the Llaguas, protested her sons' imprisonment and argued for their release. In her own testimony, Sinailín said that the maestro had no right to treat them like that; not even her master, nor the administrator, treated them that way, she said. As a result of her protest, she was given one hundred lashes, despite the fact that she was an elderly woman and had always served the hacienda and was in good standing with the bosses (*amos*). Whipping an elderly indigenous woman was seen as a serious act of injustice by the other workers, but this was not the cause of the uprising. Rather, the indigenous workers tried to use the proper legal channels to seek justice. Bárbula Sinailín, accompanied by Manuel Pombosa, went to the city of Quito to seek justice. Pombosa was probably a relative; in fact, several of the rebels were related to one another.

According to the testimonies of native witnesses, Pombosa and Sinailín returned from Quito with a legal document in their favor, possibly a letter from the protector of natives, meant for the lieutenant of Pelileo, Manuel Ojeda. Sinailín said the letter she got from the protector in Quito called for her sons' release and the firing of the maestro. She gave the letter to Ojeda, and either Ojeda or the priest notified Ruiz, the administrator. Ruiz tried to intervene in the legal process, an act that instigated the rebellion.

A week later, upon learning of Ruiz's sabotage of what they believed was a legitimate legal decision in their favor—perhaps they believed he confiscated the letter—the native workers finished their tasks early, delivered their finished products in the obraje, and left to wait on the road for Ruiz to return from Pelileo. As Ruiz was coming on horseback, the workers began to hurl stones at him. As he retreated, they began to chase him, and he tried to take refuge in the obraje chapel, with his family, along with other white officials from the obrjae and haciendas, some with their families: the silversmith, a teacher (*maestro de gramatica*), the foreman of the obraje and his wife and children, the assistant from the sugar mill, and the doorman of the obraje. The rebels broke in to the chapel. The assistant was beaten by the mob and left for dead, although he survived. The doorman tried to appeal to one of the attackers by name, telling him, "Caysaguano, we're of the same *patria* [fatherland]—what do you want to do?" According to the testimony of Mariano Curipallo, the natives gave the doorman a blow to the head, but, seeing that he had a crucifix in his hand, they let him live. Although the conflict was divided along racial lines—indigenous people against Spaniards and mestizos—the doorman was saved by a brave, individual act of compassion. Rather than allow himself to be swept up by the mob mentality, Lorenzo Paucar, an indigenous man, secretly gave a piece of clothing to the doorman to dress him "as an Indian" with a *camiseta* or *bayeta* (types of clothing) to disguise him so that he could escape through the crowd.[1]

A cacique from another town (Cusubamba), who was in Pelileo assisting Ruiz at the time, arrived later, unaware of what was going on. The rebels locked him in a room so that he couldn't call reinforcements from Pelileo. One of the rebels, Thomas Pimbo, discovered Ruiz hiding behind the altar and alerted the others. They seized Ruiz, who begged for his life and said, "My Children [*Hijos*], what do you want to do with me?"[2] He promised to forgive them and asked that they forgive him too. He specifically offered to clear a ninety-peso debt that Thomas Pimbo owed the hacienda, and he offered the others fabric (paño), cane liquor, and money. In fact, Ruiz had earlier tried to scare off the mob with a warning shot from his gun, but when they continued to chase him, he chose to run rather than shoot them. Whether this was because the gun was loaded with blanks, as one witness suggested, or because he didn't want to kill anyone is unclear.

Now, the crowd, armed with shovels, knives, and machetes, had Ruiz's rifle, and they had him captured. Ruiz's wife begged the crowd to spare her husband's life, and it seemed they were convinced. They planned to whip him, tie him to a mule, and abandon him on the bridge in Ambato. Instead, the mob violently killed Ruiz in a lynching instigated by two women: one was Bárbula Sinailín, who yelled, "Kill this King!" and the other was Marsela Tasi, a cousin of the

Llaguas and wife of a weaver in the obraje. Both women had been whipped on different occasions after acting, as mothers, on behalf of their children who were serving in the obraje. Marsela Tasi was younger than Bárbula Sinailín, sometimes described as a *muchacha* (girl) by the witnesses. Since she was a cousin of the Llaguas, the two women were related either through blood or marriage. Tasi had a previous run-in with the administrator when she went to argue on behalf of her daughter, who was being held in the obraje, subject to forced labor. When Tasi argued with the administrator for her daughter's release, she was punished with a whipping.[3] It was Marsela Tasi who drew the first blow to Ruiz's face and cut him, at which point the rest of the crowd jumped in. Raymundo Curipallo rubbed dirt on Ruiz's face and on the statue of the Virgin Mary. They mutilated Ruiz, cutting out his eyes, tongue, and teeth. When Marsela Tasi felt his chest and told the others that he still had a heartbeat, the Llaguas whipped him and then hanged him until they were sure he was dead. Ruiz's widow begged the crowed not to dump her husband's body in the Patate River, so instead they paraded around the obraje with the cadaver, dancing and singing. They returned Ruiz's body to the chapel, where they placed the body in a seated position, surrounded by four lit candles. In a ritual of reversal, they told him, "Now go ahead and say, 'Give that Indian a hundred lashes, pull down his breeches.' Go ahead and say it, King."[4]

Other Spaniards were in hiding, locking themselves in the houses of the obraje, awaiting the arrival of reinforcements to free them. The next day, Tuesday, at around five o'clock in the morning, the teniente came from Pelileo, accompanied by Dominican friars. The leaders of the rebellion proudly showed the body of Ruiz. Manuel Pombosa had a piece of paper, which he said contained an order, from the president of Quito, to bring the head of Ruiz. It's one thing to make such a claim to the other natives, in order to instigate them, but why would Pombosa say such a thing to the teniente? Did he really believe it? The fact that the leaders "bragged" to the teniente and the friars suggests that they believed they were in the right, and that the law would be on their side, or that they were so caught up in the mob violence that they were still threatening the authorities. The Dominican friars prevented the rebels from cutting off Ruiz's head, and the rebels allowed the friars to give Ruiz a proper burial. The teniente of Pelileo called for reinforcements from Ambato. On Wednesday the Spanish and mestizo officials from the obraje, as well as the teniente of Ambato, Joseph de Merizalde, were still locked up in the houses of the San Ildefonso complex. Meanwhile, according to witnesses, the rebels celebrated with conch shells (*churos*), fifes, and drums, festive and symbolic instruments that are also used to summon people. Blas Chango claimed that a native woman named María Cazachina encouraged him to join in the gathering (*concurso*), and that he told her, "It's no fiesta for there to be a drum and conch shell."[5] They celebrated all night, and into the next day, when they threatened to use the skulls of the officials as drinking vessels.[6]

As Spanish officials remained captive in their homes, surrounded by indigenous people, awaiting reinforcements from Ambato, a woman named Doña Rosa Sanchez came riding on horseback over the hills, carrying a small sword (*espadin*) and leading a squadron of women at six o'clock on Thursday morning. These Spanish and mestiza women fought back and subdued the rebels, killing an indigenous man, Andres Titi, a cousin of the Llaguas, in the process. They hanged his corpse "so that it would rot,"[7] but the friar took it down and gave it a proper burial. The women freed the Spanish officials who had been in hiding for days. About eight indigenous men and thirteen women were detained; but, at the urging of the Dominican friar, they were released. The main instigators were later arrested or rearrested; some were caught in the central sierra towns of Pujilli and Latacunga. The Dominicans spoke to officials and then assured the rest of the native workers that they would be safe and that they could return to work in the mill.

Indigenous intermediaries testified against the rebels. The indigenous labor boss of the obraje (maestrillo) testified against the others, who were bragging about their participation in the lynching. After the killing, the maestrillo said, he went the next day to the home of Blas Chango, who had Ruiz's rifle and admitted to beating Ruiz with his own weapon. The indigenous sacristan, Manuel Guaman, also testified, saying that Lucas Cujana shouted from the bell tower to the others that they had found Ruiz in the chapel. The sacristan also said that he convinced the crowd not to dump Ruiz's body in the river.

The Dominicans played a mediating role in the conflict. They buried the bodies of both Geronimo Ruiz and Andres Titi, convinced the authorities to release the natives from jail (before some were rearrested), and assured the rest of the indigenous people that it was safe for them to return to work in the obraje. Statements show the rebels' contradictory attitudes toward sacred Catholic items. Although at least one rebel rubbed dirt on the face of the statue of the Virgin Mary, other indigenous witnesses testified that they refrained from killing the doorman because they saw that he held a crucifix in his hand. Despite their trust for the friars, and what was probably genuine respect for the crucifix, they did not respect the sanctity of the chapel or the altar, upon which they spilled Ruiz's blood.

After the leaders of the rebellion were arrested, the rest of the town tried to return to normal, and the indigenous people went back to their routine of working in the obraje. Soon after, as people were preparing for the upcoming Corpus Christi celebrations, the alguacil mayor (chief constable) of Ambato sent a letter to the *teniente general* (lieutenant) recommending the prohibition of liquor sales and dancers during the festival, because the *alcalde ordinario* (indigenous official responsible for capturing criminals) had detained three indigenous prisoners, "including a cacique named Manuel Tubón who has been calling on all the Indians of this jurisdiction, inciting them to revolt on [the day of] Corpus."[8] Don Manuel Tubón was the cacique of the Guambaló, and along with the cacique three others were arrested. Word had it that the mayor of the town of Píllaro (jurisdiction of Ambato), had captured an indigenous man, allegedly one of the rebels, and that after being whipped, the suspect confessed that the natives of Pelileo were planning a general insurrection on the day of Corpus Christi against all Spaniards and mestizos, adding that the conspirators included not only workers from the obraje, but all indigenous people of the region. Another rumor said that Don Manuel Tubón had written a letter to the governor (cacique) of Píllaro, inviting him to join the uprising. At the trial of Tubón and the other suspects, several Spanish and mestizo witnesses gave statements, mostly based on hearsay, as evidence of the imminent threat of possible alliances among indigenous groups, to form a unified opposition against mestizos and Spaniards. During interrogations, the charges against the cacique and the alleged coconspirators crumbled one by one, but the testimony of the mestizos reveals their concern about the backlash they faced for having allied with the Spaniards against indigenous people. Mestizos feared that the natives would use the fiesta, and the accompanying costumed dancing, masking, and disguise, to take revenge. The trial testimonies reveal how social tensions were expressed through the cultural practices related to the fiesta. In order to understand the mestizos' fears, it is necessary to understand the nature of Corpus Christi celebrations in the Andes.

CORPUS CHRISTI

The Catholic feast day of Corpus Christi, which celebrates the body of Christ, coincided with pre-Hispanic harvest festivals, and indigenous peoples throughout the Andes incorporated it as part of their culture to the extent that it was considered an "ancient custom" of Andeans.[9] A major part of the festival involves the costumed dancers called *danzantes*, who wear feathered headdresses on their heads and bells around their ankles. Recall from chapter 3 that among the goods that María de Vera used to pay her obraje workers were bells, feathers, and ribbons for dancing in the festival. Aside from danzantes, Corpus Christi also included other costumed dancers and parodies. In 1661 a native sacristan of the bishopric of Lima denounced a Corpus Christi parody of the priest and the liturgy, which subverted the holiest symbols of Catholicism in a humorous appropriation of priestly powers.[10] Colonial Andeans also created their own rituals of memory and ancestor worship during Corpus Christi, including the performances of traditional Andean songs and dances, which were tolerated by some priests in the archdiocese of Lima.[11] In the province of Cajatambo (Peru), a 1656 idolatry trial revealed that Andean elders were telling people to abstain from salt and *aji* (Andean hot peppers) and to "pray to their ancestors" in preparation for Corpus Christi.[12] The abstention from these foods indicates that they were ritually purifying themselves for this time of ancestor worship. The colonial cultural practice of using Corpus Christi as a time to remember one's ancestors continues in the Andes. Today, Salasacas of Pelileo and Otavaleños of Imbabura province (who celebrate San Juan and San Pedro in June) commemorate their own deceased family members during the June festivities.[13]

The link between fiestas and rebellions is well established in the literature, and the mid to late eighteenth century was the "age of insurrection" in the Andes. Thierry Saignes cites two cases of plotted rebellions in the eighteenth-century Andes, both of which were originally planned for Easter Sunday but postponed until Corpus Christi.[14] Just three years before the uprising at San Ildefonso, the "rebellion of the barrios" broke out in the city of Quito during the preparations for the Corpus Christi celebrations of 1765.[15] Spanish officials in Ambato surely recalled that rebellion, as well as a rebellion much closer to home: the 1764 Ash Wednesday rebellion in Riobamba. That rebellion, led by forasteros who were resisting new attempts to incorporate them into the labor draft, involved a very large alliance of indigenous people and took on nativistic overtones. According to the corregidor, the leaders had planned to kill off the white men, take over Riobamba, and establish an independent government led by native "kings." When the Spaniards fought back, it was the indigenous rebels who took refuge in the church, using a statue of the Virgin Mary as a shield against the reinforcements. As in the San Ildefonso rebellion, and other rebellions of the central sierra, it was a priest who calmed both sides, this time by taking hold of the Eucharist. The oidor who originally published the act that caused the rebellion left Riobamba for Ambato, where he must have told disturbing stories about the rebellion, which at one point reportedly included an estimated ten thousand rebels.[16] Four years later, after the uprising in San Ildefonso, it would not be so hard for whites to imagine a massive native rebellion in the jurisdiction of Ambato. In both rebellions, whites were concerned with keeping indigenous laborers, and priests had to convince the workers that it was safe to return to their jobs.

The suspected coconspirators of the alleged Corpus Christi plot in Pelileo were known to local whites through their occupations. Manuel Tubón was a cacique, and Simon Quintuña and Miguel Condo (both from the parcialidad of Tacungas living in Pelileo) were said to be ladinos—indigenous people who were proficient in Spanish. Quintuña was a leader of the artisans (*oficial de todos los oficiales*), or at least of the tailors, and he was also *alcalde del barrio*, a type of neighborhood watchman, of the lower sector of Pelileo. The title *oficial* usually refers to a guild member who holds the rank of journeyman, but I couldn't find information on guilds in Pelileo. It is clear, though, that Simon Quintuña occupied a position of some status, as an artisan and indigenous watchman. Condo was a shearer, and the fourth suspect, Thomas Muchagalo, was a cantor in the church who had also served as alcalde ordinario.

THE ACCUSED

The four indigenous men who were detained on May 18, 1768, had each said something to mestizos that was interpreted as a threat but explained by the accused as a simple misunderstanding.[17] For example, Thomas Muchagalo was reported to have threatened another indigenous man, Mariano Ronda, telling him "that he had done something very bad by siding with the Spaniards and against the Indians, and that it was certain that they would rise up against him and the other townspeople." For his part, Muchagalo admitted that he had threatened Ronda and told him that he better not show his face on the street, but it had nothing to do with the obraje rebellion. Rather, Muchagalo said he was angry with Ronda because Ronda was married to one of Muchagalo's nieces and was making amorous advances to another niece, who was also married, and he couldn't stand him because he was a philanderer.

In the case of Miguel Condo, mestizo witnesses claimed that one night while drunk he yelled out that he was going to burn down the homes of all the townspeople. This was heard by some mestizos who had intervened to stop Condo from beating his wife during an argument. Condo said that during that argument, he threatened *his wife*, saying that he was going to burn down their home and get transferred to Quito, where he would continue in his profession as a shearer. However, this was interpreted by the mestizo townspeople as part of a planned insurgency to be carried out during the upcoming festival.

Simon Quintuña got into trouble for his role in the preparations for the upcoming fiesta. Several mestizo witnesses said that they heard that Simon Quintuña was planning to lead the natives of his sector in an uprising against Spaniards and mestizos of the town while disguised as a danzante, *matachin*, or *diablito*, all typical costumed dancers in Corpus Christi. The danzante has already been described. The diablito, or little devil, is another costumed performer, and a matachin is a type of dancer that takes on a variety of forms, from "acrobats to masked fools and courtly sword dancers."[18] Like the danzantes of Corpus Christi, their costumes sometimes included wearing bells around their legs, but in the case of the matachines they also sometimes carried swords and shields and imitated mock battles. In Europe, dancers who dressed as "wild men" and devils were also referred to as matachines.[19] A drawing by the Andean chronicler Guaman Poma de Ayala "suggests that matachine-like dancers were introduced at an early date into the southern Peruvian Andes . . . these Andean altar-dancers (or 'seises'?) dance with swords, wear feathers, and mark time with the ankle bells distinctive of the matachines and other European morisco dancers."[20]

The costumes were typical of festival celebrations in Europe and the Americas, but in 1768 the multiple associations of humorous parody with militant undertones (possibly expressed by sword fighting) loomed over the mestizos of Pelileo. The statement that Quintuña would kill Spaniards and mestizos while dressed as a matachin or diablito reflects the historical concern that symbolic expressions of subversion during fiestas could transform into political action and armed insurgence. Disguises not only mask the identity of the wearer, thereby allowing for anonymity in the act of resistance, but they also blur the boundaries between performance and action. In her study of colonial fears of indigenous disguises during the Corpus Christi celebrations in colonial Peru, Carolyn Dean shows that colonial authorities feared the political consequences of the symbolic form of costumed dancers. The dance of the Chunchos—highland parodies of "savage" Amazonian Indians—was of particular concern because "*[i]mitating*

Indians out of control and *being* Indians out of control seemed a little too alike."[21]

Officials from Pelileo recognized the danger posed by costumed dancers, and the alguacil recommended that festival dancers and the sale of liquor to indigenous people be prohibited during the 1768 celebrations because of the rumors. This particular rumor about Simon Quintuña, however, was mentioned by several witnesses and finally traced through a grapevine of local white women to Ambrosia Garsés, who was sixteen or seventeen years old. When asked the basis for her accusation that Simon Quintuña was planning to lead the natives of his sector in an uprising, she said that Simon Quintuña was going around, as alcalde of the lower sector, inviting mestizos and indios to join him on the day of Corpus, during which he would perform as a danzante or matachin, "as he was accustomed"; but since he was inviting the mestizos to the said performance, and it was "never the custom before" that mestizos attend such a function, she believed that it must be for an uprising.[22] In this climate of increased racial tension between natives and mestizos, Quintuña, in his capacity as an indigenous official, and through his very participation as a festival performer in

FIGURE 16. Costumed Dancers. Danzantes and "Forest Person." Nineteenth-Century Ecuador. From Gaetano Osculati, 1854.

disguise (whether it was as a devil, matachin, or other masked dancer), created suspicion when he invited mestizos to join him. In his own testimony, Simon Quintuña stated that he never instigated any gathering against the Spaniards and mestizos of Pelileo. Rather, he explained that since he is an oficial, a tailor by trade, and since it is the custom in this town that on the day of "Corpus of Our Lord" one of the activities is for all the craftsmen (oficiales—journeymen) to set up stands in the plaza for the procession of the *mojiganga* (paper mache dummy), he was simply inviting the other tradesmen to set up their stands in the plaza for the procession.[23] The custom was not at all unusual. George Foster reported that during Corpus Christi celebrations in Spain, artisans' guilds would carry symbols of their professions, and in Peru, the artisans (tailors, blacksmiths, shoemakers) set up "altars" in the plaza for the festivities.[24] The "procession of the mojiganga" was probably a reference to the tradition of the *mojigón*—an effigy of a grotesque giant that was part of the procession on this day. Despite this long-standing annual custom, in the political climate of racial tensions, the invitation was taken as a threat. In his role as a tailor and alcalde of the lower sector, Simon Quintuña raised suspicions of a planned gathering when he invited people to accompany him on the day of the festivities.

DON MANUEL TUBÓN

The cacique of the Guambaló, Don Manuel Tubón, was most directly associated with specific threats of revenge against mestizos. Several mestizo witnesses said that Tubón was overheard saying that the mestizos might be "very satisfied" that the Indians from the sweatshop were captured and handed over to be punished, but they better take Communion and go to confession because the day was coming when they too would be killed, decapitated, or hanged. He allegedly said this while passing by the home of a white family, although the housekeeper for that family, an indigenous woman from Quito, declared that she only heard Tubón say that it was good that the mestizos were going to confession and receiving Communion (an ambiguous message), and nothing more.[25] Furthermore, there were very specific rumors about the alleged letter that Tubón had sent to the native governor of the town of Píllaro, inviting those natives to join him in the rebellion planned for Corpus Christi.[26]

When the cacique was interrogated about warning (threatening) mestizos to confess and take Communion, because they would soon be killed, he stated under oath that on the day in question he had been walking home from visiting another indigenous person, where they had been drinking to celebrate the May Festival of the Cross. He did not recall making such a statement, and if he did, it was only because he was drunk. He admitted, however, that he might have said that the mestizos should go live in the towns and cities with the Spaniards, and not among the Indians, occupying their lands and bothering them, because he "had a tendency to say that" when he drank. While in jail, Tubón told a fellow inmate that his only intention was to get the mestizos to leave the town and go live with the Spaniards in the cities, but he never intended to rise up against them nor instigate others to rise up. When Miguel Condo was interrogated about his knowledge of Don Manuel Tubón, he reported hearing Tubón say, "I am the cacique of these Indians and of this town, and it belongs to Indians, and not to the mestizos, who should go live in the cities, villas, and asientos [Spanish urban centers]."[27] This drunken "tendency" to criticize mestizos for occupying indigenous lands increased mestizo suspicions of the cacique in this political climate of collective fear, and perhaps guilt, in the aftermath of the obraje rebellion.

The racial tensions were probably compounded by the violation of colonial laws meant to protect indigenous communities. In his study of Bolivia, Sinclair Thomson states:

> According to the Laws of the Indies, no "Spaniards"—meaning non-Indians— could reside in the towns, although this prescription was only loosely observed in the colonial period. As the eighteenth century wore on, mestizos and creoles who were looking for parcels of land, access to Indian labor, and local power increasingly infiltrated and took up residence in the town centers. Nevertheless, the Spanish Crown originally did intend to guarantee the land-base of communities and to protect Indians from the abuse of other colonial subjects, in order to ensure its own vitally important appropriation of tribute.[28]

Tubón's drunken, repeated statements regarding mestizo residence in native communities suggests a growing tension in interracial relations prior to the rebellion, but the mestizos' choice to round up the rebels for the Spanish marked a turning point in indigenous-mestizo relations.

As for the letter to the native governor of Píllaro, Tubón said that he never wrote any such letter and that he didn't even know the governor of Píllaro, and he challenged authorities to bring the governor as a witness and ask if any such letter ever existed. In fact officials did undertake an investigation and concluded that no such letter ever existed. But this detailed rumor shows a major concern for inter-indigenous alliances; it showed that the indigenous resentment in the sweatshop could spill over to the town of Pelileo, which could spill over to other towns of Ambato and spread through the region. While the Spaniards and mestizos emphasized a pan-indigenous uprising, repeatedly stating that the leaders were gathering together "all the Indians" of the region, the cacique himself emphasized ethnic and political divisions, blaming the rebellion on the Chumaquí and Pilalata Indians, not on his own parcialidad of Guambaló.[29]

Although many mestizos feared a backlash for their role in subduing the rebellion, not all were critical of Don Manuel Tubón. Several mestizo and indigenous people served as character witnesses for Tubón. They affirmed his loyalty, that he never spoke boldly to Spaniards or mestizos, that his subjects attended their religious lessons regularly, that he always paid tribute on time, and that he and his subjects were humble and obedient. The court found no evidence of a conspiracy, and the *protector de naturales* (protector of natives) asked that the accused men be released immediately, stating that prison is a horrible punishment for indigenous people "because they find themselves without communication, food, and without what is most valuable for the Indians, their innocent chicha [maize beer]."[30] The order for their release was finally signed November 4, 1768, five and a half months after their arrest.

SYMBOLS AND SUBVERSIONS

When Tubón admitted that he had a tendency to say that mestizos should go live in cities, and should not occupy indigenous lands, it was a way of voicing a criticism while maintaining the appearance of subordination and loyalty to the colonial order. There are several ways in which subordinate classes vocalize their criticism of power. The subversive message is often hidden because either the message or the messenger are disguised—for example, when someone anonymously shouts insults against authorities from a crowd, or when a person uses an expression with a double meaning.[31] Marginalized people cannot directly and publicly criticize the powerful; they must veil their criticism, which allows them to obscure the political message. Don Manuel Tubón had authority over his subjects, but caciques always had to carefully balance their obligations to their subjects with their obligations to the colonial authorities. While colonial laws prohibiting nonindigenous peoples from living in native communities were ignored, Don Manuel Tubón was careful not to assert his criticisms directly to the mestizos. Instead he expressed his discontent in the type of ambiguous expressions that are politically subversive. Tubón vocalized his true feelings with the pretext that he "was drunk" to avoid being accused of animosity toward the mestizos. In fact, three of the defendants (Tubón, Muchagalo, and Condo) said that their mestizo neighbors had misinterpreted statements they made after drinking chicha and cane alcohol during the Festival of the Cross. Tubón and perhaps the other suspects seem to have used drinking as a strategy to express one's feelings about sensitive topics without being held responsible for their statements.[32] Similarly, in their analysis of a rebellion in Igaguasi, Atacama, in 1775, Nelson Castro, Jorge Hidalgo, and Viviana Briones demonstrate the link between fiestas, drinking, memory, and rebellion. In that case, the indigenous celebrants who had "drunk" during carnival shouted that they "would expel all Spaniards from the asiento until not one remained in their lands" since the lands belonged to them and not to the king of Spain.[33] In Don Manuel Tubón's case, he was able to admit a resentment of mestizo occupation while maintaining that he was an honorable, loyal cacique whose subjects were humble and who never had any intention of instigating an uprising.

The disrespect and ridicule of authorities, costumes, drunkenness, and symbolic inversions of festivals open a space for political defiance. Another manifestation of the relationship between fiestas and rebellion is that political protests use symbols of the fiesta. For example, James Scott notes that historically in Europe, people used symbols of carnival in their political protests and rebellions.[34] In the uprising in San Ildefonso, the indigenous rebels danced, sang, and played the "churo" (trumpet shell) and drum. During his defense, Blas Chango claimed that he told one woman that "it was no fiesta" for there to be drums and trumpet shells.[35] But the shell and trumpet, which are instruments typically used to summon indigenous people to come together for the fiesta, are also "unmistakable signs of an uprising."[36]

Unlike Tubón, Muchagalo, and Condo, Simon Quintuña did not use the guise of "drunkenness" to explain his statements but rather provided an alternative meaning to the statements. He said that he was acting in his role as alcalde and as an official of the craftsmen. Year after year, journeymen, artisans, and guild members would set up stalls in the plaza or participate in the procession of Corpus Christi. Costumed dancing was also a well-known custom. So why did Quintuña's invitation to mestizos make him a suspect? The case results from the combination of characteristics of festivals and the political tensions of the time period—that is, the growing tensions between mestizos and native groups in Pelileo. In the history of Ecuador, indigenous and mestizo people sometimes joined together against the oligarchy. In this case, mestizos chose to side with the Spaniards against the indigenous people during the obraje conflict. The mestizos expected resentment on the part of their indigenous neighbors, and they heard threats in the statements made by drunken natives. They worried not only that the obraje workers would take revenge, but that it would lead to a general insurrection among all the native ethnic groups of the jurisdiction of Ambato.

Furthermore, the statements made during the trial indicated a transition phase in the ethnic composition of Pelileo, as part of the long transformation from an indigenous town to a mestizo one. In the years before the uprising in the obraje, Cicala wrote that although Pelileo was an indigenous town, it had an equal number of mestizo inhabitants.[37] Mestizos were neighbors of the indigenous residents, and they knew one another and interacted, but interracial relations were characterized by ambiguity throughout the colonial period and after independence.[38]

The indigenous suspects in this case occupied specific social positions that made them well known to Spaniards and mestizos: Tubón held the public position of cacique of Guambaló, Quintuña was an alcalde, and Thomas Muchagalo was a cantor (choirmaster) of the church. However, in Pelileo, in May 1768, the mestizo ambivalence toward their indigenous neighbors was expressed in rumors that the festival would become a native insurrection and, through their festive disguises, indigenous people would burn down the houses of their neighbors and kill Spaniards and mestizos. The fiesta, as a cultural space for interaction of different sectors of society, serves to unite people in a common celebration. But in certain sociopolitical contexts, the historical relationship between festivities and rebellions looms as a threat. Although the court found no evidence of a plot, the case against Don Manuel Tubón and others reveals that Spaniards and mestizos were aware of the link between fiestas and transgressions, and that they were at a turning point in relations between mestizos and indigenous people in the town of Pelileo.

SENTENCE OF THE REBELS

In 1769, the trial of the accused ring leaders of the killing of Ruiz was complete. Some local indigenous people had tried to help their friends during the trial by saying that the accused had been with them, helping to plough a field, for example, during the lynching of the administrator. All the accused denied being present during the violence, so they were subjected to torture. Blas Chango finally admitted to having been present, but only as a spectator, and testified to what he witnessed. The Llagua brothers, Manuel Pombosa, and Bárbula Sinailín were sentenced to death, and the court ordered their bodies to be dismembered (just outside of Quito), their parts transported to San Ildefonso, where their arms and legs would be placed along the various roads leading to the obraje and to other towns in Ambato; their heads would be placed in secure cages in front of the obraje, so that nobody could take them down. Eleven other rebels were sentenced to two hundred public lashes: one hundred to be administered along the streets of Quito, and another one hundred in Pelileo, while their crime was announced to the others. After being lashed, they would serve ten years in an obraje of Yaruqui (Riobamba). A fourteen-year-old indigenous boy who crawled through the chapel window to let the rebels in to where the Spaniards were hiding was sentenced to twenty-five lashes and five years of labor. Marsela Tasi, who delivered the first blow to Ruiz and incited the others to kill him, was to be sent to the women's prison of Santa Marta for ten years. The bodies of those who were sentenced to death were dismembered, and some of the remains were buried in the church of Chimbacalle (in Quito). The rest were transported, along with the prisoners, to Pelileo. After the first one hundred lashes had been administered in Quito, Domingo Toctaquisa could not endure the entire six-day walk to Pelileo and was left, weak and injured, in Latacunga.[39]

CONCLUSION

When the government took over the obraje, the increase in production quotas and decrease in socorros led to an argument and the punishment of two brothers. Indigenous workers tried to use established legal channels to get justice, but when they suspected interference on the part of the administrator, they violently rebelled. The killing of the administrator was specifically encouraged by two mothers who had been punished after intervening on behalf of their children who were being held in the obraje. After the rebellion, indigenous intermediaries fell under suspicion as tensions mounted during the planning of the annual Corpus Christi celebrations, an important focus for indigenous collective memory and a time of drinking and costumed dancing. Tensions from the obraje affected the way traditional indigenous costumed dancing was viewed by mestizos and Spaniards.

Don Manuel Tubón complained of the increasing mestizo occupation of indigenous towns. However, the composition of the towns had already been changing long before Tubón made his comments. Indigenous families who worked in the obraje, and their caciques, were already selling some of their family lands by the mid-eighteenth century. Selling inherited lands enabled the Pilalata and Chumaquí to pay for a family member's funeral, to meet tribute requirements, or to liberate a family member from the obraje. The next chapter traces patterns of inheritance of lands and sales between indigenous people, mestizos, and Spaniards. Through such sales, we can trace the disruptions and reemergence of indigenous communities.

CHAPTER 7

KIN, INHERITANCE, AND LAND

IN THE mid-eighteenth century some Pilalata and Chumaquí sold or transferred lands to meet their needs and help their relatives. The transfer of lands
led to the transformation of indigenous communities, and by tracing the
histories of specific land sales, we can trace changes in these communities. Land,
kinship, and community are intertwined, so a discussion of indigenous kinship
practices is necessary before presenting the details of specific land sales. In this
chapter I first look at wills and inheritance for clues about how kinship, including adoption, was conceived among families in Pelileo. In the second part of the
chapter I trace the histories of specific plots of land to reveal how the Chumaquí
and Pilalata sold lands to pay for relatives' funerals, to pay tribute, and occasionally to liberate a family member from the obraje of San Ildefonso. Finally,
I look at a land dispute involving indigenous and mestizo cousins. Although a
common story told by indigenous people today is that mestizos stole indigenous
lands, it is important to remember that first-generation mestizos inherited lands
from their indigenous mothers. After indigenous people initially lost access
to some lands during the conquest and reducciones, during the eighteenth-
century indigenous people, Spaniards, and mestizos bought and sold land to
one another. The cases presented here show both the cultural practices of the
indigenous people of eighteenth-century Pelileo and the use of land sales as a
strategy for coping with colonial pressures and meeting family obligations. The

transfer of lands was a step in the long process of community formation by which indigenous people chose two trajectories over time: some blended in with Hispanic communities and developed a mestizo identity, while others created an indigenous community and maintained an indigenous identity.

The source material for the information on inheritance and changes in land-ownership comes from eighteenth-century land disputes, which contain wills that were either copied or inserted into the record. Any late eighteenth-century dispute over a plot of land might contain one or more copies of much older wills, yielding important details about seventeenth-century kinship, inheritance practices, religious devotion, and ethnic identities. One pattern I found regards the role of religious ritual as a catalyst for economic transactions. Both natives and Spaniards exchanged land for the payment of proper funeral rites of relatives, and some designated certain lands to be used to pay for Masses for their souls or to continue the celebration of saints' feast days. Catholic priests mediated these land-for-ritual deals, facilitating the transfer of lands to whoever paid for the deceased's funeral. In order to understand transformations in ethnic identity in Pelileo, it is necessary to know who was buying and who was selling lands.

KINSHIP AND INHERITANCE: SINGLE MOTHERS, RITUAL KIN, AND ADOPTION

In his study of the Valley of Lima, Paul Charney demonstrates how the Spanish practices of will-making, dowries, and *compadrazgo* (ritual co-parenthood) helped the indigenous families adapt to and survive colonialism: "Paradoxically, these elements of the colonizers' culture, some even resembling pre-Hispanic practices, strengthened and extended the Indians' family ties and even helped them to retain access to some resources."[1] Bequeathing property to kin helps to maintain ties with one's family, community, and culture. Jane Mangan found that in wills from sixteenth-century Peru, indigenous women bequeathed items that were symbolic of indigenous culture—such as clothing and drinking vessels—to kin, including stepchildren. The practice of willing important objects that signified indigenous material culture maintained indigenous culture and kinship bonds, even among children with Spanish fathers and indigenous mothers.[2]

Wills reflect different types of relationships within native Andean families and occasionally between families from different racial categories. In chapter 2 I mentioned a case in which a Spanish woman claimed that her uncle purchased lands from his indigenous wet nurse. She suggested bonds of intimacy, but we do not have the indigenous nanny's testimony for support. There were some cases in the jurisdiction of Ambato in which Spaniards left land to indigenous servants whom they had raised in their homes, as in other parts of Spanish America.[3] A glance through the inventories of the estates of deceased Spaniards in the *Protocolos* section of the national archive in Ambato shows a seventeenth-century pattern in which black slaves were listed along with the furniture and other household items. Slaves and their children were usually named. Because they were associated with the home, people knew their names and the ages of their children. Indigenous people were listed with the land and sheep, and they were anonymous. Usually the inventory would state that the land or the flock of sheep came with "accion de indio gañan of the Puruguayes"—that is, a Puruguay worker. Perhaps because the individual workers served on a rotating basis, the Spanish property owners didn't bother to learn their names from year to year.

Some Spaniards did mention their indigenous servants by name. One example comes from the will of a sugar baron of Pelileo, which stands out for its attention to the indigenous servants. In 1683, Don Domingo de Acosta, who inherited sugarcane haciendas and sugar mills from his father (in Pingue and Guambaló), left money for the souls of the deceased native workers who had served him and his father on the hacienda. He had cane fields and a sugar mill in Pingue, as well as one piece of land near Pelileo that he purchased from an indigenous woman named Lorenza Puzo. He left this land to another indigenous woman named Pascuala Alulima, "who has served me."[4] This is just one example of how a plot of land in Pelileo could change hands between natives and Spaniards and back to other natives, who, for all we know, might have sold it later to other Spaniards in order to pay for a funeral or other expenses. To an indigenous woman named María, who had served his parents and raised two of his children, he left five wool anacos (native skirts) with lligllas (native shawls) for the service and childrearing. Although it is not stated in the will, it's possible that she or another indigenous servant was a mother to one or more of Don Domingo's out-of-wedlock children. Don Domingo's will reveals a familiarity and a host of interactions with local indigenous people, even knowing their nicknames. He bought, sold, and willed lands to and from indigenous people, and he tried to assure that they would be paid what they were owed. Such connections between indigenous people and Spaniards occurred throughout the

Andes,[5] but, given the social distance between indigenous people and whites in Pelileo in the first half of the twentieth century, cases of close interactions between Spaniards and indigenous there are significant because they prove that relations were not always hostile.

In addition to wills, baptismal records reveal information about godparenthood and single parents. The records show a number of single mothers with out-of-wedlock children. Many babies were listed only with their mother and "unknown father."[6] Out-of-wedlock children were not unusual for the colonial period. Deborah Truhan found that two out of three women in late sixteenth-century Cuenca declared in their wills that they had children out of wedlock.[7] Records for Pelileo indicate that it was still common in the eighteenth century.

In a classic study of ritual co-parenthood, called compadrazgo in Latin America, Sidney Mintz and Eric Wolf described strategies used by peasants to extend their social networks by forming ties of ritual kinship—through baptism, for example—with social superiors.[8] In Latin America, the ritual creates mutual obligations and bonds between the parents and godparents of the child, who refer to one another as *compadre* (co-father) and *comadre* (co-mother). The cultural expectations might differ when godparents are chosen from within the indigenous community rather than between indigenous people and Spaniards. When indigenous peasants chose whites, as social superiors, to be godparents, they created social capital across socioracial categories, on which they could rely for certain needs, although the nature of the relationship varied. When they selected other indigenous people to become ritual kin, they strengthened ties within indigenous communities.

Complete baptismal records for Pelileo were only available for the eighteenth century. Sometimes the indigenous godparent had the same last name as the mother; this was often the case with Comasanta women, indicating that they may have been choosing maternal relatives, thereby reinforcing indigenous kinship systems. While native Andeans in Pelileo usually chose one another as godparents, they occasionally chose Spaniards, and some Spaniards were godparents to multiple indigenous children. Doña María Orozco was a Spanish woman of Pelileo whose lands bordered lands of indigenous people. She was chosen as a baptismal godmother by several different indigenous families. Whether the godparents were Spanish, or more often, indigenous, most entries only listed a single godfather or godmother of baptism, rather than a couple, and there was no pattern according to gender: godparents of boys or girls could be male or female, although there seem to be more godmothers than godfathers.

Wills of indigenous people yield valuable information on practices of adoption and the composition of indigenous families and households from the seventeenth through nineteenth centuries. Some left lands to godchildren and adopted children. For example, in the 1673 will of Don Geronimo Toasa, cacique of the Chumaquí, he left lands to a foster daughter, Barbola Ungas, and stated that he wanted her to have them "because I raised her and none of my heirs should impede her" from having the lands.[9] The foster daughter carried the same feminine surname as the daughters that Toasa had with his wife, suggesting that the girl was adopted into the matriline. In another case, Andres Caizabanda, a Sigchos Collanas man, was raised in the home of Don Joseph Toasa (possibly Chumaquí), who was married to an elite Pilalata woman, showing how a descendant of migrants from Latacunga was incorporated into, or at least cared for by, a local indigenous elite family.[10]

Caciques as well as commoners raised foster children. An eighteenth-century land dispute in Salasaca contained the will of Geronima Culqui, who bequeathed lands to her sons, daughters, and a niece whom she raised.[11] In another case a Chumaquí woman, Rosa Guamancha, inherited lands from her mother. Rosa had one legitimate son, who was a contracted laborer in San Ildefonso, and one foster daughter whom she raised and gave her feminine surname. When Rosa made her will in 1790, she first bequeathed lands to the foster daughter, before mentioning which lands she was leaving to her son.[12] In her 1888 will Vicenta Curichumbi of Huasalata (a sector of modern Salasaca) stated that she was married to Domingo Masaquiza, but they had no surviving children together (their only daughter died). She did have four adopted children: a boy with the last name Chango and three girls who carried her last name. She stated that "they have served me in all my work" and that they were her "universal heirs."[13] She left her adopted daughters and son lands that she had inherited from her father, Estevan Masaquiza. Adoption was not only used by couples who lacked children; some indigenous families had both adopted and biological children. For example, one of the native families who sold lands to the Jesuits included biological siblings and an adopted sibling, all equal shareholders in the lands.

The above-mentioned cases show the maintenance of indigenous families and communities through adoption or child circulation among indigenous people. One case of adoption stands out for its illustration of ties of familiarity between Spaniards and indigenous people. Sometime in the late 1730s an indigenous woman, Manuela Quilligana, received a visit from her Spanish friend, Doña Gregoria Fernandez Chico. Doña Gregoria said that she was on her way to a neighboring town and stayed the night with Manuela. That night Doña Gregoria gave birth to a baby boy. Gregoria asked Manuela to take the child to her (Gregoria's) mother, promising to pay her three pesos for the errand. But when Manuela brought the child to Gregoria's mother, Doña Isabela, she didn't want him, and she told Manuela to throw him in the river or to give him to someone who would want him. Manuela now had to decide what to do with the Spanish baby, and she discussed the matter with her sister, who advised her to give the child to an indigenous compadre named Gregorio. But instead Manuela decided to give the child to Juana Comasanta, her sister's comadre, who was apparently childless. So, through this ritual kin network of indigenous women, the Spanish baby ended up with Juana Comasanta. Juana baptized the baby and she raised the child "with lots of work," and when the boy was three years old the biological father, Manuel Naranjo, came looking for his son. Juana asked him why he had abandoned his son, for which he blamed his "damned mother-in-law, a bad Christian," and said that it was his wife who abandoned the baby, and that he had been all over Quito, Tacunga, and Riobamba searching for his son. But Juana Comasanta kept the child.

When Gregoria, the biological mother, died, her mother survived her, and the son, Juan Lopez de Naranjo (who carried his biological father's last name, rather than that of his adoptive indigenous father), wanted an inventory of all Gregoria's belongings, in order to compensate Juana Comasanta. He was over fourteen but under twenty five years of age, so he was appointed a representative (tutor). The representative said that Juana Comasanta gave young Juan love and care from her heart, despite her poverty. He argued that the indigenous mother should be paid from the biological mother's estate, even though Juana Comasanta raised him out of "Christian charity," a concern that is more appropriate from his biological grandmother Doña Isabela, because, he said, he is "two times a son" (*dos veces hijo*).

Doña Isabela insisted that she had not inherited anything from her daughter, and that any money she had was spent on getting Gregoria's marriage annulled in Quito. Doña Isabela continued with an argument on the rules surrounding adoption:

> It is a Christian act for Catholics to raise abandoned children left at their doors and raise them as if they were born of their wombs and they adopt them as such, for this reason they gain legitimate custody [*dominio*] over the abandoned child, and if the natural father wants to take the child from his adoptive parents by force,

he must compensate for the [cost of] raising of the child, when the adoptive father and natural father agree on adequate compensation, the natural father can take the child; but in this case, I [Doña Isabela] have not forcibly taken the child, and didn't even know if my daughter had given birth to him or not, because from the time she got married until the day she died she was estranged from me, and I never knew that he was really my grandson until the day that the Indian woman declared that I owed her two hundred pesos . . . in no way is the child owed my belongings, even if he were the legitimate son of my daughter, as the other party claims, believing that my daughter left me something when she died . . . my daughter died quickly and violently, and didn't have time to make a will . . . besides, it's not the custom in these *reynos* to compensate those who raised the child; no judge has ever ordered that the parent pay, unless there was a contract with the adoptive parent; in these times many abandoned children have been raised without knowing who their parents had been, and when they learn who they were they don't obligate them to pay for the upbringing.[14]

According to Doña Isabela, it was her understanding that Juana Comasanta fought for, and won, the right to keep the child. She said that when Manuel Naranjo tried to get custody of his biological son, Juana Comasanta, "motivated by the love she had developed for the child," did not want to give up the three-year-old child. The two went before an ecclesiastical judge (according to Doña Isabela), who found in favor of Comasanta. Even though Naranjo had offered her twenty more pesos, on top of twenty he had paid to compensate her for what she already spent caring for the child, she didn't want to take it because "she loved him like her own son."[15] The judge found in favor of the indigenous mother. If Doña Isabela's information is correct, that means that the ecclesiastical judge favored an adoptive indigenous mother over a Spanish biological father, departing from earlier custody battles between Spanish men and indigenous women in the Andes. In early colonial Peru Spanish fathers used their legal power to take their biological mestizo children away from the indigenous mothers. In granting power to the European fathers, authorities guaranteed that the child would be raised with Spanish culture, language, and religion, rather than being raised as a Quechua-speaking Indian.[16] In this eighteenth-century case, by contrast, the ecclesiastical judge felt that the child would be better off with his adoptive, indigenous parents. In the late colonial period, secular judges of custody cases in the Audiencia of Lima began to consider people's emotional attachments to children in their decisions.[17] As someone who was "two times a son," young Juan Lopez de Naranjo never gave up his Spanish identity, which enabled him to attempt to claim his Spanish mother's estate. One would think that a child raised by Quichua-speaking parents would be culturally indigenous, but there is no indication of this in the record. Perhaps he grew up bilingual, and, given the benefits of being Spanish in colonial society, his adoptive mother might have reminded him of his white status.

While a lot of information is missing about this story, we can infer that Gregoria's mother and husband did not get along, even though the mother had initially agreed to the marriage, and that Gregoria was already estranged from her husband, and probably her mother, when she was pregnant. What was her relationship to Manuela Quilligana? The document only says that the Spanish woman and the indigenous woman were friends. It is possible that Gregoria may have already been feeling labor pains when she decided to spend the night at the home of Quilligana, perhaps needing someone to mediate with her mother. Perhaps she feared her mother's rejection of the child and thought that the indigenous woman would be able to find a home for him. In the end, Manuela Quilligana did find a home, with her sister's comadre, a childless woman who, with her indigenous husband, adopted and raised him. Both the teenaged son and his adoptive mother felt that the adoptive mother was entitled to some of Gregoria's estate as compensation for feeding, clothing, and raising the boy. This case of child circulation shows indigenous women's use of a network of kin and ritual kin to find a home for the child, as well as the relations of familiarity between Manuela and Gregoria and the bonds of affection developed between the indigenous adoptive mother and Spanish child.

Among indigenous people, relatives continued to help one another, although conflicts over inheritance also led to disputes among relatives. Lands were a resource that could be sold when money was needed, sometimes to help a family member. I now turn to cases in which relatives paid off debts in order to keep a family member out of the obraje.

FAMILY AND OBRAJE DEBTS

In chapter 3 I discussed how the textile economy affected indigenous families in Pelileo. A century after the 1661 case in which natives of Pelileo denounced the abuses that they suffered in the obraje, some were still being forced into the obraje over debt, and family members still searched for ways to liberate their loved ones from the obraje. I found two cases in which land was exchanged between indigenous people to liberate someone from the obraje. In the first case, a secondary chief of the Chumaquí took over his brother's lands and paid the brother's debt to the obraje. In the second case, land was transferred from one indigenous family to another in order to liberate a relative from the obraje.

Clemente Allan was a worker who ran away, leaving a large debt he owed to the obraje. His brother, Pedro Allan, was a principal of Chumaquí, and he took over Clemente's lands and paid off most of the debt. When Pedro made his will in 1764, he revealed his religious devotion in his will. He left land that he had inherited from his mother, Francisca Yumbulin, to pay for fiestas for Pelileo's patron saint, Saint Peter.[18] He also mentioned some money still owed to the obraje from his brother Clemente's debt, as well as the lands he had taken over from his brother, which now went to Pedro's widow. Years later, Clemente's son tried to claim his father's lands as his inheritance, but then he learned of his father's debt to the mill, and he understood that Pedro rightfully gained the lands when he assumed Clemente's debt. Nevertheless, Pedro's widow agreed to give Clemente's son a loom for weaving (worth three pesos), to make up the difference between the value of the land and the debt that was paid. In this case, the land was transferred from the descendants of one brother (Clemente) to the descendants of the other (Pedro) in order to clear the debt to the obraje.

In the second case, land was transferred between two unrelated indigenous families. In a dispute between the Bandas, descendants of a Pilalata man, and the Sailemas (indigenous people whose parcialidad is not stated), the dispute was traced back to a land exchange to liberate someone from the obraje. The Bandas had owned the lands in Nitón (see figure 10) but had a maternal half brother who had been sentenced to the obraje because he owed tribute. In order to liberate their half brother, the Bandas sold their lands to their neighbors, the Sailemas. The Banda family also had debts over weddings and funerals. Here we have another example of how the obraje affected indigenous cultural life. These ceremonial debts, necessary for the proper rites of passage of marriage and death, were compounded by the need to liberate their half brother from the obraje. The Bandas responded by transferring lands to the Sailemas and their descendants. Later, in his 1782 will, Estevan Sailema acknowledged that he obtained lands in Nitón for getting someone (the Banda brother) out of the obraje of San Ildefonso. He revealed another practice in his will: indigenous people were breeding large flocks of sheep on their own, and they could exchange these for land. Estevan Sailema left the Nitón lands, as well as lands that his mother got in exchange for fifty head of sheep, to his heirs.[19] This led to confusion a generation later, when the descendants of the Bandas and the Sailemas were fighting over the lands in 1813. Although the parcialidad of the Sailemas is not stated, there are Sailemas among the modern-day Salasaca families today.

In a third eighteenth-century case involving the obraje, a man tried to help his son by offering to work off the son's debt. In 1792 Lorenzo Chipantiza was a voluntary worker on the hacienda of Chumaquí who owed the owner, Vicente Villagomez, fifteen pesos. Lorenzo's father, Mateo, offered to work for Villagomez to settle up his son's debt. The father and son requested that Villagomez allow the father to work off the son's debt, or if that was not acceptable, at least to allow Lorenzo to pay it back gradually, through some type of payment plan. Rather than accept either proposition, Villagomez (through his mayordomo) forced Lorenzo into the obraje, where he was immediately given twenty-five lashes, forced to work as a wool beater (*vergueador*) by day, and locked in the dungeon at night. He was kept there for five months, without pay or the advancement of goods, until the protector of natives filed to have the accounts settled and to have Villagomez fined twenty-five pesos: thirteen to compensate Lorenzo for the whipping, and the rest to be used as officials saw fit.[20]

All three cases show how families relied on one another to free a member from debt servitude in the obraje. In both of the cases in which native families transferred inherited lands in order to free a relative from debt owed to the obraje, the lands went to their indigenous relatives or neighbors. There were probably cases in which indigenous people sold land to whites for the same reason: to pay off a debt and get a family member out of the obraje. Indigenous people also sold lands to Spaniards (and to other indigenous people) to pay for funerals or to pay tribute, and often the same piece of land changed ownership several times during the eighteenth century. In some cases, the elites of the Pilalata, the Changos, sold their subjects' lands to Spaniards. Sometime between 1760 and 1774, Don Fernando Chango, who had a "bad habit" of selling indigenous communal lands, sold a piece of land to a Spaniard. Don Fernando's brother, the cacique of the Pilalata, assigned that same piece of land to Juan Mayta, his subject, as a reward for his service in the labor draft. It was, after all, part of the communal lands for the Pilalata. The heirs of the Spanish buyer and the indigenous heirs of Juan Mayta fought over the land into the nineteenth century. When the indigenous litigants died, the Spanish heirs continued to fight among themselves for the land.[21] The Chango brothers, as caciques of the

Pilalata, sold other lands in the eighteenth century that were later disputed, leading to fights among the heirs well into the nineteenth century.[22]

PRIMOS: NATIVES AND MESTIZOS IN PELILEO

There is a history of Spaniards and mestizos taking over indigenous lands in the Americas. But the history is complicated by the fact that first-generation mestizos were part of indigenous families and sometimes legitimately inherited lands from their indigenous mothers. I turn now to mestizo involvement in indigenous land disputes.

Although colonial laws prohibited Spaniards, blacks, and mestizos from living among Indians, the offspring of indigenous women were heirs to their mothers' lands. Mestizos attempted to lay claim to lands from their indigenous mothers or their Spanish fathers, and when these claims put them into conflict with indigenous people, courts often ruled in favor of the natives. The following case illustrates how first-generation mestizos (the offspring of indigenous women and Spanish men) inherited lands from their mother that put them in dispute with their cousins, or *primos*.

When someone received land in exchange for paying for a funeral, their children were not always aware of the deal. Later, the children on both sides grow up, each believing that they were the rightful heirs. Among the Chumaquí in 1776, mestizo and indigenous relatives fought over a plot of land. The dispute was traced back to an agreement between indigenous relatives to give lands in exchange for paying the funeral costs of a common relative. Two mestizo brothers, Sebastian and Mariano Morales, argued that their indigenous mother, Eugenia Canin, had paid for her brother's funeral in exchange for the lands. That brother, Sebastian Aseycha, had drowned in the Patate River without leaving a will. The mestizo brothers claimed inheritance of the lands from their mother. But their indigenous cousin, Lucas, was the son of Sebastian Aseycha and believed that he was the heir to his father's lands. This was not a case of mestizos stealing lands from indigenous people, but rather of relatives fighting over which indigenous sibling (Eugenia or Sebastian) legitimately possessed the lands. The mestizo brothers died during the dispute, and their widows, white women who both used the title "Doña" to indicate their status, continued fighting against their Chumaquí in-laws for the lands. Here we witness mestizaje, or whitening, in progress: the natural sons (born out of wedlock) of an indigenous Chumaquí woman (and Spanish man?) married white women. Their descendants would then be classified as mestizos or *montañeses* (a polite term for mestizo) of Pelileo, and they would eventually split off from their Chumaquí relatives. In fact, Eugenia Canin was the daughter of a principal of Chumaquí. Eugenia owned several other plots of land that she left to her mestizo grandchildren, but the disputed plot in this case was legally granted to the indigenous heir (Lucas Aseycha), the son of Sebastian.[23]

Although the sons of Eugenia laid claim to indigenous lands through their mother, they strengthened their claims to their status as white-mestizos by marrying white women. Their children would surely not be classified as Indians, and therefore would not pay tribute like their indigenous cousins. Others laying claim to mestizo status would use marriage, in addition to biological descent, to support their claims of mestizo status to avoid paying Indian tribute. For example, in an earlier case (1752), the Meneses brothers of Pelileo petitioned for legal recognition of mestizo status. They said that they had served to defend the city of Guayaquil from British threats and paid the *alcabala*, the tax from which Indians were exempt. They produced their baptismal records (from 1722 and 1725, where they were recorded in the book of Spaniards and montañeses), and they produced witnesses to their mixed heritage as sons of an Indian woman and a Spanish man. But colonial officials were not convinced, so the Meneses would have to produce more evidence of whiteness if they didn't want to pay the Indian tribute.[24]

In petitions for legal recognition of mestizo status throughout the Audiencia of Quito, petitioners first used biological descent to prove their mestizo status. This sometimes meant that their indigenous mothers had to declare that they had a "weakness" with a Spanish man. People used cultural factors[25] as secondary evidence to support their claims of being mestizo. In the case of the Meneses brothers, several Spaniards gave statements on behalf of the Meneses brothers, saying that they were known as mestizos and that they were married to white women (*mujeres blancas*). The brothers added: "We are publicly known in this jurisdiction and town as mestizos and as such we are married to Spanish women."[26] This adds a dimension to constructions of race in the mid-eighteenth century; it is not just based on parentage and descent, but also on cultural practices of *blanqueamiento* ("whitening") by choosing to marry Spanish women. The brothers also paid the alcabala, the tax from which indigenous people were exempt.

While Spaniards testified on behalf of the Meneses, declaring that they were publicly known as mestizos, indigenous caciques testified against them. Indigenous caciques were always trying to increase their own pool of subjects, so it was in their interest to go against indigenous people who were trying to claim a mestizo identity. Manuel Ganan, the cacique of the Camayos Puruguayes (who had tried to force Carlos Masaquiza into the obraje), claimed that the Meneses brothers were Indians who belonged to his parcialidad. It was acknowledged that their mother was indigenous. The question was whether their father, Marcos, was a mestizo or an indigenous person who dressed like a mestizo. In a telling example of the connection between labor and race in colonial Quito, the cacique got other indigenous people to testify that the Meneses had been imprisoned in San Ildefonso as proof of their Indianness! If marrying white women made a man whiter, being locked in San Ildefonso proved that he was indigenous. The reason this served as proof was that they were locked in the obraje for not paying the Indian tribute, so it is a reference to their status as tribute payers that makes them indnigenous. But there is also an association between natives and sweatshop labor that was so naturalized in the colonial period that it's as if being in San Ildefonso served as evidence of one's indigenous status.

Furthermore, the cacique argued, the Meneses were listed in the tribute records of the parcialidad of Puruguayes. Not only was their mother Indian, but their father was as well; however, since the time he was a teenager, he had adopted a common strategy of wearing mestizo clothing (*traje de mestizo*) in order to "pass." Ganan said that the jurisdiction of Ambato was full of Indians from towns in Riobamba (Puruguayes). Other Spanish witnesses said that the father of the Meneses brothers was a pure Indian—a Puruguay to be exact, but because the father had been raised in the home of a Spaniard, he took the Spanish last name Meneses and donned Spanish clothing. Another witness, a native elite from Pelileo, Don Crespin Guallpa, said Marcos was the natural son of an Indian woman of Lictos; "nevertheless instead of wearing Indian clothing he dressed as a *cholo* [half-breed]."[27] Don Manuel Chango, cacique of the Pilalata, testified to the same, specifying the same "cholo" clothing. Another native witness from Pelileo, Bisente Chayugo, said that he knew Marcos Meneses (the father of the petitioners), and even though he dressed like a cholo, he paid tribute, and the said Marcos Meneses was a prisoner in the obraje of San Ildefonso for tribute.[28]

Geneological evidence of "race" in petitons for mestizo status require supplementary evidence from cultural and legal practices, including marriage to white women and payment of the sales tax. In this case, those who claimed that the petitioners were indigenous cited genealogical evidence as well as service in the obraje as evidence that the petitioner was assigned to the category of Indian tributary.

There were obvious benefits to claiming mestizo status for oneself and for one's children, especially male children who would not be subject to tribute and labor requirements. It's no wonder that the father of the Meneses brothers adopted a Spanish name and "cholo" clothing. Mestizaje transformed indigenous families and communities, as in the case of Eugenia Canin, whose grandchildren, the children of white women, would likely maintain a mestizo identity and follow a different trajectory from their Chumaquí cousins. Over the next century, Pelileo would become increasingly mestizo. Indigenous families would choose whether to follow a mestizo identity or maintain an indigenous communal identity.

CONCLUSION

Indigenous people used wills to maintain ties with their descendants, including adopted children, and to pass family lands to their heirs. Kinship practices included adoption and ritual co-parenthood, which reinforced ties among indigenous families in the community. Occasionally, such ties of ritual kinship and adoption crossed colonial racial categories. Indigenous people continued to help their family members who were stuck in the obraje, by offering to work off the debt or by selling inherited lands to pay it off. There were many land transfers in the eighteenth century as a response to cultural pressures, such as the need to pay for funerals and weddings or to pay debts or tribute obligations. While the Pilalata and Chumaquí responded to these pressures by selling lands, the Sigchos Collanas were purchasing lands from the obraje Indians as well as impoverished Spaniards. The next chapter focuses on the Sigchos Collanas' purchase of lands as a step in the historical process of reconstituting an indigenous community.

CHAPTER 8

SPANISH REVERSALS OF FORTUNE AND ANDEAN ETHNOGENESIS

I N THIS chapter I provide evidence that the Sigchos Collanas engaged in a strategy of purchasing land in Salasaca that allowed them to re-create an indigenous community. The Sigchos Collanas were the descendants of people who migrated to Pelileo in the late seventeenth and early eighteenth centuries. They might have been following an even earlier migration pattern directed by the caciques of the corregimiento of Latacunga. They were not subject to work in the obraje, but they lacked lands in the community. In the eighteenth century, they purchased lands from the Pilalata and Chumaquí as well as from Spaniards. They transformed these lands into indigenous ethnic territory, and while other parts of Pelileo became mestizo (in the nineteenth and twentieth centuries), people in Salasaca maintained a distinctive indigenous identity. By tracing the histories of specific plots of land in and around Salasaca, I show that indigenous strategies for acquiring lands were a significant step in the transformation from the multiple different indigenous groups, including the obraje Indians, to one single indigenous ethnic identification as Salasacas. Although this transformation occurred in the eighteenth and nineteenth centuries, I trace the history of land sales of specific plots going back to the seventeenth century in order to show how ownership changed. The colonial practices discussed here contributed to the modern-day ethnic compostition of Pelileo.

Some of the land that currently belongs to the Salasacas was owned by the Spanish de la Parras and their descendants, the Fiallos, until the second half of the eighteenth century. Granted to the conquistador Hernando de la Parra, a "subaltern" of Benalcázer,[1] properties passed down through generations, but by the mid-eighteenth century the heirs were fighting with one another over land and selling it off to indigenous people. In fact, before the Chumaquí had been granted to Galarza as an encomienda in 1662, they had been granted to Hernando de la Parra.[2] In some late colonial cases, different descendants of de la Parra sold the same piece of land to different Sighos Collanas/Salasaca buyers, causing Spanish inheritance disputes to spill over into the Indian sphere. The parts of Salasaca that were not owned by the Parras belonged to the Chumaquí and Pilalata. I trace the history of lands in Huasalata (also spelled Wasalata), one of the eighteen hamlet-like sectors of modern Salasaca, as well as the histories of acquisition of Catitahua (Katitawa), Manguigua, and Llicacama, all sectors within Salasaca. In figure 10 (on p. 32), the area that includes part of modern-day Salasaca is shaded, and sectors shown on the map include Huasalata on the western margin, Patoloma, and the hill Catitahua on the eastern border.

THE CREATION OF ETHNIC TERRITORY

The indigenous people living in Salasaca created an ethnic territory, but there is no evidence that they acted as a group or planned it that way when they made individual purchases in the eighteenth century. In fact, sometimes different individuals fought with one another over land that had been purchased. Recall the 1727 case of María Asuchimbo (see chapter 4), in which the Sigchos Collanas said that they did not have access to lands, and the 1743 case of Carlos Masaquiza (see chapter 5), in which he said that the Sigchos Collanas in Salasaca did not have access to communal lands in Pelileo, only those plots which they had purchased themselves. I do not know exactly when the Sigchos Collanas residents in Salasaca began purchasing land; the earliest reference I have to "Masaquiza" ownership (the most common surname of the Sigchos Collanas in Salasaca) is a 1695 reference to a plot owned by Andres Masaquiza.[3] However, Andres inherited the land from his mother, Andrea Culquiyuca. Women from local ethnic groups of Pelileo, with last names like Comasanta, Esay, Culqui and Culquiyuca did have access to land as part of their family inheritance, and some of them married Sigchos Collanas men. These women would then pass those lands on to their daughters as well as their sons, and the sons would be classified as Sigchos Collanas even though they had a mixed background. From the 1740s onward, indigenous individuals engaged in a strategy of purchasing contiguous plots of land from their neighbors in order to form one larger plot. By the nineteenth century, what started out as an individual strategy of land acquisition became, at some point, a group strategy for maintaining an indigenous space: the indigenous people in Salasaca stopped selling lands to whites and mestizos, and excluded white authorities from their community. One of the individuals who bought lands in Salasaca was Blas Jerez, who made several purchases from different people, both indigenous and Spanish.

LANDS PURCHASED BY BLAS JEREZ

The testimony of Nicholas Masaquiza about one piece of land provides a perfect example of how several different men of Sigchos Collanas origins attempted to get the same piece of land from an obraje Indian in the eighteenth century.[4] Nicholas Masaquiza, who was estimated to be about eighty years old in 1752, said that his father had purchased lands in Chumaquí and Nitón from Mateo Liguisa, a Chumaquí man who worked as a vergueador (wool beater) in the obraje. Nicholas's father possessed the lands for some time, but when the seller's daughters and heirs realized that Masaquiza had never fully paid, they repossessed the land and rented it out to Blas Jerez, another man of Sigchos Collanas origins (also said in the document to be a camayo of Latacunga). Jerez, a "resident of Salasaca," grew crops on the land he was renting from the seller's daughters, and when these two women died, the priest of Pelileo charged Jerez for their funerals in exchange for the land. So a Masaquiza of Sigchos Collanas origins attempted to buy the land but couldn't pay; another of Sigchos Collanas origins, Jerez, rented the lands and acquired them when he paid for the owner's funerals.

A third Sigchos Collanas man, Santiago Masaquiza, the nephew of Nicholas (the witness), also tried to purchase the same piece of land from someone who was not the rightful owner. Martin Teneta was a forastero of the Puruguayes who offered to sell the land to Santiago Masaquiza. Nicholas said that he warned his nephew not to buy it from Teneta, because he would find himself mired in a legal dispute. Santiago purchased the land anyway, and then he lost it to Blas Jerez. The case shows how the Sigchos Collanas as individuals were trying to buy up land in the area, making them vulnerable to fraudulent sales that led to conflicts with one another over the same piece of land. It also shows the role of priests in assigning the cost of the funeral to an indigenous person in exchange for land. This happened in several cases; the "buyer" paid the priest directly, sometimes in money, sometimes in a combination of money and grain from the land, and became owner of the (deceased's) land after paying the priest.

Blas Jerez also purchased lands in the same area from the Spaniard Francisco Rodriguez, whose father had previously purchased them in 1688 from a local native. The local native had sold the land to the Spaniard in order to meet his tribute obligation. This is one of several examples of land going from natives of Pelileo (the obraje Indians) to Spaniards in the seventeenth century, who later sold them to descendants of the Sigchos Collanas camayos living in Salasaca in the eighteenth century. In other words, in these cases, as the lands in and around Salasaca went from the obraje Indians to the Sigchos Collanas camayos, they sometimes passed through Spanish hands first. In this case the original transfer in 1688 was witnessed by Don Pedro Chango and other caciques and native officials of Pelileo, indicating their approval of the transfer of lands from natives to Spaniards as a way to cope with colonial pressures of tribute obligations. The history of ownership of these plots in Chumaquí and Nitón is as follows:

Local indigenous owner (probably Pilalata) → Father of Francisco Rodriguez (Spaniard) → Francisco Rodriguez → Blas Jerez (Sigchos Collana)

Between 1744 and 1762 Blas Jerez acquired many plots of land in and around Salasaca, either through direct purchase from the Pilalata owners, or by paying the priest for people's funerals and then getting their land in return.[5] Most of these sales were witnessed by the caciques of the Pilalata. This included lands in the Salasaca sector called Manguigua (purchased from a Pilalata man), as well as lands in Nitón and Rosario (formerly called Rumichaca). Sometimes, in the record of long land disputes that lasted years, we see ethnogenesis at the individual level, in terms of the ethnonym applied to a person. I found two cases in which the same document refers to someone as a Collana at the beginning of the case, and years later, toward the end of the case, as a "Salasaca Indian." This was the case with Blas Jerez, and with another man with the surname Masaquiza. Both cases are from the mid-eighteenth century, when there was a land grab by the Sigchos Collanas in Salasaca, indicating that they were becoming Salasacas during these years.

If the descendants of the camayos from the corregimiento of Latacunga did not originally have lands in Salasaca, and they began buying up land in the eighteenth century, possibly earlier, where were they getting the money? As I mentioned before, marriage to local landowning women would be one way that sons, still listed as Sigchos Collanas (but really of mixed ethnic heritage), would get access to their mother's lands. The case of Blas Jerez, above, gives a clue to a cultural practice that provides another strategy for getting money to purchase land. When Blas died, his widow was still involved in disputes over some of these purchased lands. Elderly witnesses for the widow, Ignacia Paredes, recalled that when the couple got married, Ignacia's parents gave her two cows for breeding, "to help with the cost of married life," and from these two cows they got up to five head of cattle, perhaps more, which they sold and used to purchase lands. In 1774 the witnesses who recalled this gift that kept on giving were both indigenous and mestizo (montañes). One indigenous witness was, like Blas Jerez, another land-buying descendant of migrants, Ventura Toainga (listed as an Indian of the Tacungas living in Salasaca). Ventura and Blas had both purchased lands in Salasaca from Pilalatas (Ventura's lands are discussed below). Ventura's recollection of Ignacia's wedding gift was more detailed than that of other witnesses: he said that her father gave her a black cow, spotted on the back side, and her mother gave her a "mulata-colored" cow, both for breeding (*de vientre*).[6]

Even if the witness (estimated to be about fifty years old at the time of his declaration) was not recalling the exact cows given at the marriage, he might be recalling a general custom of having different individuals contribute a separate gift animal. The fact that he did not say, "Her parents gave her two cows," but rather specified that the father gave one and the mother gave another, of distinct colors, might refer to a practice of gender parallelism. It also suggests a type of Andean practice by which different kin and ritual kin contribute specific gifts at marriage, such as different varieties of potatoes for the newlywed couple's fields.[7] For example, one twentieth-century practice among the Salasacas was for parents or ritual kin to give a "start-up fund" of a male and female sheep, for breeding, as a wedding gift.

Whether Ignacia's gift was part of a cultural practice, or simply an individual situation, witnesses referred to it as evidence that the lands purchased by her late husband were rightfully hers, because they were purchased with money from her cows. The bestowing of dowries was a colonial cultural practice that enabled the social reproduction of indigenous families.[8] In the case of Blas Jerez and Ignacia

Paredes, it permitted the descendants of migrants from the Latacunga region to invest in plots of land throughout Salasaca and become part of an emerging indigenous community. Just as the mother of Estevan Sailema (see chapter 7) acquired land by exchanging it for fifty head of sheep, the case of Blas Jerez and Ignacia Paredes shows that indigenous people were breeding animals in order to sell them to invest in land, or to pay for someone's funeral and acquire the deceased's land. In Blas's case, he started out renting the lands and acquired ownership by paying the priest for the owners' funerals.

The number of eighteenth-century Sigchos Collanas and Tacungas who purchased lands from obraje Indians and others in and around Salasaca are too numerous to discuss here. In the fourteen-square-kilometer community and its immediate borders, I found sixteen sales in the mid-eighteenth century, and this is only what I took from legal disptues, so the number of actual land sales is underrepresented here. I will discuss two more significant cases of land disputes in the Salasaca sectors Huasalata and Catitahua.

HUASALATA LANDS

In a seventeenth-century case, the cacique Don Pedro Chango assigned Pilalata lands in Huasalata to one of his subjects, María Criollo, in 1690. Criollo was the wet nurse and servant of a Spanish priest whom she raised, and she sold the lands to him. The priest left the lands to his niece, Theresa Fiallo, who sold them to another Spaniard, Felipe Araujo, in 1757 (discussed in chapter 2). So the history of land transfer looks like this:

María Criollo (Pilalata)⟶Spanish priest⟶Theresa Fiallo, his niece⟶Felipe Araujo (Spanish)

However, those same Pilalata lands in Huasalata have an alternative history, perhaps because the caciques of the Pilalata assigned the same piece of land to different Pilalata subjects. Agustina Hinojosa, a Pilalata woman "of the obraje of San Ildefonso," also claimed the lands, and in 1757 she and her brother sold lands called "Pato Urcu" (most likely Patoloma on figure 10, on p. 32) to Ventura Toainga (the above-mentioned Tacunga witness). Toainga bought the lands of these obraje Indians in Huasalata and Patoloma and paid for Agustina's funeral when she died. By 1779, Toainga was in a dispute with his Spanish neighbor,

Araujo, who was "intruding" on his lands. Araujo's side claimed that Indians, "as our enemies," were always trying to get at their lands.[9] In this land history the transfer is as follows:

Agustina Hinojosa (Pilalata) → Ventura Toainga (camayo Tacunga)

Both parties trace these sectors of Salasaca to the Pilalata: Araujo by way of a Pilalata wet nurse's transfer of the lands to the Spaniard she raised, Toainga by way of direct purchase from the Pilalata owners. The lands stayed with Ventura Toainga, who won the case (Araujo still owned neighboring plots). When Toainga died in 1783, the lands passed on to his widow, María Culqui.

All the indigenous buyers in the cases mentioned so far—Masaquiza, Toainga, and Jerez, of Sichos Collanas or Tacungas origins—have the last names of modern-day Salasaca families who own lands in Huasalata and other parts of Salasaca. By 1857, the Masaquizas and Toaingas were allies together against a local Spaniard, and by 1886 the "residents of Salasaca," with surnames Masaquiza, Pilla, Caizabanda, Comasanta, and Culqui, joined together in a lawsuit to get access to communal waters from the Mocha River, suggesting the fusion of several parcialidades as a single group.[10]

CATITAHUA LANDS

Catitahua (spelled Katitawa today) is a hill on the northeastern border of Salasaca. It is connected to two other hills that have sacred shrines at the top. For generations, Salasacas, including shamans, have left offerings at those shrines and prayed to God and to the mountain spirits for health, love, and success in music, spinning wool (women), weaving (men), and school.[11] One of the shrines is on a mountain known to some as "Palama" (the name varies), and it is located in a crevice alternately called Palama Cruz or Nitón Cruz. That land was probably once owned by Geronimo Toasa, a cacique of the Chumaquí, likely the same 1661 cacique in whose home the obraje workers were paid off to keep quiet and not denounce their abuses to the Quito commission. Geronimo Toasa had land in Chumaquí and in Nitón Palama (figure 17), which he left to his daughter Bernarda Ungas and nephew Joseph Toasa.[12]

The lands of Catitahua belonged to both Pilalata and Spaniards. Cecilia Comasanta, a woman of Salasaca married to a Spaniard, inherited Catitahua

FIGURE 17. View of Nitón Palama from Salasaca. Photo by José Carrasco.

lands from her aunt, Francisca Cusichimbo, in 1733. Those lands bordered lands owned by natives (with the last name Toainga) and by Spaniards. These Spaniards had previously purchased the lands from caciques.

In addition to the lands that she inherited from her aunt, in the 1730s Cecilia Comasanta had purchased several plots of land from Pilalatas. According to Don Fernando Chango, those lands had always belonged to the Pilalata, "since the time of the conquest," but they were disputed by the descendants of Hernan de la Parra. One of the descendants, Joseph de la Parra, a *beato* (a person who wore clerical habits without being part of a religious order), rented out the plots of land on Catitahua to several indigenous people who worked the land, growing barley and maize. Joseph de la Parra raised two boys of Sigchos Collanas origins. When de la Parra noticed that the native renters were marking off their plots with century plants, he sent these foster boys to uproot the plants, worrying that the indigenous renters would start to think that the plots were their own. In fact, the Pilalata did pass the lands on to their children in their wills, but they said their ancestors had possessed and worked the land for over a century. Whether the possession was legal or not, the protector of natives argued that the ancestors of those who left or sold lands to Cecilia Comasanta had possessed and worked the land for more than eighty years, and so native possession should be recognized.[13] If indigenous people were taking over lands that they had been renting from Spaniards, then this is an example in which indigenous people "beat the Spaniards at their own game."[14] In the early colonial period, Spaniards had used this same strategy to get land from natives.

Indigenous "usurpers" were not Joseph de la Parra's only problem. His relative Joan Fiallo also claimed the lands. Due to his fight with this relative, Joseph went into hiding, but he was very ill at the time. He spent his last days in the home of an indigenous person, where he died. After Joseph's death, the Fiallos continued their dispute over the lands of Catitahua, Nitón, and Chiquicha, with one another and with local indigenous people. In 1754, Cecilia Comasanta complained that Joan Fiallo was trying to take her lands in Catitahua. In their defense the Fiallos used a copy of the land grant to the sons of the conquistador, their ancestor, dating back to 1576: "Pedro and Francisco de la Parra, brothers, sons of Fernando de la Parra, deceased, who was a vecino of this city and one of the first conquistadores and settlers [pobladores] of this city and provinces of this Kingdom . . . have requested lands from Hambato to Pelileo . . . called Chiquilica [Chiquicha], which is a round mountain . . . there is a lot of land that can be given in the mountain that goes from Pelileo to Hambato."[15] In 1644, a descendant of one of those brothers was granted possession of lands between Ambato and Chumaquí, in a possession ceremony that was witnessed by three natives of Chumaquí. Now, in 1754, both the Spaniards and the Pilalata who claimed the Catitahua lands got Sigchos Collanas and Tacunga witnesses living in Salasaca to testify on their behalf. Later, in 1760, these indigenous people living in Salasaca (the Masaquizas) owned lands in Catitahua and joined the Pilalata (with the last name Quillana) to fight against Fiallo. This is another example of the collaboration of indigenous people against Spaniards.

THE DE LA PARRA FAMILY

There is no doubt that the Parras owned lands in Salasaca, from Huasalata on the western border of the community, which they sold to the descendants of the former camayos from Latacunga, to Catitahua on the eastern border, which bordered native (mostly Pilalata) communal lands. One land dispute, which at first appeared to be a case of a mestizo taking indigenous lands, turned out to be a case of a Spaniard, Joseph de la Parra, selling part of his family inheritance against the wishes of his sisters and mestizo half sibling. In 1745 Joseph de la Parra sold land in Huasalata to Gregorio Masaquiza, a "Collana Indian in Tacunga, subject of Don Francisco Hati Haja."[16] This was a transitional phase, where the mid-eighteenth-century descendants of Sigchos Collanas migrants were still classified as Collanas, but were buying lands in Salasaca.

Since Joseph's illegitimate mestizo half brother claimed part of the land, the indigenous buyer had to buy out the mestizo as well as the legitimate female heirs of de la Parra, Josepha and Lorenza de la Parra, since these were family lands. Gregorio Masaquiza ended up paying more money in order to get the land from the Parras.

The descendants of the conquistador must have already felt desperate by 1727. Some of the female cousins got into a nasty fist fight over lands in Nitón, and some of the Parras could not even afford funerals for their parents. One descendant, Gabriel de la Parra, had to rely on a Salasaca man (most likely of Sigchos Collanas origins), Isidro Jerez, to pay for his funeral and subsequent Masses for his soul; in exchange, Jerez got some of the Parra family lands in Salasaca. Those lands then passed on to Isidro's son Sebastian Jerez and daughter Rosa Quinatoa. Gabriel died without leaving a will, and unfortunately, Gabriel de la Parra's relatives sold some of the same lands to Antonio Masaquiza, causing problems between the indigenous buyers and their descendants. The priest confirmed that Isidro Jerez paid for the funeral of Gabriel, so the land stayed with the Jerez heirs.[17] The two histories are as follows:

> Gabriel (Spaniard)⟶Isidro Jerez (indigenous)⟶Sebastian and Rosa (indigenous Salasacas)

and

> Gabriel⟶his brother and nephews (Spaniards)⟶Antonio Masaquiza (indigenous Salasaca)

In 1767 a nephew of Gabriel, Joachin de la Parra, said that his father, as the rightful owner, sold the lands to Antonio Masaquiza. Joaquin was legally declared to be among the "solemn poor" and was in jail during the dispute. The other nephews of Gabriel de la Parra, Thomas and Joseph, were also legally declared to be among the solemn poor. Once someone was legally declared to be among the solemn poor, he could pursue his legal case free of charge, and the eighteenth-century courts saw hundreds of new petitions by individuals asking to be officially recognized as *pobres de solmnidad*, including many cases of Spaniards like Joachin de la Parra, who lost their fortunes. This legal declaration allowed for the maintenance of racial distinctions in eighteenth-century Quito. According to Cynthia Milton, initially "this relief measure waived normal legal fees and gave speedy resolution of court cases for economically troubled residents who could prove their honor, merit, and need, thereby sustaining their privileged position even if only for a little while longer. Pobreza de solemnidad offered a kind of 'justice by insurance' for the elite. . . . Not all the poor in colonial Spanish America were equal, and thus distinct relief measures were extended to the two republics, according them each specific rights and duties."[18]

As Milton shows, through the first half of the eighteenth century, *poverty* had a different meaning for whites than it did for indigenous people and blacks (the miserable or "wretched poor"), and the legal category helped maintain a distinction between types of poor people to maintain colonial distinctions between whites and indigenous people, regardless of economic status. What is significant in the case of Salasaca is that during this eighteenth-century increase in Spanish petitions of poverty, the formerly landless camayos in Salasaca took advantage of the opportunity to get the lands that were once granted to a conquistador. Getting land from this family who was losing its fortune was a step in the creation of ethnic territory that allowed for the ethnogenesis of the Salasacas.[19]

CONCLUSION

The decline of the original landed elites was not limited to Pelileo or even the Audiencia of Quito. In Peru, Susan Ramírez traced the eighteenth-century impoverishment of the descendants of conquistadores and the old elite and their replacement by new Spanish families, some of them immigrants from Spain.[20] What is most enlightening about the case of Pelileo is that the lands owned by the Parras were taken over by indigenous people, the descendants of economic colonists to the region. The economic and natural disasters of the eighteenth century led to the waning fortunes of some elite families. As these elites sold off everything from family heirlooms to lands,[21] the Sigchos Collanas in Pelileo took advantage of the opportunity to purchase plots from both Spaniards and local indigenous people. The evidence indicates that they sold animals and used the money either to purchase land directly or to pay the priest for the funeral of the deceased landowner, and thereby aquire the land. Another strategy was to rent a plot of land and then use the grain from that land to purchase the plot, or simply to pass the rented plot to their descendants in wills. They often tried to purchase their neighbors' plots to form a larger contiguous unit of land. Eventually, they formed a common ethnic territory with a common toponym and ethnonym. In the final chapter, I discuss the nineteenth-century process of solidification of Salasaca as a distinct, ethnic community.

CHAPTER 9
HISTORY AND CULTURAL IDENTITY

AFTER THE descendants of the Sigchos Collanas and Tacungas purchased (or took over) lands in Salasaca in the eighteenth century, the next crucial step in re-creating and maintaining an indigenous identity was to exclude whites and mestizos from the ethnic territory. Once these Salasacas had acquired land from Spaniards, Chumaquí, and Pilalata, they refrained from selling lands to whites, which made them unique for the region in the mid-nineteenth century. In the rest of Ambato, indigenous people and mestizos sold lands to each other, whereas the Salasacas only transferred lands among themselves.[1] Once they formed an ethnic territory, they moved to exclude white authorities from their community.[2]

Here I trace the ethnic transformations that occurred in Pelileo and the activities of indigenous people up to the final decades of the operation of San Ildefonso. While many Chumaquí and Pilalata adopted mestizo identities, others intermarried with the Sigchos Collanas and became part of the emerging ethnic community of Salasaca. First I begin with a discussion of the abolition of indigenous tribute in Ecuador, which allowed for the dissolution of previous ayllu/parcialidad categories and allowed indigenous people to adopt new identities. Second, I evaluate evidence of the ethnic origins of the Salasacas. Finally, I return to the situation of San Ildefonso, from the late eighteenth century to its decline in the 1890s, and present evidence that the Salasacas filled a niche to meet the local and regional needs for textiles through their weaving activities. This chapter explains how the different choices of indigenous families led to the current ethnic composition of Pelileo.

THE ABOLITION OF TRIBUTE

The abolition of tribute must have been a turning point for native peoples. It was no longer necessary for notaries to keep track of a person's parcialidad (or ayllu) and cacique for tribute purposes, so indigenous men were not required to identify with a specific group. It is important to remember that the ayllus were fluid categories anyway: the Chumaquí, Pilalata, and Guambaló married one another, but for administrative purposes, it seems that men identified with their father's parcialidad and cacique, if they knew who their fathers were. In the nineteenth century, the Indian tribute was revoked and reinstated several times in Ecuador before it was finally abolished in 1857. Even before the abolition of tribute, in nineteenth-century court cases scribes were less meticulous about recording the specific parcialidades of native plaintiffs in legal disputes, and they more often referred to them as generic "Indians of Pelileo." However, nineteenth-century tribute records by necessity continued to distinguish indigenous people by parcialidad up until the abolition of tribute.

Earlier failed efforts to abolish tribute were part of an overall goal of integrating indigenous people into Hispanic society. Many indigenous people must have embraced assimilation and the chance to become mestizos, facilitated by the loosening of parcialidad categories. Others, throughout Ecuador, resisted attempts at assimilation, maintained their indigenous identities, and re-created themselves as unique ethnic groups. In 1825, when Ecuador was part of Gran Colombia, a decree abolished official native positions "including the posts of caciques, governors, and alcaldes mayores. Colombian officials reasoned, first, that these offices were no longer needed for tribute collection, and second, that Indian communities should conform to the Hispanic pattern of town government under a council."[3] Nevertheless, in the nineteenth and early twentieth centuries, some of the people who were formerly identified as Sigchos Collanas, Tacungas, or Pilalata now joined together as Salasacas to resist white authorities in their community and to protect resources like water. Recall that the caciques of the Pilalata had the last name Chango. In the early twentieth century, Salasacas had their own indigenous governors, such as Raimundo Chango, who worked with the Catholic priests to appoint indigenous watchmen (alcaldes) and festival sponsors. By that time, they had already solidified as a single ethnic community that distinguished itself not only from their neighbors, but from the parent communities (Sigchos Collana, Pilalata, Tacunga), which Patricia Albers describes as the completion of the process of ethnogenesis.[4] Evidence suggests that by the twentieth century, the origins of the Salasacas had been forgotten, and by the 1940s historians and anthropologists began to speculate that this unique, defensive ethnic group were the descendants of mitimaes, a population that was transplanted to Ecuador from Bolivia by the Incas.

ETHNICITY OF THE SALASACAS

Based on an analysis of last names from the colonial period to the present, the evidence suggests that the ancestors of the Salasacas were from multiple ethnic groups, including local women of Pelileo, who owned lands in Pachanlica and other parts of Pelileo. Pachanlica (figure 10, on p. 32) encompassed modern-day Totoras, Benitez, and Cevallos, which all border Salasaca. Other ancestors were from the Pilalata, Chumaquí, Sigchos Collana, Tacunga, Puruguay and probably some women from the Carpinteros of the town of Quero or other mitimae groups of the region. For example, the feminine surname Culqi appears in lists of women from mitimae groups in Pelileo and is found among Salasacas today. The surname Comasanta is also found among Salasaca men and women. In the colonial period Comasanta was the feminine surname of some of the obraje families, including one of the wet nurses to the slave children. Tungurahua historian Pedro Reino Garcés traces the origins of the Salasacas to the northern Andean Quito-Panzaleos, Sigchos Collanas, and Tacungas, as well as people from Nasca, Peru (based on the last names Pilla and Pillajo), and other groups who were incorporated into the Salasacas during the colonial period.[5]

Although indigenous people from different backgrounds intermarried in Salasaca, including some local native women said to be of Pachanlica or Salasaca, the most common origin claimed by men (and some women) living in Salasaca in the eighteenth century is from Sigchos Collanas. Both the Tacungas and Sigchos Collanas have origins in the western portion of the corregimiento of Latacunga. It is possible that the Sigchos Collanas were descendants of an earlier mitimae population in Latacunga, but the term *collana* should not be assumed to refer to origins in Collasuyu, the southern quarter of the Inca empire that would include modern-day Bolivia. *Collana* could also refer to a distinguished ayllu, or a superior class of people.[6] The term "collana" was also used as a category in a tripartite system in twentieth-century Loja in southern Ecuador.[7]

The mitimae-origin theory of the Salasacas is not supported by any specific colonial reference. Whereas colonial records specifically mention the mitimae origins of the ethnic groups of Quero, no such mention is made of the Sigchos Collanas in Salasaca. Under the Incas, there were multiple ethnic groups living in Sigchos Collanas, including several mitimae populations. Some Salasaca last names, such as Anancolla, suggest origins in the southern Andes, but such origins have been overemphasized in trying to explain Salasaca uniqueness. By the time the Sigchos Collanas went to Salasaca (since the seventeenth century, if not earlier), they were probably already a mixture of multiple ethnic groups. Futhermore, there were mixtures of mitimaes and northern Andean groups throughout colonial Quito, so Salasaca would not be unique in having some mitimae ancestors. To summarize, the Salasacas cannot be said to be a homogenous mitimae group.

In fact, the Sigchos Collanas who were sent to Salasaca carried the last name of a northern Andean cacique. There is evidence that Machaquicha (a variant of Masaquiza) was the last name of a north Andean cacique of Angamarca (west of Latacunga).[8] The Masaquizas who went to Salasaca were probably from a specific group within the Sigchos Collanas. When the Madres Bernardas of Madrid had the encomienda of Sigchos Collanas people, the natives were sent all over the highlands of Ecuador, including the Chota Valley in northern Ecuador, which like Pelileo underwent a colonial economic transition from native-owned coca fields to the production of Spanish products such as sugarcane.[9] Tribute records indicate that while the Sigchos Collanas were sent as camayos to different regions, those with the last name Masaquiza were sent almost exclusively to Salasaca, with a few exceptions. The Madres Bernardas had representatives in Quito who had power of attorney over their affairs. These representatives rented out the encomienda of Salasaca at least twice, for four years each, to individual Spaniards: once in 1702 and again in 1710. In the 1702 rental contract, they were referred to as the "salasacas and collanas" of the jurisdiction of Ambato,[10] and the 1710 contract referred to the rental of "Indios Sigchos Collanas sueltos that reside in the Asiento de Hambato which by another name are called Salasacas."[11] The term *sueltos* usually referred to unincorporated natives, but the Collanas/Salasacas were clearly part of the encomienda and under the administration of the nuns' representative in Quito.

In the late eighteenth century, tribute records for Ambato and the eight towns that comprised the jurisdiction show that Ambato and Pelileo had the highest concentrations of native tribute payers, about 22 percent each (appendix 1). When looking at the origins of those natives, Pelileo had the highest concentration of Collanas: more than half (59 percent) for the jurisdiction lived in Pelileo (appendix 2). Recall that Carlos Masaquiza (see chapter 5) said that his father Simon Masaquiza and his mother Marta Jerez were from the "ayllu and parcialidad of Collanas." If the Masaquizas and others (such as the Caizabandas and Jerezes) who were sent to Salasaca did constitute a specific subgroup, this would have facilitated their ethnogenesis. Powers's study of migration and ethnogenesis in colonial Quito demonstrates how indigenous communities transformed and reproduced themselves to become the distinctive ethnic groups that we see today: "In areas where short-range migrations were prevalent and where groups of families from the same ayllu migrated to the same destination, social organization was most likely reconstituted in a new location."[12] The Salasacas fit this description.

As camayos, they were sent to specialize in some activity, but unfortunately the documents do not specify what they were doing. They were not designated for obraje service, either in Sigchos (which had its own obraje) or in Pelileo. Although records show a few individual workers named Masaquiza in the payment records of San Ildefonso, they are not listed as Sigchos Collanas. Rather, in the 1660s, the obraje worker Diego Masaquiza was listed as a "Royal Crown Indian" and a Guambaló, Alonso Masaquiza as a "camayo of Pelileo," and Andres Masaquiza as belonging to the "ayllu of don Ventura" (probably of the Chumaquí); another Andres Masaquiza was listed as a "native of Ambato of the ayllu of don Juan Saca" and had worked in the obraje since 1622.[13] The lack of any other document referring to a Don Juan Saca is puzzling, and it is possible that Andres Masaquiza invented it. The earliest Masaquiza in the payment record is from 1619. These men might have been either runaways who incorporated themselves into different local ethnic groups of Pelileo or members of the Sigchos Collanas camayo colony who left Salasaca and joined other groups, perhaps through marriage.

The encomienda designation of the indigenous peoples of colonial Quito shaped their fates. The Pilalata and Chumaquí, of Galarza's encomienda, and the Guambaló of an encomienda of the Royal Crown suffered forced labor in the obraje of San Ildefonso in the seventeenth century. The Sigchos Collanas of Salasaca were of the encomienda of Madrid-based Madres Bernardas del

Santisimo Sacramento. In Salasaca they were governed by a secondary chief who maintained allegiance to the Hati dynasty in Latacunga. As a group they were not forced into the obraje. So what were they doing?

Karen Powers and I suggested the possibility that colonial-era Sigchos Collanas may have been sent as camayos to Salasaca to process cabuya plant (*Furcraea andina*) fiber into sacks for the transportation of textiles from San Ildefonso.[14] Cicala reported cabuya fiber processing in Pelileo for the mid-eighteenth century,[15] and, almost a century later, a group of Salasacas protesting the tithe said that making sacks from cabuya fibers was the only way they had to support their families, because their lands were dry and their animals were sickly.[16] Still, we are speculating on mid-colonial economic specialties based on nineteenth-century activities, but for all we know the sack making might have been taken over by Salasacas in the nineteenth century, as trade between the highlands and the coastal port of Guayaquil increased. Another possibility is that the camayos specialized in the production of cochineal, the parasite to the prickly pear cactus plant that produces a natural red or purple dye. Cochineal is still cultivated in Salasaca today, and a 1761 report describes this activity in the jurisdiction of Hambato; it could have been Salasaca.[17]

FROM PARCIALIDAD TO PARISH

Nineteenth-century legal documents for Pelileo reveal a shift in identification from a people under the government of a native elite and parcialidad (even if they are physically dispersed in various locations) to an identification with a place. Nineteenth-century marriage records for the parishes of Chumaquí and Guambaló show a mixture of whites (*blancos*) and indigenous people, whereas Salasaca (an "annex" of the parish of Pelileo at the time) was strictly indigenous.[18] Identification with one's parish—Guambaló, Chumaquí, or the *matriz* (mother parish) of Pelileo—would facilitate assimilation into Hispanic culture and eventual status as mestizos, while Salasaca, by contrast, became the name of the ethnic group associated with the indigenous annex.

In the "mestizos" section of the National Archive of Ecuador, there are very few official petitions for mestizo status from Pelileo. Rather, it seems that people outside of Salasaca simply did not maintain a distinctive indigenous identity. Aside from Church records that show mixed communities in the other parishes of Pelileo, Reino Garcés found that lands in the modern canton of Cevallos (formerly called Capote) overlapped with Salasaca, but the Salasaca families who lived there did not maintain an indigenous identity. Although they have the same last names as modern Salasaca families, and share the same ancestors, they assimilated with Hispanic, mestizo culture. They did not maintain an ethnic attire, nor did they keep up the Quichua language.[19]

Some Salasacas told me that some of the mestizo inhabitants of the neighboring parishes know Quichua but are "ashamed to speak it," in contrast to the Salasacas who proudly maintain an indigenous, Quichua-speaking identity. This supports the argument that Salasaca became a "safe haven" for people who wanted to maintain an indigenous identity. In our analysis of Salasaca ethnogenesis, Karen Powers and I suggested some possible advantages of maintaining an indigenous identity in the nineteenth century, but we also cautioned against assumptions that identity is always a political project or must have some economic benefit.[20] Using James Scott's notion of "cultural refusal,"[21] we argued that some people value their cultural identity in and of itself, regardless of perceived economic or political benefits or drawbacks. In the northern Andes, these choices led to divergent identities as white-mestizo or indigenous. There is some evidence that in the early twentieth century, after San Ildefonso closed, the Salasacas supplied local and regional markets with coarse textiles. I close this chapter with reports on San Ildefonso in the late eighteenth and nineteenth centuries.

THE FINAL DECADES OF SAN ILDEFONSO

THE LATE EIGHTEENTH CENTURY

During a 1777 inspection of the obraje, when it was still under the administration of the Temporalidades branch of government, officials undertook an inspection of the obraje and asked the native workers about any problems. The workers did not complain specifically about the administrator or maestro, but they mentioned some of the same ongoing problems throughout the history of obrajes in Quito: accounts hadn't been settled, they were paid in clothing, and the daily quotas were too high for them to complete. Their wives and children still helped them in the obraje, but male workers said that this was voluntary. Unlike the problems of the previous century, the native workers said that they never missed Mass or religious instruction, and they were granted time off for festivals, in accordance with Crown policy. Although the mill had a dungeon

and stocks, the workers said that such punishments were only used for "delin-
quents" (there were four there from Otavalo at the time of the inspection). To
protect the native workers, the 1777 inspectors prohibited the administrator
from advancing clothing (*ropa de castilla*) against the workers' salaries unless the
workers requested it, and then it had to be valued at the current market price.
They lowered the quota for the spinners and threatened the administrator with
a fine if he did not comply.[22]

Late eighteenth-century natural disasters affected the cost of maintaining
the obraje. Much of the food that was grown on the haciendas associated with
San Ildefonso was used to feed the workers in the obraje. After disastrous floods
in 1783, there was a shortage of food, and the administrator had to purchase food
at high prices.[23] After an earthquake of 1797, parts of the obraje were destroyed
and a recommendation was made to move it closer to Chumaquí. The report
on the destruction provides a description of Pelileo in 1798. The foggy hill of
Nitón was used for sheep pasture and for growing barley and potatoes. The lands
around the obraje were poor quality. "The obraje Indians have their huts made
of vara [probably cane or reed stalks] and earth, covered with straw, which they
inhabit with their families and they cultivate [food] for themselves which is the
custom and the way to keep them, which they call situating them [*asitionando*]
for the agricultural work on the haciendas and manufacture in the obraje, for
without them nothing is made or produced."[24] The description is in accordance
with the structure of the *huasipungo* system, in which native Andean families
were allowed to have their huts and a small patch of land on which to grow
food in exchange for their labor on the hacienda (or, in this case, the obraje-
hacienda complex).

As in the seventeenth century, administrators looked for ways to force people
into the obraje, with the compliance of the indigenous labor boss called the
maestrillo. As late as 1795 Nicolas Pilagasi, the indigenous maestrillo of the
obraje, destroyed the crops of two Chumaquí natives: Pedro Guato and Beatris
Ungas. These were lands in Salate that they had inherited from their families,
and they had been supporting themselves and paying their tribute with the produce from those lands. The obraje administrator, José Valenzuela, claimed that
the lands belonged to the obraje, and that all Indians who lived on the lands had
to work for the obraje. The Chumaquí petitioners, he said, obtained the lands
as huasipungos (sharecroppers), and once they stopped working for the obraje,
they had to vacate the lands, unless they could prove otherwise. Although the
administrator of San Ildefonso said that the indigenous plaintiffs had to either

prove property ownership, submit to work in the obraje, or vacate the lands, he did not have a strong case that the Salate lands belonged to the obraje. In fact, he conceded that Pedro Guato and Beatris Ungas might be the rightful owners of the land, but even if they were, he said the existence of *indios sueltos* (those living freely without working in the obraje) caused problems for the haciendas of San Ildefonso: they set a bad example for the other Indians. The administrator said that they were drunks and corrupted the other Indians, and furthermore they were taking sugarcane.[25]

Indigenous people continued to attempt to get justice through the legal channels available to them. In 1799 a worker, Andres Masaquiza, perhaps a Salasaca volunteer worker, filed a complaint against the maestro of San Ildefonso. Masaquiza complained that the maestro whipped him. Several Chumaquí coworkers made statements on behalf of the maestro that Masaquiza was a drunk, of bad temperament, and not liked by his coworkers.[26] The available evidence indicates that although people were still punished in the late eighteenth century, the level of coercion and imprisonment in San Ildefonso was not nearly as bad as it was in the seventeenth century.

CONTRACTION OF THE TEXTILE INDUSTRY

The silver mines of Potosí faced an economic downturn, with reverberations for the northern Andean textile market, which supplied cloth to economic centers of Lima and Potosí. Competition from imported European cloth and other economic problems in the textile industry led to a "contraction"[27] of the obraje economy by the late eighteenth century, with some obrajes closing for good. Although San Ildefonso remained open, by 1795 textiles were no longer being sent to Lima or Quito but were either sold directly in the region, sold to merchants, or used to pay the workers.[28] In 1800, Don Agustín Valdivieso, an obraje owner originally from Loja (southern Ecuador) but living in Quito, purchased San Ildefonso and its adjacent haciendas from the Temporalidades. Profits were down, and the obraje had not completely recovered from the damage done by the 1797 earthquake. By then, San Ildefonso was not very lucrative, but it remained in the Valdivieso family for some time. A tribute record from 1823 (which still records four indigenous men who identified as "Nasca") lists the obraje as belonging to the heirs of Valdivieso, and it shows many Pilalata and Chumaquí still working there, along with others from the central sierra.[29] Between 1820 and 1860 there was an intrusion of foreign imports that cut into the textile market. At the same time, the growing cacao trade led to increased migration of labor from the highlands to the coast.

In 1885, San Ildefonso was the only obraje left in the province of Tungurahua, and it continued to produce wool textiles, while indigenous people were also making their own textiles. The *jefe político* (political boss) of Pelileo reported: "The indigenous people of Salasaca manufacture a wool cloth that they call lliglla which they prefer to the best European paño, and they not only weave it for their own use but they also sell it for 3 or 4 sucres per vara."[30] After the introduction of machinery in 1890, the workers' quotas for spinning wool was doubled from one to two pounds per day, and the workers went on strike. After days of pleading by the jefe político of Pelileo, some went back to work, while others quit.[31]

Historian Hernan Ibarra suggests that the Salasacas replaced the textile production that was lost after San Ildefonso attempted to modernize in 1890. He found evidence of Salasacas producing *jerga*, the coarse twill cloth that used to be manufactured in the obraje ("porque la jerga que elaboraba el obraje, aparece siendo producido por los Salasacas en 1920").[32] It's possible that the Salasacas were selling cloth to the local people who used to buy it from San Ildefonso. After the construction of the railroad to Guayaquil facilitated highland-coastal commerce, new commercial opportunities developed in the province of Tungurahua. In the 1920s, one merchant, Elias Garcés, would purchase jerga from the Salasacas to sell in Manabí on the coast.[33]

By the second half of the twentieth century, Salasacas were mainly weaving cloth for their own use, and some continue to do so to this day. Men were the traditional weavers in Salasaca, making women's skirts (anacos), coarse wool shirts pinned at the shoulders (*pichu jerga*), shawls (bayetas), and men's ponchos[34] on Spanish-style looms, using wool spun by the women.[35] Men (and now some women, too) weave the women's elaborate belts called *chumbis* on the backstrap loom, with designs for which the Salasacas are known.

CONCLUSION

If Ibarra is correct that the Salasacas took over the jerga production for Pelileo, then this is a case in which the Sigchos Collana, the one indigenous group that was exempt from work in the obraje, took over the lands from, and intermarried with, the obraje Indians and remained a free (not bound to an hacienda) indigenous community in the nineteenth century. Later, they filled a niche to supply a merchant with coarse, twill cloth. From the late nineteenth century through the first half of the twentieth century, priests, government officials, and Ecuadorian writers consistently described the Salasacas as defensive and closed off to outsiders. The intrigue of this "traditional" group of people led to erroneous assumptions that they were a homogenous mitimae group that occupied territory since the time of the Incas. But the evidence shows that the Salasacas were part of the same processes of migration, intermarriage, and ethnogenesis that occurred throughout Ecuador as indigenous people re-created their communities and cultural identities.

CONCLUSION

PELILEO TODAY is known as the "blue city" because it is a center of white-mestizo-owned workshops that produce blue jeans and other denim clothing. Relations between the Salasacas and white-mestizos are much improved, and in 2004 the people of Pelileo elected (and later reelected) an indigenous Salasaca, Dr. Manuel Caizabanda, to be their mayor. Dr. Caizabanda and his family proudly display their indigenous identity by continuing to wear Salasaca ethnic attire.

The past diversity of Pelileo's peoples that populated the region around the textile mill remains a hidden story to most. Through the chapters presented here, I attempted to uncover some of this history and to capture the indigenous historical experience through the stories of Andean men and women and their varied responses to the challenges they faced. The different responses to those challenges, and the various strategies for reconstituting family and community, explain the current cultural identity of Pelileo's indigenous people.

Eric Wolf showed how the world system, as an integrated economy, affected local cultures.[1] Europeans who never lived in the Americas benefited from the labor of indigenous Americans and African peoples, who toiled on plantations, in mines, and in sweatshops in the Americas. The encomienda system, in which the Crown granted Spaniards rights to indigenous labor, affected the fates of indigenous people. The Duke of Uceda had an encomienda of Sigchos Collanas, which he granted to an order of nuns based in Madrid. Evidence indicates that one particular group among the Sigchos Collanas was sent to Salasaca, starting perhaps in the seventeenth century and continuing to migrate there in the early eighteenth century. In contrast, the seventeenth-century Chumaquí and Pilalata, as part of the encomienda of Antonio Lopez de Galarza, were forced to serve in his wife's obraje. The Guambaló belonged to an encomienda of the Crown but were also forced into the obraje by their caciques.

In the northern Andes, the need to supply South American mining centers with cloth led to a textile boom in the Audiencia of Quito. Here I traced the cultural history of the indigenous families around one large textile mill, and I uncovered the voices of the workers and the strategies they used to cope with hardships. People drew on culture as a resource to cope with the harsh obraje labor system, including relying on kin and Andean institutions of reciprocal labor. People also relied on the obraje to acquire ceremonial items to celebrate the rituals that held meaning for them: bread for the Day of the Dead; wax candles; and bells, feathers, and ribbons for the costume of the Corpus Christi dancers. The indigenous experience of the obraje was part of indigenous cultural history of Pelileo.

Indigenous people responded to the pressures of the textile economy and other colonial pressures in different ways, from small, everyday domestic acts to the larger, cultural transformation of ethnogenesis. Different individuals responded by running away and abandoning their families; by using the legal system to attempt to get justice; by adapting as best they could; by helping family members pay their debts to the obraje, plough their fields, or meet their quotas; or, in 1768, by violently rebelling. Some sold lands to pay tribute; a few tried to pass as mestizos by dressing differently and marrying white women. Others, like Ignacia Paredes, used a wedding gift to breed animals for sale and invest in lands and, with other land buyers, formed a new community. Throughout the nineteenth century, especially after the abolition of tribute, keeping the native parcialidades straight was not as important to government officials. Eventually, people came to identify as residents of a place rather than as members of a particular ayllu and parcialidad, and mixed communities like the center of Pelileo and the annexes of Chumaquí and Guambaló eventually blended with Hispanic culture. But not Salasaca. By excluding whites from their territory, those in Salasaca maintained an indigenous culture and identity. The former obraje Indians chose two divergent paths. While some native Pilalata and Chumaquí chose to become white-mestizo, others chose, along with the Sigchos Collanas, to join the emerging indigenous community of Salasaca.

Like other self-identifying indigenous peoples of modern highland Ecuador, the Salasaca consider themselves a pure, homogenous blood group. The Saraguro and Cañari from the southern Ecuadorian Andes can be compared with the Salasaca.[2] The province of Loja, like the province of Tungurahua, was diverse and mobile during the colonial period, but by the second half of the twentieth century, "only Saraguro retains a clearly identifiable, quichua-speaking Indian population."[3] Despite being the result of historical processes of migration, intermarriage, and ethnogenesis, some, including the Saraguro themselves, speculate that the Saraguro might be the descendants of a mitimae population that has maintained their identity and location for five hundred years as a way to explain their cultural distinctiveness. However, as Minchom states: "[T]he survival of the Indian communities in Saraguro doubtless owed much to their cultural vitality and inner strength as well as to more objective conditions relating to land ownership, etc."[4] The cases of the Saraguro and Cañari provide evidence that, despite different local histories, the process of ethnogenesis described for Salasaca is part of a more general pattern that gave rise to the modern-day ethnic groups of highland Ecuador. As in southern Ecuador, the ethnohistory of Pelileo reveals a dynamic history of a racially and ethnically diverse town. From this diversity, one group of indigenous people, the Salasacas, resisted the historical process of "whitening" and re-created themselves as a distinctive cultural group.

The ethnohistory of Pelileo gives us a more nuanced understanding of the history of Quito's textile economy by revealing the actions of ordinary men and women as they tried to make a life for themselves, as well as the interactions between people who were classified into different socioracial categories. Through the "farm and factory" complex, the owners of the textile mill also owned the haciendas and ranches on which sheep were raised to produce the raw material for Quito's famous paños. The practice of debt peonage enabled different owners to shift indigenous labor from estate to mill, although this was seen most clearly under the ownership of María de Vera, when shepherds were charged for the miscarried fetuses of sheep and sent to the obraje. What did this mean for the indigenous laborers and their families? Seventeenth-century shepherds were locked in the mill and could not go home to their families; in a failed attempt to keep his son out of the obraje, an eighteenth-century father offered to work off his son's debt on the hacienda; and natives of Pelileo sold off plots of land, which they inherited from their grandmothers, mothers, and fathers, to liberate indebted family members from the obraje, thereby depriving their descendants of those lands.

Although this is a study of one town, it gives us insight into historical and cultural processes that occurred throughout the Audiencia de Quito—from the adaptation of indigenous families to an exploitative labor system driven by Quito's textile market, to the buying and selling of lands between Spaniards and natives, and finally to the choice of some groups to resist whitening and re-create themselves as unique indigenous ethnic groups. While there are regional differences, many of the events I presented here were occurring throughout colonial Quito. San Ildefonso is probably only distinguished by the large number of slaves present during the seventeenth century, but the labor conditions for the indigenous people were similar throughout the highlands. Reports from different caciques and colonial officials, from different times and places in the Audiencia, show that indigenous families throughout highland Ecuador experienced the obraje system the same way: with debt servitude, shackles, hunger, and brutal, forced labor. It is likely that their responses to those experiences were similar to the ones described by the Pilalata, Chumaquí, and Guambaló—such as a mother who sent her little girl to accompany the son that was taken to the obraje, a wife's choice to help her husband meet his quota so that he wouldn't run away and abandon the family, and a man's reliance on kin networks to get a substitute in the obraje when he needed to plough his fields or attend a funeral.

In this context of exploitation that pitted racial groups against one another, the record reveals rare glimpses of people's compassion for others and relationships with people of other racial groups. We see this in references to acts of compassion such as a black slave's hidden resistance to whipping an indigenous man, a Spaniard who paid off an obraje worker's debt, an indigenous man who disguised a Spaniard as a native to save his life during a revolt, a Spanish man who left money for the souls of his indigenous servants, and an indigenous woman who adopted and loved the Spanish child she raised. I do not want to imply that interracial bonds of affection were rare in the Andes; indeed, scholars have analyzed numerous examples. But it is important to study the nature of interracial relations within the particular context of the shadow of a large obraje that exacerbated racial tensions.

The early twentieth-century isolation between Salasacas and white-mestizos, noted by many writers and the Salasacas themselves, masks a hidden history of interactions between social groups. The historical presence of blacks in seventeenth-century Pelileo is even more masked, and their voices have been silenced. I have attempted to recover what I could from Andean testimonies about the indigenous historical experience. By telling the stories of native

Andeans, I hope to give a sense of their history, how their lives were affected by the obraje economy and colonial policies, and the strategies they used to survive, to keep their families together, and, for some, to re-create their cultural identity.

FIGURE 18. Salasacas at the Cemetery for the Day of the Dead, 2012. Courtesy of the Jimenez Masaquiza Family.

APPENDIX 1

Tributary Population in the Nine Districts of Ambato

I N THE late eighteenth century, the villa of Ambato included nine districts: Ambato and eight towns around the center. Pelileo hosted 22 percent of the adult male tributary population, about the same as Ambato, while the rest was scattered throughout the other towns. In 1779 there were a total of 3,780 indigenous tribute payers living in the villa of Ambato. The tributary population was dispersed as follows:

Ambato	827
Pelileo	825
Quisapincha	627
Santa Rosa	458
Píllaro	286
Yzamba	233
Tisaleo	228
Patate	169
Quero	127

Source: AGI Quito 447: "Tributos de Ambato."

APPENDIX 2

Tributary Population: Sigchos Collanas in the Jurisdiction of Ambato in 1787

B
Y 1787, tribute records not only included the number of tributary Indians, but broke down the origins among Riobamba, Quito, Tacungas, and Sigchos Collanas. In those records, Pelileo had the highest number of Sigchos Collanas (166), followed by Ambato, which had 55 "Sigchos Collanas and Angamarcas" grouped together:

Ambato	55
Pelileo	166
Quisapincha	3
Santa Rosa	23
Píllaro	8
Yzamba	0
Tisaleo	9
Patate	12
Quero	7

Total Collanas: 283; about 59 percent lived in Pelileo.

Source: AGI Quito 447: "Tributos de Ambato."

NOTES

INTRODUCTION

1. ANE Obrajes 8-X-1661 fol. 192r.
2. Aurora Gómez-Galvarriato, "Premodern Manufacturing," 378.
3. Cushner, *Farm and Factory*, 94.
4. Gómez-Galvarriato, "Premodern Manufacturing," 377.
5. AGI Quito 13, R. 13, No. 38; 1666-11-15: "Estado de la encomienda de Pelileo." Digital document accessed through PARES.
6. ANE Obrajes 1666 fol. 170r.: "Causa criminal iniciada a fines de 1665 por el oidor don Luis Joseph Merlo de la Fuente." This document is catalogued under "obrajes," caja 7 expediente 1, "Quito, 1666, 1008 folios," and is not listed with a more specific date.
7. Cicala, *Descripción histórico-topográfica*, 397.
8. Cicala, *Descripción histórico-topográfica*, 397.
9. Cicala, *Descripción histórico-topográfica*, 400.
10. Told by witnesses throughout the document in ANE Obrajes 8-X-1661.
11. Cicala, *Descripción histórico-topográfica*, 401.
12. Cicala, *Descripción histórico-topográfica*, 402–3.
13. See Hardwick, Pearsall, and Wulf, introduction to "Centering Families in Atlantic History."
14. See the American Anthropological Association project: "Race: Are We So Different?" at http://www.understandingrace.org/home.html.
15. A discussion of all the different colonial classifications of people (castas) in Latin America is beyond the scope of this book. For one rare, early eighteenth-century

example of the use of other terms in Ambato, see Corr, "Race and 'Metaphysical Accidents.'" The complexity of racial classifications, including casta categories, and the manipulation of such categories, is covered in the chapters of *Imperial Subjects*, edited by Fisher and O'Hara. See also Mörner, *Race in Latin America*; Rappaport, *Disappearing Mestizo*; Schwartz, "Colonial Identities and the *Sociedad de Castas*." For a discussion of race in Ecuador, see Rahier, "Blackness, the Racial/Spatial Order"; Weismantel, *Cholas and Pishtacos*; N. Whitten and D. Whitten, *Histories of the Present*, chap. 3; N. Whitten and Corr, "Imagery of Blackness" and "Indigenous Constructions of 'Blackness.'"

16. From Whitten and Corr, "Imagery of Blackness."

17. Minchom, *People of Quito*, 198–99.

18. Lane, "Haunting the Present," 90–91.

19. A. Guerrero, "Administraction of Dominated Populations," 282.

20. Casagrande, "Strategies for Survival," 264–65.

21. Stutzman, "*El Mestizaje*."

22. Bryant, *Rivers of Gold*, 3.

23. For one example, see the discussion of slave-indigenous relations in Nueva Granada in Soulodre-La France, "Whites and Mulattos."

24. Tardieu, "Negros e indios," 547.

25. Salomon, *Native Lords of Quito*, 122.

26. "Yngas Carpinteros." ANE/T Juicios Ambato 25-V-1721.

27. Graubart, *With Our Labor and Sweat*, 168–69.

28. Casagrande, "Strategies for Survival"; Martínez, "La condición actual."

29. Wolf, *Europe and the People without History*.

30. Powers, *Andean Journeys*.

31. Norman E. Whitten Jr. highlights the role of symbols of contrast to create and maintain identity in the process of ethnogenesis in his essay "Ethnogenesis."

32. For a comprehensive analysis of the significance of textiles in expressing ethnic identity in modern Ecuador, see Rowe, ed., *Costume and Identity*.

33. Barth, *Ethnic Groups and Boundaries*.

34. I counted 143 indigenous individuals who gave declarations in the first phase of the investigation (ANE Obrajes 8-X-1661). The investigation was suspended during the change of president in Quito, then resumed in 1665 and concluded in 1666. While I cite a number of testimonies from that second phase, I did not count the exact number of additional witnesses from the 1666 document (ANE Obrajes 1666), which is 1,008 folios, but between the two documents the number of indigenous witnesses exceeds 150.

35. Some argue that private property ownership in the modern sense didn't exist under the Incas (see Ramírez, *World Upside Down*, chap. 3). Although Quechua might lack terms for property ownership, it does have a possessive marker *–pa* (or *–pak* in Quichua). For example, *Inkapa(k) chakra* would translate as the "Inca's field." Whether this would refer to the actual plot of land or the product (the plants) in precontact times is a matter of debate. Even if people in the preconquest Andes

only had rights to the product of a piece of land, and not the actual plot as property, by the early colonial period indigenous people were buying, selling, and bequeathing specific plots of land. My statement that the Inca owned coca fields in Pelileo is based on Frank Salomon's writing on the "Auqui," heir to Atahualpa: "Lands he held in private ownership . . . reflect the pre-Hispanic locale of his 'crown' lands," and again, "The 'Auqui' owned lands on the outskirts of Quito, in Puéllaro, Peruchuo, Yaruquies, Pelileo, and Cumbayá. . . . The Cumbayá property, largest and best of his private lands, was still known as Hacienda el Auqui in the nineteenth century" (*Native Lords of Quito*, 171). Linda Newson also reports on local lords who received lands as gifts from the Inca: "As late as 1601 the cacique of Chambo owned three coca chacras in Pelileo" (*Life and Death in Early Colonial Ecuador*, 47).

36. For a discussion on the anthropology of caring and empathy, see Ortner, "Dark Anthropology," 60. See also Das, "Engaging the Life of the Other."

CHAPTER 1

1. Lehman, "Andean Societies and the Theory of Peasant Economy."
2. Stadel, "Del Valle al Monte." For a description of the páramo Andes, see Hess, "Moving Up—Moving Down," and Salomon, *Native Lords of Quito*.
3. Salomon, *Native Lords of Quito*.
4. AGI Quito 47, No. 14. Digital document accessed through PARES.
5. ANE Indígenas 2-XI-1754.
6. Gomezjurado Zevallos, "El vecindario," 18.
7. Anónimo, "Descripción de los pueblos," 55. The numbers are a combination of the number of tributary Indians reported, and the *cushma*, or nontributary indigenous people, such as women and children. Jaime Costales cites a similar report from a different secondary source with slightly different numbers. Costales, "El obraje de San Ildefonso," 65.
8. ANE Indígenas 4-VII-1641.
9. Powers, *Andean Journeys*, 81–105.
10. Reino Garcés, *Documentos*, 62. One of the descendants of the Anasca, an elite named Don Mateo Inga Anasca, married a Comasanta woman. Comasanta is a feminine surname found among local indigenous women of Pelileo throughout the colonial period, and it remains a surname in Salasaca to this day. Reino Garcés also traces the last name Pillajo to migrants from Nasca, Peru. *La Comarca de Capote*, 70.
11. In tribute records from 1705 to 1711, Doña Francisca Anasca (also spelled de la Nasca) is listed as cacica of forasteros of Pelileo. ANE/T Juicios 1705.
12. Powers, *Andean Journeys*, 88.
13. Salomon, *Native Lords of Quito*, 171.
14. Newson, *Life and Death*, 47.
15. ANE/T Protocolos 2 Juan de Castro 1605–25.
16. ANE/T Protocolos 2 Juan de Castro 1605–25.

17. ANE/T Protocolos 2 Juan de Castro 1605–25.

18. Ortiz de la Tabla, "El obraje."

19. ANE Quito Indígenas 2-III-1680.

20. Reino Garcés, *Documentos*, 56–57.

21. Hirschkind, "The Enigmatic Evanescence of Coca."

22. ANE Obrajes 1666 fol. 462r. For information on Don Francisco Hati, see Powers, *Andean Journeys*, 83–84.

23. Testimony of Don Andres Llugsa, cacique of Patate, in ANE Obrajes 1666 fol. 449r.–450v.

24. This last recommendation is in accordance with Jesuit policy for putting blind indigenous men in intermediary roles; see Durston, *Pastoral Quechua*, 285. In other towns of the jurisdiction of Ambato, there are references to a blind town crier and a blind harpist, which were official civil and Church positions for indigenous people.

25. See Quilter and Urton, *Narrative Threads*; Salomon, *Cord Keepers*.

26. AGI Quito 69. The order is transcribed by Ortiz de la Tabla in "Las ordenanzas," the English translation of which is provided in Salomon, *Cord Keepers*, 118, citing Costales de Oviedo.

27. Salomon, *Cord Keepers*, 118.

28. AGI (digital) Quito, 9, R. 7, No. 52; 1604-4-4: "Miguel de Ibarra sobre diversos puntos" (IV, image 10). Community obrajes, in theory, were for the benefit of the indigenous people, so that they could pay their tribute. In practice, the workers suffered as much there as in privately owned obrajes.

CHAPTER 2

1. Peña Montenegro, *Itinerario para párrocos de indios*, 400.

2. In his report to the Crown, Merlo de la Fuente said that Galarza and his wife had the obraje for thirty years without following any regulations. Based on the statement, I estimated that the stories from this chapter and the next took place between 1630 and 1666. AGI Quito, 13, R. 13, No. 38; 1666-11-15: "Estado de la encomienda de Pelileo y agravios a sus indios." Digital document accessed through PARES.

3. AGI Quito, 13, R. 13, No. 38; 1666-11-15. Digital document accessed through PARES.

4. The original testimonies can be found in ANE Obrajes 8-X-1661; ANE Obrajes 1666; and they are summarized in AGI Quito 13, R. 13, N. 38; 1666-11-15. Digital document accessed through PARES.

5. Reino Garcés, *El componente africano colonial en Tungurahua*.

6. Anónimo, "Descripción de los pueblos," 57.

7. Tyrer, "Demographic and Economic History," 172.

8. Testimony of the alcalde Juan Challay of the Camayos, in ANE Obrajes 1666 103r-v.

9. J. Costales, "El obraje de San Ildefonso," 123.

10. The hacienda system of the central sierra of Ecuador benefited from the uncompensated labor of women and children throughout the nineteenth and early twentieth centuries, and nineteenth-century indigenous men filed legal complaints that their wives were not compensated for the labor that they contributed to the hacienda. O'Connor, *Gender, Indian, Nation*, 173.

11. Brutal treatment of workers, which would leave them incapacitated from working, if not dead, might seem counterproductive, but there are other historical examples of overseers torturing their workers to death. Slaves were tortured to death, even though the owners had paid money for them (see Price, *First Time*, 45–47, for example). Although some foremen were more sadistic than others, the general description is consistent with reports from other obrajes during the seventeenth and eighteenth centuries, which supports the credibility of the testimonies.

12. AGI Quito 1666-11-15, image 35. Digital document accessed through PARES.

13. AGI Quito 1666-11-15, image 36.

14. ANE Obrajes 8-X-1661 fol. 291v.: "[A] visto este testigo es que quando se solian juntar a pilar lana para juntar manteca entre los negros y yndios cardadores imprimadores si alguno para suplir la lana que les suele faltar para ajustar sus tareas o suelen con tostado u otras cossas que sus mujeres les solian llebar de comer compran a escondidas unos a otros algún poquillo de lana rreparandolo alguno de dhos negros les dava de moxicones o bofetadas diciendo que como hazian esso la hacienda de su amo."

15. ANE Obrajes 1666 fol. 123r.

16. Tardieu, "Negros e indios," 546. Another witness said that he believed that the blacks robbed the Andeans due to hunger; ANE Obrajes 1666 fol. 242v.

17. Testimony of Francisco Corcha, in ANE Obrajes 8-X-1661 fol. 222r.

18. I follow Karen Powers in defining the Spanish sphere as the haciendas, mines, and obraje enterprises. *Andean Journeys*, 8.

19. Testimony of Andres Chango, in ANE Obrajes 1666 fol. 491r.

20. Testimony of Juan Challay, alcalde of obraje, in ANE 1661 fol. 101–11.

21. The motivation for the foreman, and sometimes the owners, to ensure Masses for the souls of indigenous people who died in the obraje is not clear. It might have been the responsibility of Spaniards to give Christian burials to indigenous people who died in their service, but the obraje owners and administrator ignored many responsibilities, such as giving workers time off for feast days, or ensuring that children attended religious lessons. So why pay for funerals or Masses? One reason might have been to appease the family so that they wouldn't complain to the priest or an outside authority; another possibility is a genuine religious belief or fear of divine retribution.

22. ANE Obrajes 1666 fol. 444v-r.

23. ANE Obrajes 1666 fol. 468r.

24. ANE Obrajes 1666 fol. 468r.

25. Tardieu, "Negros e indios."

26. Testimony of Joan Yancha, in ANE Obrajes 8-X-1661 fol. 302v.

27. Tardieu, "Negros e indios." Slaves who served in the obrajes of New Spain did not accept their position of servitude, as revealed in blasphemy trials; slaves lashed out with blasphemous language after their quotas were increased to extreme levels or after particularly severe punishments. Proctor, "Afro-Mexican Slave Labor."

28. Bryant, *Rivers of Gold*, 29.

29. ANE Obrajes 8-X-1661 fol. 206r-v.

30. Testimony of Andres Quilcacuri, in ANE Obrajes 8-X-1661 fol. 261v.

31. Tardieu, "Negros e indios," 542.

32. Tardieu, "Negros e indios," 542.

33. Rowe, "Costume in Southern Pichincha Province," 176.

34. ANE Obrajes 8-X-1661 fol. 311r.

35. Davis, *Travels*, 93–94, cited in Fildes, *Wet Nursing*, 141.

36. Phelan, *Kingdom of Quito*, 267.

37. Burdick, *Blessed Anastácia*, 48.

38. Testimony of Don Gabriel Centeno, in ANE Obrajes 1666 fol. 179v.

39. Testimony of María Comasanta, in ANE Obrajes 8-X-1661 fol. 93.

40. When the cacique gave his testimony, he said he had an aunt named Luisa who had nursed many black children, and who had just finished nursing two children at the time of his declaration. ANE Obrajes 8-X-1661 fol. 350r.

41. ANE Obrajes 8-X-1661 fol. 162r-v.

42. ANE Obrajes 8-X-1661 fol.162r-v.

43. Tardieu, "Negros e indios," 544.

44. See, for example, Lane, "Africans and Natives," 176.

45. Burdick, *Blessed Anastácia*, 175.

46. Premo, *Children of the Father King*, 105–7.

47. Price, *First Time*, 47.

48. My speculation is based on research on the history of wet-nursing, and my own fieldwork in Pelileo in a modern-day indigenous community at a time when the women were not using diapers or bottles. I recognize the danger and inaccuracy of projecting modern indigenous practices onto past peoples, but for lack of information I am suggesting possible scenarios. For studies of wet-nursing, see Fildes *Wet Nursing*; Sherwood, *Poverty in Eighteenth-Century Spain*; Sussman, *Selling Mothers' Milk*.

49. Premo, "Familiar."

50. Premo, "Familiar."

51. Tardieu, "Negros e indios," 546.

52. Bryant, *Rivers of Gold*, 2–3.

53. Reino Garcés, *El componente africano*, 27–28. The older will is copied into a document from 1701, but María de Vera had already passed away by the time of the 1661 inquest.

54. Bryant lists Bañon among the many ethnic monikers of Qutio's slave populations. *Rivers of Gold*, 98.

55. O'Toole, *Bound Lives*, 139.

56. ANE Obrajes 1666 fol. 495r-v.
57. Cushner, *Farm and Factory*, 137.
58. Tardieu, "Negros e indios," 538.
59. "[L]a coxia quando avian de azotar por ambas lados entre negro y indio el dho negro Chinchico quien muchas vezes de compación quando el dho maestro no estava atento a los dhos azotes los pegava en el suelo, o ablandava mucho la mano, y este testigo tambien llevo tres vezes segun se aquerda con el dicho azote de verga." ANE Obrajes 8-X-1661 fol. 306r.
60. See the work of Scott, *Weapons of the Weak* and *Domination and the Arts of Resistance*.
61. See the discussion in Soulodre-La France, "Whites and Mulattos."
62. See the work of Trouillot, *Silencing the Past*.
63. Gauderman describes a case in Quito in which an obraje owner used a black slave woman to punish the indigenous workers. Some slaves even had their own indigenous servants; *Women's Lives in Colonial Quito*, 76, 89. On the other hand, some native caciques petitioned the Council of Indies to grant them permission to have African slaves; Lane, *Quito 1599*, 58. The situation was different in the city of Quito, where indigenous couples chose blacks to be their children's godparents; Schwartz and Salomon, "New Peoples," 463.
64. Premo, "Familiar."

CHAPTER 3

1. Trouillot, *Silencing the Past*, 23.
2. There is abundant and ongoing scholarship exploring the role of indigenous intermediaries. Yanna Yannakakis explores the complex position of different native intermediaries in colonial Oaxaca in *The Art of Being In-Between*. The position of native elites and office holders in the Andes is discussed by David Cahill and Blanca Tovías in their introduction to *Élites indígenas en los Andes*. Frank Salomon explains the role of northern Andean chiefdoms under the Incas in *Native Lords of Quito*, while Karen Powers shows the rise of chiefly dynasties and intruder caciques in colonial Quito in *Andean Journeys*. John Charles's book *Allies at Odds* explores the role of native Church assistants in the Andes. See also Alcira Dueñas's "Introduction: Andeans Articulating Colonial Worlds."
3. ANE Obrajes 8-X-1661 fol. 290r.
4. ANE Obrajes 8-X-1661 fol. 274r.
5. I use the colonial spelling (*quipo* or *quipocàma*) to refer to the social position, and the modern spelling (*khipu*) to refer to the actual cord used for accounting, following Quilter and Urton, *Narrative Threads*.
6. Testimony of Doña María Mulmuquis, in ANE Obrajes 1666 fol. 508r.
7. ANE Obrajes 8-X-1661 73r.
8. ANE Obrajes 8-X-1661 186r-v.
9. bell hooks is the correct spelling of this scholar's name.
10. hooks, "Homeplace," 176.

11. hooks specifically calls on the "Contemporary black struggle" to "honor this history of service just as it must critique the sexist definition of service as women's 'natural' role." "Homeplace," 176.

12. Icaza, *The Villagers (Huasipungo)*, 25.

13. Emilia Ferraro shows how the hearth of indigenous homes continues to serve as an intimate space symbolizing cooperation, reciprocity, and family unity, which is sustained by female kin. *Reciprocidad, don y deuda*, 180.

14. ANE Obrajes 8-X-1661 fol. 236v.

15. Gualpamullo blamed his wife's miscarriage on the shock of seeing him get whipped. ANE Obrajes 8-X-1661 fol. 237r.

16. Testimony of Geronimo Cuxana, in ANE Obrajes 1666 fol. 509r.

17. See Salomon, *Cord Keepers*, 118–19, for a discussion of how Inca accountants could parlay their role into a political position in early colonial Peru. Although the quipocamas of Galarza's haciendas did not deal with Inca wealth, one can see how they used their roles to gain a favorable political position. For an example of the use of a khipu on a nineteenth-century hacienda, see Hyland, "Ply, Markedness, and Redundancy."

18. ANE Religiosos 4-IV-1661; AGI Quito 1664-6-17.

19. Tardieu, "Negros e indios," 537.

20. AGI Quito 7.

21. Testimony of Luisa Unsinguil, in ANE Obrajes 1666 fol. 77r.-78r.

22. Testimony of Favian Sunsu, in ANE Obrajes 1661 fol. 111r.

23. Ramírez, *World Upside Down*.

24. Powers, *Andean Journeys*, 150.

25. Monsalve, "Curacas pleitistas."

26. ANE Obrajes 8-X-1661 fol. 83r.-84v. Tintin said that the girl was more or less ten, but she was described as "una hermanilla menor," a younger sister, of the ten-year-old brother, and the mother said she was "tierna," so she was probably less than ten years old. Tintin said she went "para que cuydasse en darle de comer." I don't know the location of the dock or source of salt to which he was referring; one possibility is the town of Baños.

27. AGI Quito 1666-11-15, image 37. Digital document accessed through PARES.

28. ANE Obrajes 1666 fol. 500r.

29. Although his subjects were working on Galarza's hacienda, they belonged to the encomienda of the maestre de campo Don Pedro de Ocaeta.

30. ANE Obrajes 1666 fol. 507r.-508v.

31. Testimony of Don Gonsalo Puzia y Alomaliza, in ANE Obrajes 1661 fol. 344r.

32. Testimony of Pablo Yumbay, in ANE Obrajes 1661 fol. 68r.

33. Testimony of Jacinto Curillo, in ANE Obrajes 1661 52r.-54v.

34. ANE Obrajes 8-X-1661 fol. 333v.

35. ANE Obrajes 1666 fol. 640v.

36. AGI Quito 1666-11-15. Digital document accessed through PARES.

37. Testimony of Pedro Toctaquisa, in ANE Obrajes 8-X-1666 fol. 190v.

38. Testimony of Geronimo Moposita, in ANE Obrajes 8-X-1661 fol. 336v.
39. ANE Obrajes 8-X-1661 fol. 233r.-234v.
40. ANE Obrajes 8-X-1661 fol. 233r.-234v.
41. ANE Obrajes 8-X-1661 fol. 233r.-234v.
42. Burns, *Into the Archive*, 125.
43. Burns, *Into the Archive*, 133–34. Burns cautions researchers to think more about the production of archives. Nevertheless, she shows that despite the multiple voices and formulaic language imposed on native legal statements, the documents can represent a "rare, subaltern perspective, even the voices of people unable to represent themselves in writing." Most testimonies from the 1661 investigation do not seem overly embellished. In addition to Quichua terms for positions such as *atalpacama* (one who takes care of chickens), and items such as *cocabi* (sack lunch), other Quichua terms were occasionally incorporated into the record. In a testimony about the workers' quotas being increased, the Quichua slipped through, and the scribe recorded that weavers were given "seis cargas de lana de tarea quando *ñaupa* heran solas quatro" (six loads of wool when ñaupa [before] it was only four). ANE Obrajes 1666 493v.
44. Valderrama Fernandez and Escalante Gutierrez, *Andean Lives*, 3.
45. Tardieu, "Negros e indios," 546.
46. Tardieu, "Negros e indios," 546.
47. Saporta Sternbach, "Re-membering the Dead"; Gugelberger and Kearney, "Voices for the Voiceless."
48. The testimonies of Toctaquisa, from the hacienda of Chumaquí, and Condori, from the hacienda of Ipolongo in the town of Quero, are the only testimonies I found from this case that compare the situation of the indigenous people of Pelileo to historical examples of Christian captivity. Spanish dramas, literature, and ballads told stories of Christian captivity by Moors and Turks, but according to Fernando Operé, such traditions were rare in Spanish America. Indigenous people were probably most familiar with the idea of "Moors" through festive dramas and dances representing Christians and Moors, which were readily appropriated by indigenous cultures in the Americas. Or perhaps the priests were discussing Christian captivity in their sermons. The example of the Jívaros (Xivaros) stands out against these comparisons with old-world captive taking. The Jívaros were the Shuar people of the Ecuadorian Amazon who led a rebellion in 1599 in which they captured Spanish women. Some later reported white, bearded Jívaros, which were attributed to these captive women. Operé, *Indian Captivity in Spanish America*, 203; see also Lane, *Quito 1599*, 54. On the Jívaro, see Harner, *Jívaro*, xiii; Taylor, "La invención del Jívaro"; Bollaert, "On the Idol Human Head of the Jívaro," 12.
49. Block, *Ordinary Lives*, 2.
50. Testimony of Marta Pancha, ANE Obrajes 1661 fol. 158r.
51. Counihan, "Mexicanas' Food Voice," 181.
52. Counihan, *A Tortilla Is Like Life*, 99. Elizabeth Newman also gives detailed attention to women's food work by suggesting possible historical scenarios of daily life,

based on her archeological research in Puebla, Mexico. *Biography of a Hacienda*, 160–61.

53. Emma-Jayne Abbots reports that guinea pig was a special delicacy since pre-Columbian times. "It Doesn't Taste as Good," 207.

54. The following testimionies are from ANE Obrajes 7 1666 fol. 41v.-45r.

55. Testimony of Miguel Caizatassi inANE Obrajes 1661 fol. 199r.

56. Holtzman, "Food and Memory."

57. ANE Obrajes 1661 fol. 55r.-58v.

58. ANE Obrajes 8-X-1661 fol. 56v.

59. I say this because in another testimony Mateo Almagro of the Camayos Puruguayes of Pelileo said that his father Don Xptobal Almagro was owed money for the time that he served as an alcalde in the obraje when it was owned by María de Vera's father. ANE Obrajes 1661 fol. 193r.

60. ANE Obrajes 8-X-1661 fol. 58r.

61. Testimony of Geronima Chunchugna, niece of Jacinto Quibisa, in ANE Obrajes 8-X-1661 fol. 55r.

62. "[N]o querian ir a verlos y socorrerlos al dho obraxe por no ser conosidos lo a oydo dezir en diferentes ocaciones a los mismos yndios lamentandosse de que aun sus parientes los negavan en no quererlos yr a ver al dho obraxe ni a socorrerlos en sus necesidades y hambres por no ser conosidos." Testimony of Joan Yancha, in ANE Obrajes 1661 fol. 306r.

63. Testimony of Augustín Hambacho, in ANE Obrajes 1666 fol. 417r.

64. ANE Obrajes 1666 fol. 187r.

65. Testimony of Augustín Hambacho, in ANE Obrajes 1666 420r.

66. ANE Obrajes 8-X-1661 fol. 231r., 164r.; ANE Obrajes 1666 fol. 177r.

67. ANE Obrajes 8-X-1661 289r-v.

68. ANE Obrajes 8-X-1661 fol. 60r-v.

69. ANE Obrajes 8-X-1661 fol. 291v.

70. ANE Obrajes 8-X-1661 fol. 145r. Witnesses did not always give specific ages, but sometimes referred to the sons as *tiernos* (tender), which I gloss as "very young."

71. ANE Obrajes 1661 fol. 227r.

72. ANE Obrajes 1661 fol. 295r.

73. Saporta Sternbach, "Re-membering the Dead," 93.

74. Cushner, *Farm and Factory*, 102.

75. J. Costales, "El obraje de San Ildefonso," 148.

76. Cushner, *Farm and Factory*, 102.

77. See Powers, *Andean Journeys*, 82–84.

CHAPTER 4

1. Gomezjurado Zevallos, "El vecindario," 18–19.

2. Kennedy Troya and Fauria Roma, "Obrajes en la Audiencia de Quito," 155–57.

3. ANE Religiosos 1675-III-V.

4. ANE Religiosos 20-VI-1693.

5. Anónimo, "Descripción de los pueblos," 56.

6. Carpinteros were exempt from the mita according to Gregorio Guallachamen. ANE Obrajes 1666 fol. 432r.

7. Although eighteenth-century baptismal records put the Salasacas and forasteros into one section, they were different groups. Those labeled Salasacas had the names of the Sigchos Collanas (such as Masaquiza), while most of those labeled as forasteros had different last names.

8. ANE Indígenas 1-VII-1695.

9. Alchon, *Native Society*, 94. Alchon's source refers to San Ildefonso by its older name, the obraje of Pilatos.

10. Silverblatt, *Moon, Sun, and Witches*, 31–39.

11. Salomon, *Native Lords of Quito*, 133.

12. Belote and Belote, "Gender, Ethnicity, and Modernization."

13. See Muñoz Bernand, "Estratégias matrimoniales"; Reino Garcés, *Tisaleo indígena en la colonia*, 106.

14. Cited in Burgos Guevara, *Primeras doctrinas*, 449. I thank Deborah Truhan and Karen Powers for this reference.

15. Karen Powers, pers. comm.

16. Graubart, *With Our Labor and Sweat*, 158–61.

17. Powers, *Women in the Crucible of Conquest*, 45–46.

18. Lane, *Quito 1599*, 93.

19. Garrett, "In Spite of Her Sex."

20. ANE Cacicazgos 14-XII-1709.

21. ANE Cacicazgos 14-XII-1709.

22. Daza, master's thesis, forthcoming.

23. For comparison with a Mesoamerican seating of a cacica, see Terraciano, *Mixtecs of Colonial Oaxaca*, 160–62.

24. Ceremonial stools are still used by Quichua-speaking Amazonian shamans in Ecuador as a "seat of power," when they take the hallucinogenic "soul vine" (*ayahuasca*) and deal with the spirit world; N. Whitten and D. Whitten, *From Myth to Creation*, 36–41. Some colonial Andean stools were decorated with Amazonian symbols; Cummins, *Toasts with the Inca*, 302–3.

25. ANE Cacicazgos 5-VI-1710.

26. ANE Cacicazgos 14-XII-1709 fol. 16r.

27. See O'Phelan Godoy, "Tiempo inmemorial."

28. Cummins, *Toasts with the Inca*, 302.

29. Thomson, *We Alone Will Rule*, 42.

30. ANE Cacicazgos 14-XII-1709 fol. 21r.

31. ANE Cacicazgos 6-VII-1712 fol. 17r.

32. ANE Cacicazgos 6-VII-1712 fol. 58r-v.

33. ANE Cacicazgos 6-VII-1712 fol. 59r.

34. ANE Indígenas 6-V-1743. I found one other eighteenth-century reference to a cacica of Pelileo. Doña Margarita Polo del Aguila governed a Royal Crown sector; it is not clear whether these were natives of an expired encomienda or descendants of forasteros. She inherited the cacicazgo from her late husband, the cacique Don Joseph Perez de la Nasca. De la Nasca was the last name of the seventeenth-century caciques who rounded up "vagabonds" and incorporated them into a Crown parcialidad, so these Royal Crown Indians were probably descendants of those forasteros, including some who claimed origins in Cuzco (see chapter 1).

35. ANE Indígenas 15-II-1712.

36. The Duke of Uceda held several encomiendas in the Audiencia de Quito, and he granted some, including the Sigchos Collanas, to the Monjas Bernardas to support their religious order. See Ortiz de la Tabla, *Los encomenderos*, 113–14.

37. ANE Cacicazgos 1-I-1728.

38. Perhaps due to a scribe's mistake in recording the last name.

39. ANE Cacicazgos 1-I-1728fol. 13r.

40. ANE Cacicazgos 1-I-1728 fol.18r-v.

41. ANE Cacicazgos 1-I-1728 fol.18r-v.

42. Daza, master's thesis, forthcoming.

CHAPTER 5

1. Andrien, *Kingdom of Quito*, 56–58.

2. Cicala, *Descripción histórico-topográfica*, 402.

3. AGI Quito 133, No. 26; 9-VIII-1737: "Jose de Araujo to Crown."

4. Caption by J. Guerrero, in *Imágenes del Ecuador del Siglo XIX*, 97.

5. AGI Quito 144, No. 50: "Manuel Gregorio de la Cerda: Perjuicios que sufre la provincia."

6. See Uzcátegui Andrade, *Los Llanganates*.

7. Moreno Yánez, *Sublevaciones indígenas*, 86.

8. Salomon, Native Lords of Quito, 105.

9. Silverblatt, *Moon, Sun, and Witches*, 197–210.

10. AGI Quito 144, No. 50: "Manuel Gregorio de la Cerda: Perjuicios que sufre la provincia."

11. Cushner, *Farm and Factory*, 93.

12. Cushner, *Farm and Factory*, 103.

13. ANE Obrajes 1-II-1760.

14. Nicholas Cushner, who had access to some Jesuit archives, said that there were no baptismal or other records of Jesuit slaves, and he found no information on slaves in Pelileo during the Jesuit holdings. *Farm and Factory*, 136–37.

15. ANE Indígenas 12-VII-1727.

16. ANE/T Notarías Segunda 30-IX-1795.

17. AAQ González Suárez boxes 6–7.

18. Cushner, *Farm and Factory*, 207n1.

19. Andrien, *Kingdom of Quito*, 125–26.
20. ANE Indígenas 9-III-1743.

CHAPTER 6

1. Testimony of Manuel de Heredía, in ANE Criminales 20-V-1768 fol. 14v.
2. Testimony of Petrona Salazar (wife of the sugar mill assistant), in ANE Criminales 20-V-1768 fol. 18v.
3. José María Coba Robalino wrote in his 1929 *Mongrafía general* (p. 273) that the instigators were one family, sent to the obraje as prisoners from Píllaro, and that the administrator was forcing himself on the daughter, who was chained in the obraje with her father. It's possible that he is referring to Marcela Tasi, who tried to get her daughter out of the obraje, but his statements that five people were executed (the mother, father, two sons, and a daughter), and that the family was from Píllaro, are not supported by the trial record.
4. Moreno Yánez, *Sublevaciones indígenas*, 121.
5. Testimony of Blas Chango, in ANE Criminales 20-V-1768 fol. 113r.
6. Testimony of Manuel Ojeda, in ANE Criminales 20-V-1768 fol. 27v.
7. Testimiony of Phelipe Llagua, in ANE Criminales 20-V-1768 fol. 47v.
8. ANE/T Notarías Primera 20-V-1767.
9. Minchom, *People of Quito*, 91.
10. Charles, *Allies at Odds*, 148–50. According to Charles, such parodies were common in the colonial period. The mimicry of sacred symbols in the seventeenth-century performance described by Charles is very similar to the modern Salasaca *mondongo misa* performed as part of the funeral rites, in which priests' powers are both mocked and appropriated. See Corr, *Ritual and Remembrance*; Wogan, *Magical Writing*.
11. Durston, *Pastoral Quechua*, 61–64.
12. Charles, *Allies at Odds*, 60.
13. Corr, *Ritual and Remembrance*, 98; Wibblesman, *Ritual Encounters*, 112.
14. Sainges, "Quechua-Aymara Heartland," 125.
15. McFarlane, "The Rebellion of the Barrios"; see also Black, *Limits of Gender Domination*.
16. Moreno Yánez, *Alzamientos indígenas*, 24.
17. ANE/T Notarías Primera 20-V-1767 fol.16r.
18. Harris, *Aztecs, Moors, and Christians*, 230.
19. Harris, *Aztecs, Moors, and Christians*, 232–33.
20. Poole, "Accomodation and Resistance," 114.
21. Dean, *Inka Bodies*, 58 (emphasis in original).
22. ANE/T Notarías Primera 20-V-1767 fol.13v.-14r.
23. ANE/T Notarías Primera 20-V-1767 fol.17v.-18r.
24. Foster, *Culture and Conquest*, 207n6.
25. ANE/T Notarías Primera 20-V-1767.

26. Coba Robalino reported that sometime between 1730 and 1760 there was a rebellion in Píllaro in which the natives threatened to poison the water of the whites. If this is true, it might explain the fear of connections between native leaders in Pelileo and Píllaro. *Monografía general*, 212.
27. ANE/T Notarías Primera 20-V-1767 fol. 19r.
28. Thomson, *We Alone Will Rule*, 22.
29. ANE/T Notarías Primera 20-V-1767.
30. ANE/T Notarías Primera 20-V-1767 fol. 38v.
31. Scott, *Domination and the Arts of Resistance*, 139.
32. I have undertaken many years of ethnographic fieldwork among the Salasacas, who sometimes refer to drinking as "putting on memory," meaning that one drinks to the point of "remembering" angry sentiments that they normally repress, but which they openly speak about when drinking. Drinking today is seen as positively conducive to expressing repressed resentments; when one refuses alcoholic beverages, he might be pressured to drink only enough to "put on memory" and say what he really feels.
33. Castro, Hidalgo, Briones, "Fiestas, borracheras, y rebeliones," 82.
34. Scott, *Domination and the Arts of Resistance*, 181.
35. ANE Criminales 20-V-1768.
36. Moreno Yánez, "Chambo 1797," 397. Yanna Yannakakis writes of the use of horns and drums as calls to war in an eighteenth-century Zapotec rebellion, and she says that native intermediaries in Oaxaca were often described as sources of conflict in both native and Spanish accounts. *The Art of Being In-Between*, 68.
37. Cicala, *Descripción histórico-topográfica*, 392.
38. A. Guerrero, "Administration of Dominated Populations," 280–81.
39. ANE Criminales 20-V-1768 171v.

CHAPTER 7

1. Charney, *Indian Society*, 147.
2. Mangan, *Transatlantic Obligations*, 139.
3. Premo, "Familiar."
4. ANE Pobreza 28-XI-1704.
5. For example, some encomenderos of sixteenth-century Peru expressed guilt for having exploited the labor and resources of their indigenous subjects, and they left resources for Masses for their souls; Ramírez, *World Upside Down*, 66. Other Spaniards of sixteenth-century Peru left money or goods to be used as dowries for their indigenous servants; Mangan, *Translatlantic Obligations*, 127–28. During the seventeenth-century sugar boom on the north coast of Peru, one landowner paid for the building of a church for indigenous people; Ramírez, *Provincial Patriarchs*, 193. See also Premo, "Familiar."
6. Salasacas told me that there was confusion about last names among some people due to a practice that single mothers used. "In the past," probably the first half of the twentieth century, single mothers would ask a male friend to stand in as the

"father" of the baby during the baptismal rite, saying, "Shutichibai" (Please baptize/ give a name). In some cases, the child was the result of an affair with a married man, so the young woman would avoid involving the biological father. The last name on the baptismal record would then be the surname of the male friend who pretended to be the child's father, while other legal documents may have listed the child with a different last name.

7. Truhan, "Mi última y postrimera voluntad," cited in León G. and Mora, "Poder y amor."

8. Mintz and Wolf, "An Analysis of Ritual Co-Parenthood."

9. "[A] mi hija que lo crie en mi poder a una chiquilla que se llama Barbola Ungas." He also referred to her as "mi muchacha." Will of Geronimo Toasa, 1673, copied into ANE Cacicazgos 6-VII-1712.

10. ANE Cacicazgos 5-VI-1710. While Andres Caizabanda might have been either a servant or foster child of the cacique, he maintained his Sigchos Collanas status.

11. ANE Indígenas 12-XI-1754. The lands were in Llicacama, a sector of modern-day Salasaca.

12. ANE/T Notarías Segunda 20-IV-1809.

13. ANE/T Juicios 6-XI-1888.

14. ANE/T Notarías Primera 19-X-1754.

15. ANE/T Notarías Primera 19-X-1754.

16. Mangan, "Moving Mestizos."

17. Premo, *Children of the Father King*, 179–210.

18. ANE/T Notarías Segunda 11-I-1803.

19. ANE/T Notarías Segunda 19-I-1813.

20. ANE Indigenas 16-VIII-1792.

21. ANE/T Juicios 20-VIII-1779.

22. ANE/T Notarías Segunda 6-VIII-1814.

23. ANE/T Notarías Primera 7-XII-1776.

24. ANE Mestizos 7-III-1752.

25. In Mesoamerica and the Andes, this could include factors such as clothing and occupation. See Graubart, *With Our Labor*, 121–57; Fisher and O'Hara, *Imperial Subjects*; Rappaport, *Disappearing Mestizo*.

26. ANE Mestizos 7-III-1752.

27. This "cholo" clothing is specified as "cotón de bayeta y calson de lo mismo," or color-printed cotton cape and pants (breeches).

28. ANE Mestizos 7-III-1752.

CHAPTER 8

1. Castillo Jácome, citing Isaias Toro Ruiz, lists white residents of Ambato in 1615, including "Juan de la Parra, Francisco y Hernando de la Parra, hermanos quiteños, nietos de Hernando de la Parra, subaltern de Benalcasar." Castillo Jácome, *Historia de la Provincia de Tungurahua*, 192.

2. Gomezjurado Zevallos, "El vecindario," 18.
3. From a will copied into the case of Cecilia Comasanta, in ANE Indígenas 12-XI-1754.
4. ANE/T Notarías Primera 11-III-1752.
5. ANE/T Notarías Primera 11-III-1752.
6. ANE/T Notarías Primera 11-III-1752.
7. Lambert, "Bilaterality in the Andes."
8. See Charney, *Indian Society*; Mangan, *Transatlantic Obligations*.
9. ANE/T Juicios 19-II-1777.
10. ANE/T Protocolos fol. 7–8: "15 enero de 1886–diciembre 1887."
11. Corr, *Ritual and Remembrance*, 148–56; Wogan, *Magical Writing*, 152.
12. 1673 will copied into ANE Cacicazgos 6-VII-1712.
13. ANE Indígenas 12-XI-1754.
14. Corr and Powers, "Ethnogenesis," 17.
15. ANE Indígenas 12-XI-1754.
16. ANE/T Notarías Primera I-VII-1745.
17. ANE/T 18-V-1767.
18. Milton, "Poverty and Politics of Colonialism," 597.
19. The Masaquizas were accused of another strategy to get lands in one case between indigenous heirs. The Caiza family (Pilalata) owned lands in Chumaquí, Nitón, and the sector of Salasaca called Cochapamba. In an 1809 land dispute, one descendant of the Caizas, Juan Guatomillo, accused other indigenous people of being Masaquizas who changed their last name to Caiza in order to get at the lands. The accuser does not present any evidence to support his accusation. ANE/T 20-IV-1809.
20. See Ramírez, *Provincial Patriarchs*.
21. Milton, "Poverty and Politics of Colonialism," 601.

CHAPTER 9

1. Ibarra, "Cambios agrarios," 162.
2. Ibarra, "Cambios agrarios," 216–19.
3. Van Aken, "Lingering Death of Indian Tribute," 442.
4. Albers, "Changing Patterns of Ethnicity."
5. Reino Garcés, *Documentos*, 146.
6. Corr and Powers, "Ethnogenesis," 15. According to R. T. Zuidema, *collana* means "first, most prominent"; *Ceque System*, 3. Hugo Burgos Guevara says that Sigchos was divided into Hatun Sigchos and Collana Sigchos, with the Collana being the nobles, which he says would have conquered the original population of Hatun Sigchos; *El guaman, el puma y el amaru*, 330. Salomon also found ayllus labeled "collana" among the "yumbos" west of the Andes. *Los yumbos, niguas, y tsátchila*, 79.
7. Martin Minchom cites Linda Belote, who identified three nonlocalized ranked "strata called *Quintos, Collanas* and *Secundeles*." Minchom, "Making of a White Province," 34.

8. Navas de Pozo, *Angamarca*, 83–84.

9. Feijóo, *El 'Valle Sangriento.'*

10. Reino Garcés, *Historias de tinta y polvo*, 68.

11. "Arendamiento de la Encomienda de Salasaca a favor del Alferes Don Phelis Flores." ANE/T Protocolos 27: "Juan Antonio Balezuela 1706–1710."

12. Powers, *Andean Journeys*, 80.

13. ANE Obrajes 1661 caja 5, exp. 1., fol. 870.

14. Corr and Powers, "Ethnogenesis."

15. Cicala, *Descripción histórico-topográfica*, 393.

16. ANE/T Notarías Tercera 29-IV-1854.

17. AGI Quito 278, R. 2, No. 15, 1761.

18. Libro de Matrimonios 1869–85, Casa Parroquial Pelileo.

19. Reino Garcés, *La Comarca de Capote*, 69. The place known as the Playas of Cevallos was formerly Andignato-Pachanlica. A similar process occurred among people on the Ecuadorian-Colombian border: "[T]hese northern Ecuadorian peasants do not consider themseselves to be indigenous at all, whereas their cousins in Nariño [Colombia] aggressively and passionately assert their native identity." Rappaport, "Carchi Province (Ecuador) and the Department of Nariño (Colomiba)," 119. As in the case of the Salasacas, indigenous territory went hand in hand with political autonomy.

20. Corr and Powers, "Ethnogensis."

21. Scott, *Art of Not Being Governed*, 19–20.

22. ANE Obrajes 12-XII-1777.

23. Borchart de Moreno, *La Audiencia de Quito*, 231.

24. ANE Obrajes 30-I-1798.

25. ANE/T Notarías Segunda 30-IX-1795.

26. ANE/T Notarías Segunda 2-3-1799. It seems that half of the document is missing. In a legal case, each side brings witnesses to give statements on their behalf. In this record, only the witnesses for the maestro appear. If the case were complete, it should contain the statements of indigenous witnesses for Masaquiza.

27. While some historians describe the "collapse" of the textile industry, others refer to it as a "contraction," since many obrajes continued to operate through the late nineteenth century. See Kennedy Troya and Fauria Roma, "Obrajes en la Audiencia de Quito," 165.

28. Borchart de Moreno, *La Audiencia de Quito*, 234.

29. ANE Tributos 1823: "Libro Publico Cobranza de Indígenas de Ambato 1823."

30. Ibarra, "Tierra, mercado y capital," 135.

31. Ibarra, "Tierra, mercado y capital," 89.

32. Ibarra, "Tierra, mercado y capital," 179.

33. Ibarra, "Tierra, mercado y capital," 176.

34. To full the men's ponchos, men roll up the cloth, put it in boiling water, remove it, and then several of them together roll it under their feet, and then they repeat the process. In 1991 I attended a "fulling party," in which a man asked his brother and

friends to help full the poncho, an all-day event for which his wife and mother provided food.

35. For a full description of Salasaca textiles, see Miller, "Salasaca," and Rowe, "Costume in Cotopaxi, Tungurahua, and Bólivar Provinces."

CONCLUSION

1. See Wolf, *Europe and the People without History*.

2. See Belote and Belote, "From the Incas to OPEC"; Hirschkind, "History of the Indian Population"; Ogburn, "Becoming Saraguro"; and Truhan, "Repopulating the Countryside."

3. Minchom, "Making of a White Province," 33. In the case of Loja, Minchom argues that it was the descendants of migrants who became white-mestizos, whereas in Salasaca, it was the descendants of migrants (the camayo colony) who maintained an indigenous identity.

4. Minchom, "Making of a White Province," 35.

GLOSSARY

The following terms are defined in accordance with their context of use in this book.

ALCAIDE. Mill guard.

ALCALDE. Indigenous official.

ALCALDE DE LA DOCTRINA. Indigenous official charged with enforcing native attendance to Catholic religious lessons (doctrina). Also called *fiscal*.

ALCALDE ORDINARIO. In indigenous communities, the native official charged with detaining criminals.

ALGUACIL. Constable.

AUDIENCIA. Colonial court composed of a president and judges; the geographic area of the jurisdiction.

AYLLU. Indigenous social group usually based on kinship but also used for administrative sectors of indigenous people. Synonymous with *parcialidad*.

CACICA. Female native lord or chief.

CACICAZGO. Hereditary chiefdom.

CACIQUE. Native lord or chief.

CAMAYO. Economic colonist. Native delegate who lived outside of the community of origin to produce goods for the home community.

CAPORAL. Labor boss. The black overseer who punished indigenous workers.

CHICHA. Maize beer.

CORREGIDOR. Spanish colonial administrator of a jurisdiction.

CORREGIMIENTO. Jurisdiction within an Audiencia.

CRIOLLO. A person of Spanish parentage born in the Americas.

DOCTRINA. Indigenous parish. Also, Christian religious lessons taught to indigenous people.

ENCOMENDERO. A Spaniard granted rights over the labor of certain indigenous groups.

ENCOMIENDA. Grant of natives to a Spaniard. Sometimes referred to the area where the native laborers resided.

FORASTERO. An outsider. Nonlocal native living in the community.

GAÑAN. Laborer contracted on a yearly basis.

HACIENDA. Landed estate.

MAESTRILLO. Indigenous work supervisor of an obraje.

MAESTRO. Spanish or mestizo foreman of the mill.

MAESTRO DE CAPILLA. Chapel master.

MAYORDOMO. Estate manager.

MINGA. Andean collective labor.

MITA. Labor draft of indigenous men between the ages of eighteen and fifty.

MITIMAES. Transplanted population. A group of people forcibly relocated from one area of the Inca empire to another.

MONTAÑES. Originally used for the offspring of a Spanish man and Inca noblewoman. A polite term for mestizo. Also a low-class Spaniard.

OBRAJE. Textile mill.

OFICIAL. Journeyman.

OIDOR. Judge.

PAÑO. High-quality wool fabric.

PÁRAMO. High-altitude grasslands of the northern Andes.

PARCIALIDAD. Administrative sector of natives. Used interchangeably with *ayllu.*

PATACÓN. Silver coin (peso).

PRINCIPAL. Secondary chief.

PROTECTOR DE NATURALES. A Spanish colonial attorney meant to represent indigenous people.

PUEBLO. Town.

QUICHUA [*kichwa*]. Variant of Quechua, the language of the Inca state, spoken in the northern Andes.

QUIPO. Also spelled *khipu* and *quipu*. An Andean record-keeping device using cords and knotted strings. Also short for *quipocama*.

QUIPOCAMA. A native accountant who keeps records on a *quipu*. In Pelileo, the title of the indigenous supervisors who kept track of the number of animals assigned to a shepherd and the number of days worked.

REAL. One-eighth of a peso.

RECOGEDOR. Guard who brings laborers to the mill.

SEMANERO. Rotating position of African slaves who supervised indigenous workers in the mill for eight days.

SOCORRO. Advances of food and clothing to a native worker against his work account.

TAREA. A unit of work; the quota that native workers were expected to produce.

TENIENTE. Lieutenant. Assistant to the corregidor.

TRIBUTE. A tax that indigenous men were required to pay.

VAGAMUNDO. "Vagabond." Another name for forastero. A native who fled his home community.

VECINO. Spanish resident of a town.

REFERENCES

PRIMARY SOURCES

Archivo Arzobispal de Quito (AAQ)
Archivo General de Indias (AGI)
Archivo Histórico de la Curia de Ambato (ACA)
Archivo Nacional del Ecuador (ANE). Sections: Cacicazgos, Criminales, Indígenas, Mestizos, Obrajes, Pobreza, Religiosos, Tributos.
Archivo Nacional del Ecuador, Tungurahua (ANE/T, located in Ambato). Sections: Protocolos, Notarías Primera, Notarías Segunda, Notarías Tercera
Casa Parroquial Pelileo, Libro de Matrimonios 1869–1885
Portal de Archivos Españoles (PARES) pares.mcu.es

PUBLISHED SOURCES

Abbots, Emma-Jayne. "'It Doesn't Taste as Good from the Pet Shop': Guinea Pig Consumption and the Performance of Transnational Kin and Class Relations in Highland Ecuador and New York City." *Food, Culture, and Society* 14, no. 2 (2011): 205–23.

Albers, Patricia. "Changing Patterns of Ethnicity in the Northeastern Plains, 1780–1870." In *History, Power, and Identity: Ethnogenesis in the Americas 1492–1992*, edited by Jonathan D. Hill, 90–118. Iowa City: University of Iowa Press, 1996.

Alchon, Suzanne Austin. *Native Society and Disease in Colonial Ecuador*. New York: Cambridge University Press, 1991.

Andrien, Kenneth J. *The Kingdom of Quito, 1690–1830: The State and Regional Development*. New York: Cambridge University Press, 1995.

Anónimo. "Descripción de los pueblos de la jurisdicción del corregimiento de Villar Don Pardo en la provincial de los puruhaes." In *Relaciones histórico-geográficas de la Audiencia de Quito siglo xvi-xix Tomo II*, edited by Pilar Ponce Leiva, 48–70. Quito: Abya-Yala, 1994 [1605].

Barth, Fredrik. *Ethnic Groups and Boundaries*. Long Grove, IL: Waveland Press, (1969) 1998.

Belote, Jim, and Linda S. Belote. "From the Incas to OPEC: A Process of Andean Ethnogenesis." Unpublished manuscript, Department of Sociology and Anthropology, University of Minnesota-Duluth, n.d.

———. "Gender, Ethnicity, and Modernization: Saraguro Women in a Changing World." In *Multidisciplinary Studies in Andean Anthropology*, edited by V. J. Vitzhum, 101–17. Michigan Discussions in Anthropology, vol. 8. Ann Arbor: University of Michigan, 1988.

Biblioteca Digital Hispánica. http://www.bne.es/es/Catalogos/BibliotecaDigitalHispanica/Inicio/index.html.

Black, Chad T. *The Limits of Gender Domination: Women, The Law, and Political Crisis in Quito, 1765-1830*. Albuquerque: University of New Mexico Press, 2010.

Block, Kristen. *Ordinary Lives in the Early Caribbean: Religion, Colonial Competition, and the Politics of Profit*. Athens: University of Georgia Press, 2012.

Bollaert, William. "On the Idol Human Head of the Jivaro Indians of Ecuador." *Royal Anthropological Institute* 2 (1863): 112–18.

Borchart de Moreno, Christiana. *La Audiencia de Quito: Aspectos económicos y sociales (siglos XVI-XVIII)*. Quito: Banco Central del Ecuador, 1998.

Bryant, Sherwin K. *Rivers of Gold, Lives of Bondage: Governing Through Slavery in Colonial Quito*. Chapel Hill: University of North Carolina Press, 2014.

Burdick, John. *Blessed Anastácia: Women, Race, and Popular Christianity in Brazil*. New York: Routdledge, 1998.

Burgos Guevara, Hugo. *El Guaman, el puma y el amaru: Formación estructural del Gobierno Indígena en Ecuador*. Quito: Abya-Yala, 1995.

———. *Primeras doctrinas en la Real Audiencia de Quito 1570-1640*. Quito: Abya-Yala, 1995.

Burns, Kathryn. *Into the Archive: Writing and Power in Colonial Peru*. Durham, NC: Duke University Press, 2010.

Cahill, David, and Blanca Tovías, eds. *Élites indígenas en los andes: Nobles, caciques y cabildantes bajo el yugo colonial*. Quito: Abya-Yala, 2003.

Casagrande, Joseph B. "Strategies for Survival: The Indians of Highland Ecuador." In *Cultural Transformation and Ethnicity in Modern Ecuador*, edited by Norman E. Whitten Jr., 260–77. Urbana: University of Illinois Press, 1981.

Castillo Jácome, Julio. *Historia de la Provincia de Tungurahua*. Ambato: Offsworth Editores, 1990.

Castro F., Nelson, Jorge Hidalgo L., and Viviana Briones B. "Fiestas, borracheras, y rebeliones: Introducción y transcripción del expediente de averiguación del tumulto acaecido en Ingahuasi, 1777." *Estudios Atacameños* 23 (2002): 77–109.

Charles, John. *Allies at Odds: The Andean Church and Its Indigenous Agents, 1583–1671.* Albuquerque: University of New Mexico Press, 2010.

Charney, Paul. *Indian Society in the Valley of Lima, Peru, 1532–1824.* Lanham, MD: University Press of America, 2001.

Chiriboga, Lucía, and Silvana Caparrini, eds. *Identidades Desnudas: Ecuador 1860–1920.* Qutio: Abya-Yala, 1994.

Cicala, Mario. *Descripción histórico-topográfica de la provincia de Quito de la Compañía de Jesus.* Quito: Biblioteca Ecuatoriana "Aurelio Espinosa Pólit," 1994 [1771].

Coba Robalino, José María. *Monografía general del cantón Píllaro.* Quito: Prensa Católica, 1929.

Coronel Feijóo, Rosario. *El 'valle sangriento': De la coca indígena a la hacienda jesuita en el Chota, 1580–1700.* Segunda edición. Quito: Corporación Editora Nacional, 2015.

Corr, Rachel. "Race and 'Metaphysical Accidents' in Colonial Quito." Paper presented at the Third Biennal Conference of the Society for Amazonian and Andean Studies University of Central Florida, Orlando, October 26–27, 2013.

———. *Ritual and Remembrance in the Ecuadorian Andes.* Tucson: University of Arizona Press, 2010.

Corr, Rachel, and Karen Vieira Powers. "Ethnogenesis, Ethnicity, and 'Cultural Refusal': The Case of the Salasacas in Highland Ecuador." *Latin American Research Review* 47, Special Issue (2012): 5–30.

Costales, Jaime. "El obraje de San Ildefonso." Tesis de licenciatura, Facultad de Ciencias Humanas, PUCE, Quito, 1979.

Costales, Pieded Peñaherrera de, and Alfredo Costales Samaniego. *Los Salasacas: Investigación y elaboración,* vol. 8. Quito: Instituto Ecuatoriano de Antropología, 1959.

———. "Tungurahua," *Llacta* no. 13. Quito: Instituto Ecuatoriano de Antropología y Geografía, 1961.

Counihan, Carole. *A Tortilla Is Like Life: Food and Culture in the San Luis Valley of Colorado.* Austin: University of Texas Press, 2009.

———. "Mexicanas' Food Voice and Differential Conscouisness in the San Luis Valley of Colorado." In *Food and Culture: A Reader,* 3rd ed., edited by Carole Counihan and Penny Van Esterik, 172–86. New York: Routledge, 2013.

Cummins, Thomas. *Toasts with the Inca: Andean Abstraction and Colonial Images on Quero Vessesls.* Ann Arbor: University of Michigan Press, 2005.

Cushner, Nicholas P. *Farm and Factory: The Jesuits and the Development of Agrarian Capitalism in Colonial Quito 1600–1767.* Albany: State University of New York Press, 1982.

Das, Veena. "Engaging the Life of the Other: Love and Everyday Life." In *Ordinary Ethics: Anthropology, Language, and Action,* edited by Michael Lambek, 376–99. New York: Fordham University Press, 2010.

Davis, J. *Travels of Four Years and a Half in the United States of America during 1798, 1799, 1800, and 1802.* New York: n.p., 1909.

Daza, Paula. Master's thesis, Facultad Latinoamericano de Ciencias Sociales, Quito, Ecuador, forthcoming.

Dean, Carolyn. *Inka Bodies and the Body of Christ: Corpus Christi in Colonial Cuzco, Peru.* Durham, NC: Duke University Press, 1999.

Dueñas, Alcira. "Introduction: Andeans Articulating Colonial Worlds." *The Americas* 72, no. 1 (January 2015): 3–17.

Durston, Alan. *Pastoral Quechua: The History of Christian Translation in Colonial Peru, 1550–1650.* Notre Dame, IN: University of Notre Dame Press, 2007.

Ferraro, Emilia. *Reciprocidad, don y deuda: relaciones y formas de intercambio en los Andes ecuatorianos.* La comunidad de Pesillo. Quito: Abya-Yala, 2004.

Fildes, Valerie A. *Wet Nursing: A History from Antiquity to the Present.* New York: Basil Blackwell, 1988.

Fisher, Andrew B., and Mathew D. O'Hara, eds. *Imperial Subjects: Race and Identity in Colonial Latin America.* Durham, NC: Duke University Press, 2009.

Foster, George M. *Culture and Conquest: America's Spanish Heritage.* New York: Wenner-Gren Foundation for Anthropological Research, 1960.

Garrett, David T. "'In Spite of Her Sex': The Cacica and the Politics of the Pueblo in Late Colonial Cusco." *The Americas* 64, no. 4 (2008): 547–81.

Gauderman, Kimberly. "A Loom of Her Own: Women and Textiles in Seventeenth-Century Quito." *Colonial Latin American Review* 13, no. 1 (2004): 47–63.

———. *Women's Lives in Colonial Quito: Gender, Law, and Economy in Spanish America.* Austin: University of Texas Press, 2003.

Gómez-Galvarriato, Aurora. "Premodern Manufacturing." In *The Cambridge Economic History of Latin America Volume 1: The Colonial Era and the Short Nineteenth Century,* edited by Victor Bulmer-Thomas, John H. Coatsworth, and Roberto Cortés Conde, 357–94. New York: Cambride University Press, 2006.

Gomezjurado Zevallos, Javier. "El vecindario blanco mestizo en Pelileo en 1847 y tenencia de tierra en el sector." In *Bases para la historia social de Pelileo,* 12–21. Quito: Corporacion Sociedad Amigos de la Genealogía, 1998.

Graubart, Karen B. *With Our Labor and Sweat: Indigenous Women and the Formation of Colonial Society in Peru, 1550–1700.* Stanford, CA: Stanford University Press, 2007.

Guerrero, Andrés. "The Administration of Dominated Populations under a Regime of Customary Citizenship: The Case of Postcolonial Ecuador." In *After Spanish Rule: Postcolonial Predicaments of the Americas,* edited by Mark Thurner and Andrés Guerrero, 272–309. Durham, NC: Duke University Press, 2003.

———. *La semántica de la dominación: el concertaje de indios.* Quito: Ediciones Libri Mundi, 1991.

Guerrero, Juan Agustín. *Imágenes del Ecuador del siglo XIX.* Compiled with an introduction by Wilson Hallo. Quito: Ediciones del Sol, 1981.

Gugelberger, George, and Michael Kearney. "Voices for the Voiceless: Testimonial Literature in Latin America." *Latin American Perspectives* 18, no. 3 (1991): 3–14.

Hardwick, Julie, Sarah M. S. Pearsall, and Karin Wulf. "Introduction: Centering Families in Atlantic Histories." *William and Mary Quarterly* 70, no. 2 (2013): 205–24.

Harner, Michael J. *The Jívaro: People of the Sacred Waterfalls*. Berkeley: University of California Press, 1972.

Harris, Max. *Aztecs, Moors, and Christians: Festivals of Reconquest in Mexico and Spain*. Austin: University of Texas Press, 2000.

Hess, Carmen G. "'Moving Up—Moving Down': Agro-Pastoral Land Use Patterns in the Ecuadorian Paramos." *Mountain Research and Development* 10, no. 4 (1990): 333–42.

Hirschkind, Lynn. "The Enigmatic Evanescence of Coca from Ecuador." *Ethnobotany Research and Applications* no. 3 (2005): 97–106.

———. "History of the Indian Population of Cañar." *Colonial Latin American Review* 4, no. 3 (1995): 1311–342.

Holtzman, Jon D. "Food and Memory." *Annual Review of Anthropology* 35 (2006): 361–78.

hooks, bell. "Homeplace: A Site of Resistance." In *Philosophy and the City*, edited by Sharon M. Meagher, 175–83. Albany: SUNY, 2008.

Hyland, Sabine. "Ply, Markedness, and Redundancy: New Evidence for How Andean Khipus Encoded Information." *American Anthropologist* 116, no. 3 (2014): 643–48.

Ibarra, Hernán. "Cambios agrarios y conflictos étnicos en la sierra central (1820–1930)." In *Estructuras agrarias y conflictos sociales en la sierra central (1820–1930)*, edited by Instituto de Investigaciones Económicas (IIE), 143–263. Quito: IIE, PUCE, CONUEP, 1990.

———. "Tierra, mercado y capital comercial en la sierra central: el caso de Tungurahua 1850–1930." Master's thesis, Facultad Latinoamericano de Ciencias Sociales, Quito, 1987.

Icaza, Jorge. *The Villagers (Huasipungo)*. Carbondale: Southern Illinois University Press, 1964.

Kennedy Troya, Alexandra, and Carmen Fauria Roma. "Obrajes en la Audiencia de Quito: Un caso studio: Tilipulo." *Boletín Americanista* 37 (1987): 143–202.

Lambert, Berndt. "Bilaterality in the Andes." In *Andean Kinship and Marriage*, edited by Ralph Bolton and Enrique Mayer, 1–27. Washington, D.C.: American Anthropological Association, 1977.

Lane, Kris. "Africans and Natives in the Mines of Spanish America." In *Beyond Black and Red: African-Native Relations in Colonial Latin America*, edited by Matthew Restall, 159–84. Albuquerque: University of New Mexico Press, 2005.

———. "Haunting the Present: Five Colonial Legacies for the New Millennium." In *Millennial Ecuador: Critical Essays on Cultural Transformations and Social Dynamics*, edited by Norman E. Whitten Jr., 75–101. Iowa City: University of Iowa Press, 2003.

———. *Quito 1599: City and Colony in Transition*. Albuquerque: University of New Mexico Press, 2002.

Lehman, David. "Introduction: Andean Societies and the Theory of Peasant Economy." In *Ecology and Exchange in the Andes*, edited by David Lehman, 1–26. Cambridge: Cambridge University Press, 1982.

León G., Natalia Catalina, and Cecilia Méndez Mora. "Poder y amor: Articulaciones e instituciones familiares en la larga duración, Ecuador." In *La Familia en Iberoamérica*

1550–1980, edited by Pablo Rodriguez. Bogotá: Universidad Externado de Colombia, 2004.

Mangan, Jane. "Moving Mestizos in Sixteenth-Century Peru: Spanish Fathers, Indigenous Mothers, and the Children in Between." *William and Mary Quarterly* 70, no. 2 (April 2013): 273–94.

———. *Transatlantic Obligations: Creating the Bonds of Family in Conquest-Era Peru and Spain*. New York: Oxford University Press, 2016.

Martínez, Nicolás. "La condición actual de la raza indígena en la provincia de Tungurahua." In *Indianistas, indianófilos, indigenistas: entre el enigma y la fascinación: Una antología de textos sobre el "problema" indígena*, edited by Jorge Trujillo, 209–43. Quito: Abya-Yala, (1916) 1993.

McFarlane, Anthony. "The 'Rebellion of the Barrios': Urban Insurrection in Bourbon Quito." *The Hispanic American Historical Review* 69, no. 2 (May 1989), 283–330.

Miller, Laura. "Salasaca." In *Costume and Identity in Highland Ecuador*, edited by Anne Pollard Rowe, 126–44. Seattle: University of Washington Press, 1998.

Milton, Cynthia. "Poverty and Politics of Colonialism: 'Poor Spaniards,' Their Petitions, and the Erosion of Privilege in Late Colonial Quito." *Hispanic American Historical Review* 85 no. 4 (2005): 595–626.

Minchom, Martin. "The Making of a White Province: Demographic Movement and Ethnic Transformation in the South of the Audiencia de Quito (1670–1830)." *Bulletin de l'Institut Francais d'Études Andines* 12, nos. 3–4 (1983): 23–39.

———. *The People of Quito, 1690–1810*. Boulder, CO: Westview Press, 1994.

Miño Vaca, Reinaldo. "Los obrajes de Santo Tomás y San Ildefonso: Su levantamiento." In *Bases para la historia social de Pelileo*, 23–36. Quito: Corporacion Sociedad Amigos de la Genealogía, 1998.

Mintz, Sidney W. *Caribbean Transformations*. New York: Columbia University Press, 1989.

Mintz, Sidney W., and Richard Price. *The Birth of African-American Culture: An Anthropological Perspective*. Boston: Beacon Press, 1976.

Mintz, Sidney W., and Eric R. Wolf. "An Analysis of Ritual Co-Parenthood (Compadrazgo)." *Southwestern Journal of Anthropology* 6, no. 4 (Winter 1950): 341–68.

Monsalve, Martín. "Curacas pleitistas y curas abusivos: conflicto, prestigio, y poder en los andes coloniales, Siglo VII." In *Élites indígenas en los andes: Nobles, caciques y cabildantes bajo el yugo colonial*, edited by David Cahill and Blanca Tovías, 159–74. Quito: Abya-Yala, 2003.

Moreno Yánez, Segundo E. *Alzamientos indígenas en la Audiencia de Quito 1534–1803*. Quito: Abya-Yala, 1987.

———. "El 'Formulario de las ordenanzas de indios': Una regulación de las relaciones laborales en las haciendas y obrajes del Quito colonial y republicano." *Ibero-amerikanisches Archiv, Neue Folge* 5, no. 3 (1979): 227–41.

———. *Sublevaciones indígenas en la Audiencia de Quito*, 3rd ed. Quito: PUCE, 1985.

———. "Una rebelión indígena anticolonial: Chambo 1797." In *Contribución a la etnohistoria ecuatoriana*, edited by Segundo Moreno Y. and Udo Oberem. Quito: Instituto Otavaleño de Antropología, 1981.

Mörner, Magnus. *Race Mixture in the History of Latin America*. Boston: Little, Brown, 1967.

Muñoz Bernand, Carmen. "Estratégias matrimoniales apellidos y nombres de pila: Libros parroquiales y civiles en el sur del Ecuador." In *Antropología del Ecuador*, edited by Segundo Moreno, 223–44. Quito: Abya-Yala, 1996.

Navas de Pozo, Yolanda. *Angamarca en el siglo XVI*. Quito, Ecuador: Abya-Yala, 1990.

Newman, Elizabeth Terese. *Biography of a Hacienda: Work and Revolution in Rural Mexico*. Tucson: University of Arizona Press, 2014.

Newson, Linda. *Life and Death in Early Colonial Ecuador*. Norman: University of Oklahoma Press, 1995.

O'Connor, Erin. *Gender, Indian, Nation: The Contradictions of Making Ecuador, 1830–1925*. Tucson: University of Arizona Press, 2007.

Ogburn, Dennis E. "Becoming Saraguro: Ethnogenesis in the Context of Inca and Spanish Colonialism." *Ethnohistory* 55, no. 2 (2008): 287–319.

Operé, Fernando. *Indian Captivity in Spanish America*. Translated by Gustavo Pellón. Charlottesville: University of Virginia Press, 2001.

O'Phelan Godoy, Scarlet. "Tiempo inmemorial, tiempo colonial: Un estudio de casos." *Procesos: Revista Ecuatoriana de Historia* 4 (1993): 3–20.

Ortiz de la Tabla Ducasse, Javier. "El obraje colonial ecuatoriano." *Revista de Indias* (1977): 471–541. Madrid: CSIC.

———. "Las ordenanzas de obrajes de Matias de Peralta para la Audiencia de Quito, 1621." *Anuario de Estudios Americanos* 33 (1976): 875–931.

———. *Los encomenderos de Quito, 1534–1660: Origen y evolución de una elite colonial*. Sevilla: Escuela de Estudios Hispano-Americanos, 1993.

Ortner, Sherry B. "Dark Anthropology and Its Others: Theory Since the Eighties." *Hau: Journal of Ethnographic Theory* 6 (1): 47–73.

Osculati, Gaetano. *Esplorazaione delle regioni equatoriali lungo il Napo ed il fiume delle Amazzoni*. Milan: Fratelli Centenari, 1854.

O'Toole, Rachel Sarah. *Bound Lives: Africans, Indians, and the Making of Race in Colonial Peru*. Pittsburgh: University of Pittsburgh Press, 2012.

Peña Montenegro, Alonso de la, and C. Baciero. *Itinerario para párrocos de indios*. 2 vols. Madrid: Consejo Superior de Investigaciones Científicas, (1668) 1995.

Phelan, John Leddy. *The Kingdom of Quito in the Seventeenth Century: Bureaucratic Politics in the Spanish Empire*. Madison: University of Wisconsin Press, 1967.

Poole, Deborah A. "Accomodation and Resistance in Andean Ritual Dance." *The Drama Review* 34, no. 2 (1990): 98–126.

Powers, Karen Vieira. *Andean Journeys: Migration, Ethnogenesis, and the State in Colonial Quito*. Albuquerque: University of New Mexico Press, 1995.

———. *Women in the Crucible of Conquest: The Gendered Genesis of Spanish American Society, 1500–1600*. Albuquerque: University of New Mexico Press, 2005.

Premo, Bianca. *Children of the Father King: Youth, Authority, and Legal Minority in Colonial Lima*. Chapel Hill: University of North Carolina Press, 2005.

———. "Familiar: Thinking beyond Lineage and across Race in Spanish Atlantic Family History." *The William and Mary Quarterly* 70, no. 2 (2013): 295–316.

Price, Richard. *First Time: The Historical Vision of an Afro-American People*. Baltimore: Johns Hopkins University Press, 1983.

Proctor, Frank T. "Afro-Mexican Slave Labor in the Obrajes de Paños of New Spain, Seventeenth and Eighteenth Centuries." *The Americas* 60, no. 1 (July 2003): 3–58.

Quilter, Jeffrey, and Gary Urton, eds. *Narrative Threads: Accounting and Recounting in Andean Khipu*. Austin: University of Texas Press, 2002.

Rahier, Jean Muteba. "Blackness, the Racial/Spatial Order, Migrations, and Miss Ecuador 1995–96." *American Anthropologist* 100, no. 2 (1998): 421–30.

Ramírez, Susan. *Provincial Patriarchs: Land Tenure and the Economics of Power in Colonial Peru*. Albuquerque: University of New Mexico Press, 1986.

———. *World Upside Down: Cross-Cultural Contact and Conflict in Sixteenth-Century Peru*. Stanford, CA: Stanford University Press, 1996.

Ramos Gómez, Luis. "La situación del indio de obraje en la ciudad de Quito según la visita realizada en 1743 por el presidente José de Araujo." *Revista Española de Antropología Americana* 28 (1998): 151–68.

Rappaport, Joanne. "Carchi Province (Ecuador) and the Department of Nariño (Colomiba)." In *Costume and History in Highland Ecuador*, edited by Ann Pollard Rowe and Lynn A. Meisch, 119–29. Austin: University of Texas Press, 2011.

———. *The Disappearing Mestizo: Configuring Difference in the Colonial New Kingdom of Granada*. Durham, NC: Duke University Press, 2014.

Reino Garcés, Pedro Arturo. *Documentos para la historia colonial de Tungurahua*, tomo I. Ambato: Maxtudio, 2009.

———. *El componente africano colonial en Tungurahua*. Ambato: Universidad Técnica de Ambato, 2012.

———. *Historias de tinta y polvo*. Ambato: Editorial Maxtudio, 2013.

———. *La Comarca de Capote: Cevallos*. Cevallos, Tungurahua: I. Municipio de Cevallos, 2004.

———. *Tisaleo indígena en la colonia*. Ambato: Editorial Maxtudio, 2002.

Rowe, Anne Pollard. "Costume in Cotopaxi, Tungurahua, and Bólivar Provinces." In *Costume and History in Highland Ecuador*, edited by Ann Pollard Rowe and Lynn A. Meisch, 224–42. Austin: University of Texas Press, 2011.

———, ed. *Costume and Identity in Highland Ecuador*. Seattle: University of Washington Press, 1998.

———. "Costume in Southern Pichincha Province." In *Costume and History in Highland Ecuador*, edited by Ann Pollard Rowe and Lynn A. Meisch, 169–223. Austin: University of Texas Press, 2011.

Rueda Novoa, Rocío. *El obraje de San Joseph de Peguchi*. Quito: Abya Yala–Tehis, 1988.

Sainges, Thierry. "Quechua-Aymara Heartland (1570–1780)." In *The Cambridge History of Native Peoples of the Americas*. Vol. 3, *South America*, edited by Frank Salomon and Stuart B. Schwartz, part 2, pp. 443–501. Cambridge University Press, 1999.

Salomon, Frank. *The Cord Keepers: Khipus and Cultural Life in a Peruvian Village*. Durham, NC: Duke University Press, 2004.

———. *Los yumbos, niguas, y tsatchila o "colorados" durante la colonia Española*. Quito: Abya-Yala, 1997.

———. *Native Lords of Quito in the Age of the Incas*. New York: Cambridge University Press, 1986.

Saporta Sternbach, Nancy. "Re-membering the Dead: Latin American women's 'Testimonial' Discourse." *Latin American Perspectives* 18, no. 3 (1991): 91–102.

Schwartz, Stuart B. "Colonial Identities and the *Sociedad de Castas*." *Colonial Latin American Review* 4, no.1 (1995): 185–201.

Schwartz, Stuart B., and Frank Salomon. "New Peoples and New Kinds of People: Adaptation, Readjustment, and Ethnogenesis in South American Indigenous Societies (Colonial Era)." In *The Cambridge History of Native Peoples of the Americas*. Vol. 3, *South America*, edited by Frank Salomon and Stuart B. Schwartz, part 2, pp. 443–501. Cambridge: Cambridge University Press, 1999.

Scott, James C. *The Art of Not Being Governed: An Anarchist History of Upland Southeast Asia*. New Haven, CT: Yale University Press, 2009.

———. *Domination and the Arts of Resistance: Hidden Transcripts*. New Haven, CT: Yale University Press, 1990.

———. *Weapons of the Weak: Everyday Forms of Peasant Resistance*. New Haven, CT: Yale University Press, 1985.

Sherwood, Joan. *Poverty in Eighteenth-Century Spain: The Women and Children of the Inclusa*. Toronto: University of Toronto Press, 1988.

Silverblatt, Irene. *Moon, Sun, and Witches: Gender Ideologies and Class in Inca and Colonial Peru*. Princeton, NJ: Princeton University Press, 1987.

Soasti, Guadalupe. "Obrajeros y comerciantes en Riobamba (s.XVII)." *Procesos: Revista Ecuatoriana de Historia* 1 (1991): 5–22.

Soulodre-La France, Renée. "'Whites and Mulattos: Our Enemies': Race Relations and Popular Political Culture in Nueva Granada." In *Beyond Black and Red: African-Native Relations in Colonial Latin America*, edited by Matthew Restall, 137–58. Albuquerque: University of New Mexico Press, 2005.

Stadel, Christoph. "Del Valle al Monte: Altitudinal Patterns of Agricultural Activities in the Patate-Pelileo Area of Ecuador." *Mountain Research and Development* 6, no. 1 (1986): 53–64.

Stutzman, Ronald. "El Mestizaje: An All-Inclusive Ideology of Exclusion." In *Cultural Transformations and Ethnicity in Modern Ecuador*, edited by Norman E. Whitten Jr., 45–94. Urbana: University of Illinois Press, 1981.

Sussman, George D. *Selling Mothers' Milk: The Wet-Nursing Business in France 1715–1914*. Urbana: University of Illinois Press, 1982.

Tardieu, Jean-Pierre. 2012. "Negros e indios en el obraje de San Ildefonso. Real Audiencia de Quito. 1665–1666." *Revista de Indias* 72, no. 255 (2012): 527–50.

Taylor, Anne Christine. "La invención del Jívaro: Notas etnográficas sobre un fantasma occidental." In *Antropología del Ecuador*, edited by Segundo Moreno, 277–89. Quito: Abya-Yala, 1996.

Terraciano, Kevin. *The Mixtecs of Colonial Oaxaca: Ñudzahui History, Sixteenth through Eighteenth Centuries*. Stanford, CA: Stanford University Press, 2001.

Thomson, Sinclair. *We Alone Will Rule: Native Andean Politics in the Age of Insurgency*. Madison: University of Wisconsin Press, 2002.

Trouillot, Michel-Rolph. *Silencing the Past: Power and the Production of History.* Boston: Beacon Press, 1995.

Truhan, Deborah L. "'Mi últimada y postrimera boluntad.'Trayectorias de tres mujeres andinas: Cuenca, 1599–1610." *Revista histórica* 15, no.1 (July 1991): 121–55.

———. "Repopulating the Countryside: Rural Forasteros in the Corregimiento de Cuenca During the Seventeenth Century." Paper presented at the Andean Studies Committee meeting of the Conference on Latin American History, New York, January 4, 1997.

Tyrer, Robson Brines. "The Demographic and Economic History of the Audiencia de Quito: Indian Population and the Textile Industry,1600–1800." PhD diss., University of California Berkeley, 1976.

Uzcátegui Andrade, Byron. *Los Llanganates y la tumba de Atahualpa.* Quito: Abya-Yala, 1992.

Valderrama Fernandez, Ricardo, Carmen Escalante Gutierrez, eds. *Andean Lives: Gregorio Condori Mamani and Asunta Quispe Huamán.* Translated from the Quechua with Annotations and a Revised Glossary by Paul H. Gelles and Gabriela Martinez Escobar. Austin: University of Texas Press, 1996.

Van Aken, Mark. "The Lingering Death of Indian Tribute in Ecuador." *The Hispanic American Historical Review* 61, no. 3 (1981): 429–59.

Weismantel, Mary. *Cholas and Pishtacos: Stories of Race and Sex in the Andes.* Chicago: University of Chicago Press, 2001.

Whitten, Dorothea S., and Norman E. Whitten Jr. *From Myth to Creation.* Urbana: University of Illinois Press, 1988.

Whitten, Norman E., Jr. "Ethnogenesis." In *The Encyclopedia of Cultural Anthropology,* edited by D. Levinson and M. Ember, 407–10. New York: Henry Holt, 1996.

Whitten, Norman E., Jr., and Rachel Corr. "Imagery of Blackness in Indigenous Myth, Ritual, and Discourse," in *Representations of Blackness and the Performance of Identities,* edited by Jean Muteba Rahier, 213–33. Westport, CT: Bergin and Garvey, 1999.

———. "Indigenous Constructions of 'Blackness.'" In *Histories of the Present: People and Power in Ecuador,* edited by Norman E. Whitten Jr. and Dorothea Scott Whitten, 45–64. Urbana: University of Illinois Press, 2011.

Wibbelsman, Michelle. *Ritual Encounters: Otavalan Modern and Mythic Modernity.* Urbana: University of Illinois Press, 2009.

Wogan, Peter. *Magical Writing in Salasaca: Literacy and Power in Highland Ecuador.* Boulder, CO: Westview Press, 2004.

Wolf, Eric. *Europe and the People without History.* Berkeley: University of California Press, 1982.

Yannakakis, Yanna. *The Art of Being In-Between: Native Intermediaries, Indian Identity, and Local Rule in Colonial Oaxaca.* Durham, NC: Duke University Press, 2008.

Zuidema, R. T. *The Ceque System of Cuzco: The Social Organizaiton of the Capital of the Inca.* Leiden: E. J. Brill, 1964.

INDEX

adoption, 24, 139, 143–46, 152

Africans: interactions with native Andeans, 15–16, 23, 38–64 passim; origins of slaves, 60–61

alcaldes, 36, 66, 73, 88, 166, 167; de la doctrina, 9, 44, 70–71

Amazonian region, 82, 116, 193n48; ceremonial stools from, 195; parodies of Indians from, 130

ayllus, 16–17, 98–99, 104, 165, 166, 168, 169

Bernardas, (nuns), Madres del Santisimo Sacramento de Madrid, 30, 108, 168, 169, 196n36

blacks. *See* Africans

blanqueamiento, 13, 150

cacicas: administrative duties and, 103, 107; colonial laws regarding, 107; disputes with caciques, 102–10; and land ownership, 34; pre-Hispanic existence of, 102; seating of (*see* ceremonies, investiture)

caciques: abolition of position, 166; complaints filed by, 71, 100; conflict with blacks, 52; and forced labor of subjects, 41, 45, 73–74, 100, 119; foster children of, 143; imprisonment of, 74; intermediary position of, 66, 72, 87, 134; and land sales, 33–35, 117, 148–49, 156, 160, and status symbols, 72; suspected of plotting rebellion, 132–34

camayos: as coca specialists, 33; description of, 28–29; designations of, 30, 109, 110, 168, 169, 170; lands purchased by, 156, 157, 163

Cañari people, 98, 178

cabuya, 10, 86, 170

ceremonies, investiture, 98, 103–4, 110

chicha: see maize beer

children: and obraje labor, 9, 20, 35, 40, 41, 63, 70–71, 73, 76, 84, 88, 91, 92, 114, 171; out-of-wedlock, 142; slave: 51 52, 54, 59, 60, 61. *See also* wet nurses

Chota, Valley of, 30, 168

Cicala, Mario, 6–11, 113, 136, 170

clothing: of caciques, 72, 104; festival, 93; and ethnic identity, 17, 19, 176; mestizo, 151; native, 52, 78, 124, 140; of slaves, 53, 60

ABOUT THE AUTHOR

Rachel Corr is associate professor of anthropology at the Wilkes Honors College of Florida Atlantic University. She has conducted ethnographic fieldwork in Ecuador since 1990. She is the author of *Ritual and Remembrance in the Ecuadorian Andes*.